A Research Agenda for Gender and Tourism

Elgar Research Agendas outline the future of research in a given area. Leading scholars are given the space to explore their subject in provocative ways, and map out the potential directions of travel. They are relevant but also visionary.

Forward-looking and innovative, Elgar Research Agendas are an essential resource for PhD students, scholars and anybody who wants to be at the forefront of research.

Titles in the series include:

A Research Agenda for Sustainability and Business
Edited by Sally V. Russell and Rory W. Padfield

A Research Agenda for Gender and Leadership
Edited by Sherylle J. Tan and Lisa DeFrank-Cole

A Research Agenda for Human Rights and the Environment
Edited by Dina Lupin

A Research Agenda for Skills and Inequality
Edited by Michael Tåhlin

A Research Agenda for East Asian Social Policy
Edited by Misa Izuhara

A Research Agenda for Organised Crime
Edited by Barry Rider

A Research Agenda for Gender and Tourism
Edited by Erica Wilson and Donna Chambers

A Research Agenda for Gender and Tourism

Edited by

ERICA WILSON

Professor of Tourism, Southern Cross University, Australia

DONNA CHAMBERS

Professor, Cultural and Creative Industries, Department of Arts, Northumbria University, UK

Elgar Research Agendas

Edward Elgar PUBLISHING

Cheltenham, UK • Northampton, MA, USA

Published by
Edward Elgar Publishing Limited
The Lypiatts
15 Lansdown Road
Cheltenham
Glos GL50 2JA
UK

Edward Elgar Publishing, Inc.
William Pratt House
9 Dewey Court
Northampton
Massachusetts 01060
USA

A catalogue record for this book
is available from the British Library

Library of Congress Control Number: 2023931304

This book is available electronically in the **Elgar**online
Geography subject collection
http://dx.doi.org/10.4337/9781789902532

MIX
Paper from
responsible sources
FSC® C013056

ISBN 978 1 78990 252 5 (cased)
ISBN 978 1 78990 253 2 (eBook)

Printed and bound in Great Britain by TJ Books Limited, Padstow, Cornwall

Contents

Contributors

Rafiah Almathami is a PhD candidate at the University of Queensland. Her research interests include gender diversity, culture, society and mixed workplace environments, particularly in the tourism and entertainment contexts. Rafiah has published peer-reviewed works on women in events and festivals and spoken on the topic at a few academic conferences and non-academic events. She is also a reviewer for *Tourism Recreation Research* and *Tourism Management Perspectives*. She is currently exploring the challenges and opportunities faced by Saudi women in the tourism and entertainment industries in Saudi Arabia as part of her PhD research.

Sandeep Basnyat is Assistant Professor at the Macao Institute for Tourism Studies, Macao, China. He holds a PhD degree in Tourism from the University of Otago. Sandeep's research areas of interest include employee relationships; human resource management; work and working conditions; and emotion, emotional labour and labour sustainability in the tourism and hospitality industry.

Claudia Becerra-Gualdrón is a PhD candidate at Wageningen University & Research in the Netherlands and holds a Master's degree in Economics from the Universidad Pedagógica y Tecnológica de Colombia. She is interested in gender studies especially in tourism in Colombia and Latin America. In her PhD, Claudia is analysing the different ways women navigate gender power relations and their interconnections at home and at work. Her work has a specific focus on qualitative feminist methodologies.

Donna Chambers is Professor of Cultural and Creative Industries at the University of Northumbria in the UK. She is a critical tourism scholar who is interested in how people and places are represented primarily through cultural and heritage tourism, postcolonial and decolonial epistemologies, and in how Black women are represented in tourism through the lens of Critical Race Theory and Black feminism. Donna is currently an Associate Editor for *Annals of Tourism Research*, and a Managing Editor for *Leisure Studies*.

Karolina Doughty is Assistant Professor in Cultural Geography at Wageningen University & Research in the Netherlands. Her central research focus has been on interactions between place and wellbeing, with a particular interest in everyday interactions and experiences, often relating to the broader themes of conviviality and belonging. Karolina's research utilizes qualitative, participatory, and audio-visual modes of enquiry, focusing on narratives, emotions, and sensory perceptions. Her work has primarily contributed to literatures on therapeutic landscapes, geographies of sound, and everyday mobilities.

Elspeth Frew, PhD, is Associate Professor in the Department of Management and Marketing in the La Trobe Business School, La Trobe University, Melbourne. She has 30 years of experience as a university academic, researcher, and educator in tourism and event management. Elspeth's research interest is in cultural tourism, with a particular focus on: dark tourism; industrial tourism; and event and attraction management. She has published work in these areas as journal articles, book chapters, and edited books.

Fernando Almeida García is Associate Professor at the University of Málaga, Spain, Department of Geography, School of Tourism. His research is focused on tourism and regional planning and urbanism, sustainable development, economic development and tourism policy. He belongs to the research group 'Territory and Tourism' (SEJ-402). Fernando has published many papers on these subjects. He has collaborated in several international projects with European and Latin American universities. Also, he worked professionally for the government department of tourism in Santiago de Compostela and Melilla (Spain).

Abolfazl Siyamiyan Gorji is a PhD candidate at the Faculty of Tourism at the University of Málaga, Spain. His research interests include destination image, tourist behaviour, residents' attitudes towards tourism, gender studies, and social media in tourism.

Seyedasaad Hosseini is a PhD candidate at the Faculty of Tourism at the University of Málaga, Spain. His research interests include tourist experience, tourist behaviour, gender studies, destination image, and sustainable tourism.

Jess Sanggyeong Je is a PhD candidate in the Department of Tourism, Sport and Hotel Management, Griffith University, Australia. Jess is interested in gender issues, intersectionality framework, and critical tourism studies. For her PhD thesis, she is examining the effectiveness of diversity and equality initiatives in tourism organizations under the supervision of Associate Professor Catheryn Khoo and Dr Elaine Chiao Ling Yang.

Rafael Cortés Macías has a PhD in Geography from the University of Málaga,

Spain. He is Professor of Human Geography at the University of Málaga in the Department of Geography. He teaches the degree in Tourism and the master's in Tourism Management and Planning Faculty of Tourism. As part of the research developed as a member of the research group 'Territory and Tourism' (SEJ-402), Rafael emphasizes the study of the relationships between tourism, impacts and territorial planning, within both the national and international contexts.

Judith Mair is Associate Professor in Tourism at the UQ Business School, University of Queensland, Australia. Judith's work aims to understand and enhance the positive impacts of tourism and events on the communities and societies which host them. She is working on a number of projects in fields including Olympic Games legacies, the links between events and social connectivity (including social capital, social cohesion, and social justice), and assessing the potential impacts of climate change on the tourism and events sector.

Carmen Pau Ka Mun graduated from Macao Institute for Tourism Studies, Macao, China. Carmen's research interests include employee relations, human resource management, and employment conditions in the tourism and hospitality industry.

Brooke Porter, PhD, is a specialist in development strategy. Brooke currently works as an instructional designer building content addressing development and resource management strategy. Her past research has explored development and environmental management and education strategies in lesser-developed regions. Brooke has worked in various roles with non-governmental organizations (NGOs), international aid agencies, and academic institutions across the globe.

Helene Pristed Nielsen is Affiliated Associate Professor at the Faculty of Social Sciences, University of the Faroe Islands. Her research interests revolve around intersections between gender, mobility and place, as well as methodological questions about how to best research gender (in)equality. Previous publications include the edited volume *Gender and Island Communities* (with Firouz Gaini) published by Routlegde in 2020, as well as the report *Equality in Isolated Labour Markets* (with Erika Anne Hayfield and Steven Arnfjord) published by TemaNord in 2020.

Heike Schänzel is Associate Professor in the School of Hospitality and Tourism at Auckland University of Technology, New Zealand. Her research interests include inter-generational relationships and wellbeing, experiential aspects, social sustainability, and social justice issues. She is passionate about the more equitable facilitation of sociality and meaningful experiences within the context of tourism. Heike is an Associate Editor for the *Journal of Tourism Futures* and has co-edited the books *Femininities in the Field* and *Masculinities in the Field.*

Margreet van der Burg is senior scholar in gender studies/history. Since 2002, Margreet has taught and researched gender in food, agricultural and rural research and development at Wageningen University in the Netherlands. From her early work she became known as the Dutch pioneer in agriculture-related history from a women's and gender perspective. Margreet's recent work aims at advancing international gender issues and approaches, both through an intersectional perspective as well as by re-positioning them within mainstream histories and their representations in cultural heritage and media.

Erica Wilson is Professor of Tourism and Pro Vice Chancellor (Academic Innovation) at Southern Cross University in Lismore, Australia. Erica's doctoral thesis was a gendered analysis of Australian women's solo travel experiences. Her research interests focus on critical tourism and pedagogy, gender and tourism, women's travel, and sustainable tourism in protected areas. Erica is on the editorial advisory boards for *Hospitality and Society*, *Journal of Tourism and Development*, and the *Annals of Leisure Research*.

Elaine Chiao Ling Yang, PhD, is Senior Lecturer at Griffith University, Australia. Elaine's research investigated various issues pertinent to women in tourism as workers, entrepreneurs, and travellers. She has also published extensively on Asian tourism and solo consumers. Elaine's goal is to work on projects that bring positive changes to women and marginalized groups in tourism and hospitality. She has worked with Tourism Australia, the Australian Department of Foreign Affairs and Trade, and other organizations on consultancy and funded projects.

Acknowledgements

In 2019, when we accepted the task of editing a text aimed at articulating a research agenda for gender and tourism, we scarcely realized what seismic events awaited us the following year! It is a well-rehearsed truism that the world came to a literal standstill due the COVID-19 pandemic and at the time of writing we are still suffering the negative consequences of this tumultuous event. Add to this a host of environmental disasters and tremendous upheavals occasioned by movements for social justice (particularly racial and gender justice) and we recognize the urgency of engaging with critical discourses and practices to address these adverse occurrences. It is an understatement to say that trying to organize our own lives while at the same time coordinating contributions from academics across the globe in such a turbulent environment was challenging. Indeed, in seeking to complete this text we suffered a series of setbacks including dealing with the personal and professional consequences of COVID-19, destructive flooding (twice), and a host of other painful events which are too many to recount here!

Yet we were determined to deliver what we believed (and still do) to be a necessary and timely text that will add significant value to the relatively small cadre of work on tourism gender research. We couldn't have done so without the tremendous support from our friends and family and to them we owe a debt of gratitude. Thanks also to the wonderfully diverse contributors who endeavoured to, and often succeeded in, meeting the deadlines we set even though they too were undoubtedly experiencing their own crises. To them we would like to say that without your great contributions this book would not have been possible.

Finally, we would like to acknowledge the ongoing support and advice from Stephanie Hartley, Senior Assistant Editor from Edward Elgar Publishing, whose patience with our many shifting and missed deadlines for delivery of the final copy is very much appreciated. There are of course many others who should be acknowledged, and we apologize for any omissions – but know that we appreciate you all. It goes without saying but we will do so anyway – any errors or omissions in the final version are solely our responsibility.

Erica Wilson and Donna Chambers
August 2022

1 Introduction to *A Research Agenda for Gender and Tourism*

Erica Wilson and Donna Chambers

1. Opening Thoughts

Tourism is gendered – its past, present and future (Chambers et al., 2017; Pritchard, 2017; Swain, 1995). In line with the philosophy of the Elgar Research Agenda series, in this volume we *look forward*, imagining, exploring and challenging the ways that gender intersects with and impacts on tourism, and how it will continue to do so. We highlight emerging research in the field, and the methods and methodologies that are – or that need to be – at the forefront of gender-aware tourism research. At the same time, it is relevant to *look back*, to understand the key developments in the study of gender and tourism that have led us to where we are now.

As critical, feminist researchers, long interested in and dedicated to the study of gender in tourism, we were delighted to be invited to edit this collection. We were pleased to be provided the privilege and opportunity to give ongoing voice to gender in the context and study of tourism. Little did we know how challenging it would be! In putting out a call for papers to the scholarly community in 2020, we wrestled with its timing and, ultimately, with the relevance and reach of such an academic book. We watched the world around us change irrevocably with the advent of COVID-19, grappling with the death and loss incurred by the greatest health crisis of our time. The pandemic has touched us, like everyone, personally and professionally, but we are both fortunate to have our health, employment and relative freedoms.

In 2020, in the early stages of considering this book, the world also witnessed the resurgence of the Black Lives Matter movement, precipitated by the brutal murder of George Floyd by the police in the United States city of Minneapolis. This event, which was live-streamed and accessed by an international audience, launched an explosion of worldwide anti-racism protests, focused on exposing and dismantling the historic and continued structural inequalities, human rights abuses and injustices faced by people of colour, both in the USA and across the globe. Higher education institutions have been forced to confront their very purpose and foundation, and the perennial and firmly rooted issues of whiteness, white privilege and racism in the academy have been brought to the surface (c.f. Arday & Mirza, 2018). At the same time, the #metoo movement was increasingly drawing worldwide attention to sexual harassment and gender-based violence, including in tourism, travel, and academe.

Thus, at the outset, contributing to a scholarly tourism publication at a time of global distress and upheaval, felt uncomfortable and morally challenging. We wrestled with our own critical, feminist identities, positionalities and epistemologies. For Donna, as a woman of colour living and working in academia in the United Kingdom, she contended yet again with the stark reality of the extent of marginalization and oppression of women of colour within Western societies – most recently the pandemic highlighted more deleterious effects and affects at the intersection between race, gender, and class (c.f. Gregory, 2022; Schneider, 2020). While she had initially explored issues of power in the context of heritage (her PhD had taken a discursive approach to the link between the English nation and heritage), she has subsequently extended this to examine issues of representational power in wider contexts, drawing on post/decolonial theories and more recently critical race theory and Black feminism. She considers her thinking and approach as now more radical in the face of the continued erasure of Black women's voices, and she has engaged more intensely with activist agendas. For Erica, as a white scholar, she wanted to move beyond yet more research on Western women travellers (the topic of her PhD and early research), particularly at this time of these multiple crises, and to allow for diverse voices to be acknowledged, heard and published. Working with Donna and based on insights from other colleagues' work in critical tourism, she was aware that gender and tourism were not just about 'women' and 'men' (or white women and men), but about the intersectionalities among gender, race, class, sexuality, and power.

Reflecting upon these issues, we started to think that perhaps a book on gender and tourism is more relevant and important than ever? Black lives matter. Gender matters. Tourism and the freedoms to move matter. We watched COVID-19 unfold as a feminist, gendered and racialized issue, as the 'boundaries' of home, work and leisure dissolve further, and new gender gaps and biases appear. We watched as the virtual halting of global tourism has impacted negatively on women, men, and local communities dependent on the tourism industry. In the end, we went forward in agreement with our fellow critical colleagues (Aitchison, 2005; Small, Harris & Wilson, 2017) that gender and feminism must remain relevant in tourism studies, and perhaps even more so now.

While recent bibliometric analyses reveal some small increases in the *numbers* of gender-focused studies in tourism, the field is still marginalized and there is much work to do in fully engaging with gender-aware, feminist ontologies, epistemologies and methodologies (Chambers et al., 2017; Figueroa-Domecq et al., 2015; Small, Wilson, & Harris, 2017). As editors, we wanted to contribute to a 'gender ignition' in tourism research, rather than retreat to a 'gender stagnation', as Figueroa-Domecq and her colleagues (2015, p. 98) have put it. As self-confessed gender igniters, we share these authors' imagining of a future gender and tourism research, of 'take-off and expansion', where through a book such as this and at a time such as this, we might 'open up new vistas for gender-aware research and the gaps in tourism's knowledge canon are addressed, enriching and broadening tourism's methodological base' (p .98). Figueroa-Domecq et al's scenario of 'stagnation and continued marginalization' (p. 98) was not desirable or acceptable to us: one where tourism fails to engage with gender-aware and feminist epistemologies, and where researchers remain obsessed with biological and simplistic sex differences (Chambers & Rakić, 2018; Figueroa-Domecq et al, 2015).

2. Gender and Tourism: A Shifting Research Agenda

The study of gender and tourism has certainly burgeoned and matured over recent decades, but in many ways remains a nascent area of inquiry. We share Eger, Munar and Hsu's (2022) view that scholarship has moved well beyond the basic question of whether gender matters in tourism; rather, we should be asking ourselves questions like 'How does gender matter? What is the relationship between gendered cultures, behaviours and worldviews? What is or will become of sustainability in tourism?' (p. 1495).

Thus we will avoid in this introductory chapter explicating an extended history of the individual concepts of 'gender' and 'tourism', and of the feminist 'waves'. However, it is necessary to offer our reflexive position on gender, and then to briefly outline the development of key research trajectories in the field. 'Gender' is a concept widely attributed to second-wave feminism, when the distinction between sex (the biological determination of male and female) and gender (the social construction of normative male and female roles) was emphasized (Curthoys, 1994; Oakley, 1972). Gender refers to the descriptors of 'masculine' and 'feminine', not as immutable structures, but as constantly changing categories shaped by social and cultural factors (Lather, 1991). De Beauvoir's (1989/1949, p. xii) renowned assertion that 'one is not born, but rather becomes a woman' encapsulates a broad feminist viewpoint that gender is a social construction. Feminist authors such as Oakley (1972) maintain that in patriarchal societies, attributes of males are valued more highly than are attributes of females. The sex/gender, or nature/nurture, concept stands as an important hallmark of the contemporary feminist movement (Curthoys, 1994). For the purposes of our research and this book, we take the standpoint that gender is a social construction, which 'refers to a system of culturally constructed identities, expressed in ideologies of masculinity and femininity, interacting with socially structured relationships in divisions of labour and leisure, sexuality, and power between women and men' (Swain, 1995, pp. 258–9).

Kinnaird and Hall's (1994, p. 24) 'gender-aware' framework in tourism, published close to three decades ago and the first of its kind to do so, still provides a helpful overarching structure for how we approach gender in tourism research:

1. The activities and processes associated with tourism development are constructed out of gendered societies;
2. Gender relations both inform, and are informed by, the practices of all societies. Therefore, economic, social, cultural, political and environmental aspects of tourism-related activity interact with the gendered nature of individual societies and the way in which gender relations are defined and redefined over time; and
3. Discussions of gender and gender relations are concerned with issues of power and control, and are political relations at the household, community and societal levels … tourism revolves around social interaction and social articulations of motivations, desires, traditions and perceptions, all of which are gendered.

Essentially, this framework explicitly recognizes that we do not live – nor conduct our research – in a gender-free society, and that all aspects of society, culture and power are inherently gendered. Kinnaird and Hall (1994) were some of the earliest scholars to write on this topic, and to explicitly acknowledge the impact of gender in tourism.

3. Phases of Scholarship: Gender and Tourism

To outline the evolution of gender in the study of tourism, we utilize Henderson's (1994) five-phase approach in leisure studies, which was added to in various advancements by Aitchison (2001) and Swain (1995) in the context of tourism (see Table 1.1). Each of these phases will now be discussed in turn, with regard to their applicability to tourism research. It should be noted that while these frameworks are useful for demonstrating the tracts of thought development, the 'reality' of gender is of course much more complex, nuanced and interlinked with many other social facets.

3.1 Womanless phase: Invisibility of Women and Gender

The first of Henderson's five stages is the 'invisible' or 'womanless' scholarship phase. Here, tourism and tourism research are 'gender blind' (Warner-Smith, 2000, p. 33). This stage is reflected in many of the early sociological models expounded in the 1970s and 1980s, which assumed a universal (that is, white male) experience of travel. Women's voices – and certainly women of colour and other non-majority groups – were virtually non-existent. As a result, early sociological discourses of tourism and travel have been rightly criticized as 'male-centric' and Anglocentric, and ensured the ongoing invisibility of women (Aitchison, 1996; Veijola & Jokinen, 1994;).

The masculinized, heteronormative language used in other early academic tourism writings further contributed to women's invisibility. Male archetypal heroes such as the wandering Ulysses are put forward as representing the experiences of all tourists, as seen in Pearce's (1988) *The Ulysses Factor*. Ulysses is chosen as reflective of the traits of the modern tourist: 'he is a liar, he is arrogant, grasping, he bears grudges, and above all, he is self interested' (p. 226). Krippendorf (1997, p. 38) refers to the 'motives of the mobile leisure-*man*' (emphasis added). If gender and the sexed body are not made explicit in tourism studies, then the tourist remains masculine, white and dominant by default; women and other voices remain subsumed within the dominant male gaze and paradigm (Westwood, Pritchard & Morgan, 2000).

3.2 Compensatory Phase: Adding Women to Tourism Research

Henderson's next phase refers to 'compensatory' scholarship, also known as the 'add women and stir' stage. Here, research is predominantly male-defined but women are 'at least' acknowledged. In the compensatory phase, women may be added to research, but their perspectives are usually considered only as

Table 1.1 A revised framework of gender and tourism scholarship

Phase of Scholarship	Description	Application to Tourism Research
1st: Invisible/ Womanless	Men's experiences and perspectives are regarded as universal; women are not explicitly acknowledged and their experiences are subsumed under the male experience.	Dominant perspective in the early years of tourism's development as an academic field of study (starting around 1972). No studies addressing women or gender can be found in the tourism journals around this time.
2nd: Compensatory/'Add Women'	Otherwise known as the 'add women and stir' phase; mostly male-defined, but women are acknowledged, without reference to broader gendered contexts.	First articles specifically on women in tourism begin to appear, essentially 'adding' women (white women) to the discourse of tourism and travel. Considers women's perspectives only as relative to males e.g.: • Smith (1979): *Women: The taste-makers in tourism* • Zalatan (1998): *Wives' involvement in tourism decision processes*
3rd: Bifocal/Sex Differences	Emphasizes sex differences between men and women; again, usually without reference to wider gendered contexts.	Research which stresses descriptive differences between men and women's tourist behaviour. Again, women are seen as relative to men, e.g.: • Myers & Moncrief (1978): *Differential leisure travel decision-making between spouses* • Ryan, Henley & Soutar (1998): *Gender differences in tourism destination choice*
4th: Feminist/ Women-Centred	Women and their lives are the focus of research; feminist aims often clearly explicated (eg. women's oppression emphasized).	Tourism research starts to deliberately foreground women as tourists and hosts. Emergence of some gendered, feminist epistemologies and methodologies, e.g.: • Small (1999): *Memory work: A method for researching women's tourist experience'* • Bolles (1997): *Women as a category of analysis in scholarship on tourism*

Phase of Scholarship	Description	Application to Tourism Research
5th: New/Gender Scholarship	'Multifocal' and 'relational', moving beyond sole focus on women. Explores women's and men's experiences with a specific focus on socialization and gender relations.	Tourism research which examines both men's and women's perspectives, with the aim of positioning their experiences within a gendered lens: • Swain (1995): *Gender and tourism: Special edition of the Annals of Tourism Research* • Kinnaird & Hall (1994): *Tourism: A gender analysis*
6th: Critical Gender Scholarship	Gender is fluid, dynamic, changing. Intersectionality; critical, poststructural, post/anti colonial; transdisciplinary perspectives.	Critical tourism research critiques fixed and limited notions of gender, sexuality and identity; opens up multiple perspectives, opportunities and voices about the intersection of gender with culture, race, social and economic position, sexuality, femininities and masculinities; empowerment. Encourages feminist, critical, reflexive, alternative epistemologies, methodologies and methods e.g.: • Pritchard et al. (2007): *Tourism and gender: Embodiment, sensuality, and experience* • Chambers et al. (2017): *Interrogating gender and the tourism academy through an epistemological lens* • Figueroa-Domecq et al. (2015): *Tourism gender research: A critical accounting*

Notes: Adapted and extended Henderson (1994b) and supported by ideas from Aitchison (2001) and Swain (1995)

relative to men's (Henderson, 1994). In the late 1970s and into the 1980s, the first articles on women began to appear in the tourism literature, essentially 'adding' women to the discourse. Women as a topic of travel and tourism emerged most prominently, perhaps, through Valene Smith's (1979) paper, *Women: The taste-makers in tourism*'. A study conducted a decade later by Hawes (1988) discussed the travel-related profiles of older women. These types of studies considered women as a new and homogenous market segment, to which tourism marketers should pay heed (Bartos, 1989).

By extension, the compensatory style of tourism research is also seen when women's travel behaviour is described and singled out, but is still considered only in relation to their husbands, partners or families (e.g. Zalatan, 1998). While compensatory studies have at least mentioned and considered women's experience, they have not done much for furthering our understanding of the wider socio-cultural, gendered and political structures which result in women's subordination and which constrain their experience. As Deem (1995, p. 264) has noted in this context, 'taking gender seriously means much more than noticing the existence of women.'

3.3 Bifocal Phase: The Sex Differential in Tourism

Following on from the compensatory phase is the 'bifocal' stage, also referred to as the 'sex differences' or 'dichotomous difference' phase. Henderson (1994) identifies the bifocal phase as one that emphasizes chiefly the differences between the sexes with regard to leisure or travel behaviour. Perhaps one of the most prominent examples of the bifocal stage in tourism research is a study by Myers and Moncrief (1978) which compared the heteronormative travel decision-making behaviour of husbands and wives. In furthering the sex differential, Ryan, Henley and Soutar (1998), investigated the differences between men and women in tourism destination choice-making, while McGehee, Loker-Murphy and Uysal (1996) examined the difference in motivations between male and female pleasure travellers.

This pursuit for male–female difference becomes problematic for several reasons when examined from a feminist/gendered perspective. Firstly, merely noting differences between the sexes may be informative but ultimately cements the essentialist male/female dichotomy. Furthermore, such an approach may indirectly 'promote the status quo in that it usually ignores the different constraints and opportunities to which women and men are exposed' (Norris & Wall, 1994, p. 58). A second related problem is that when so-called differences are found, or not found, these results are not situated within the societal contexts which create them (Kinnaird & Hall, 2000; Swain, 1995). Sex difference research makes little real contribution to a true gendered understanding of any research or phenomenon, when not grounded in these wider contexts. Such perspectives only work to further fix essentialized notions of 'man' and 'woman' and stagnate gender research rather than advance it (Figueroa-Domecq et al., 2015). Tourism research today continues to limit and misappropriate the term 'gender' to studies which do not move beyond the biological sex differential (Small, Wilson, & Harris, 2015).

3.4 Women-Centred Phase: Emerging Feminist Contributions

The 'women-centred' or 'feminist' phase refers to research which 'examines the experiences of women not in relation to men necessarily but in an attempt to understand the importance and meaning of women's lives' (Henderson, 1994, p. 125). This fourth phase moves beyond both compensation and difference to investigate women specifically, and often more explicitly grounded within a feminist perspective. Here, issues of gender, embodiment and power are explored (Veijola & Jokinen, 1994), and tourism researchers increasingly acknowledge that they can 'take nothing for granted' and that 'knowledge is always situated and ... implicated in complex power relations' (Byrne & Lentin, 2000, p. 31).

Rather than merely 'adding' women to an already androcentric study, a number of studies emerging in the 1990s and 2000s, began to address women's experiences of tourism of their own accord, not merely in terms of how they were different from men (Fullagar, 2002; Gibson & Jordan, 1998; Harris & Ateljevic, 2003; Small, 1999). Assumptions are challenged about women's experiences being homogenous. Indeed, continuing to focus on women *only*, without paying attention to intra-sex differences or to women's relationships with men, has left some wondering if this has resulted in a 'ghettoization' of gender studies (Deem, 1999). To ensure a path out of this ghetto, researchers needed to incorporate new gendered and feminist theories and frameworks.

3.5 New Gender Phase: Gender-Aware Tourism Research

The fifth phase, referred to at the time as 'new' or 'gender scholarship', signifies a stage in which both women's and men's experiences are related to a broader societal context in an effort to create a richer picture of society and human behaviour. Gender scholarship signals a progression from mere observations about differences in sex, as exemplified in the bifocal phase, to analysis and interpretation of why gendered differences exist.

Three important works produced in the mid-1990s brought 'gender' issues to the forefront of the tourism research agenda. These were a literature synthesis prepared by Norris and Wall (1994) called *Gender and tourism*, a special edition on gender and tourism in the *'Annals of Tourism Research'*, edited by Margaret Byrne Swain (1995) and a book edited by Kinnaird and Hall (1994) titled *'Tourism: A Gender Analysis'*. While emphasising women's experience as producers and consumers of tourism, these publications also pointed to the interaction of gender with other important social factors, such as ethnicity, class and race.

Here, we see research on how tourists encounter the gendered travel experience, how they interact with host cultures and how they interact with other tourists (Dahles, 2002; Wilson & Little, 2005). There is also an emergence of research on 'gendered hosts', specifically shining a light on the inequities for women in tourism labour (e.g. Cukier, Norris & Wall, 1996; Momsen, 1994; Wilkinson & Pratiwi, 1995) or in sex tourism (Pritchard, 2001). This phase also saw a body of work on how tourism can enhance women's status and access to paid employment, creating a sense of empowerment and financial independence (Scheyvens, 2000; Swain, 1989).

3.6 Critical Gender Phase: Diversity and Intersectionality

We posit here a sixth phase, which encapsulates more contemporary thinking on gender and tourism. This stage sees a move well beyond second- and even third-wave feminist studies focussed solely on women (and primarily white, Western women), reflecting an increasingly critical, self-reflexive, diverse and intersectional approach. As Eger, Munar and Hsu (2022) argue, 'the marginalization of gender studies in tourism is generally due to the misconception of this field as dealing "only" with "women's issues"' (p. 1459). Embodying the 'critical turn' in tourism scholarship, which emerged in the early to mid-2000s (Ateljevic et al., 2005; Ateljevic et al., 2007; Pritchard et al., 2007; Wilson, Harris & Small, 2008), we see researchers recognizing gender as a complex, ever-changing, mutable concept, warranting ongoing critique and problematization. Studies of women are still important and central, but must be grounded in a wider socio-cultural, feminist, and political milieu, recognising multiple perspectives, sexualities, and positionalities.

In this phase, we hear voices from the Majority World, from people of colour and from diverse sexualities, contributing to a long overdue, largely overlooked body of scholarship. This work has highlighted the gaps inherent in existing gender tourism research, and the opportunities present to open up new ways of knowing and doing. Chambers and Rakić (2018) argue that 'tourism gender research has … failed to take sufficient account of the complex intersectionalities between gender and a host of identifications including race, class, sexuality and age' (p. 145). Scholars in this phase wish to articulate, rather than disarticulate, a full conceptualization of gender into the study of tourism (Figueroa-Domecq et al., 2015). Select examples emblematic of the critical gender phase are studies focusing on gender in the tourism academy (Chambers et al., 2017; Figueroa-Domecq et al., 2015; Khoo-Lattimore et al., 2019; Nunkoo et al., 2020); gender, employment and enterprize (Figueroa-Domecq et al., 2020; Pritchard, 2017); gender and sustainable tourism (Alarcón & Cole, 2019; Eger, Munar, & Hsu, 2022; Ferguson, 2011); gender-based violence and the tourist experience (Devine & Ojeda, 2017; Vizcaino, Jeffrey, & Eger, 2020); LGBTQI+ perspectives (Ong, Vorobjovas-Pinta, & Lewis, 2020; Waitt & Markwell, 2006); and masculinities in tourism (Thurnell-Read & Casey, 2015).

This phase also sees scholars actively engaging with and drawing important insights from feminist epistemologies, reflexive positioning, post- and anti-colonial studies, alternative methodologies, non- and anti-positivist methods, and different ways of writing (Bakas, 2017; Chambers, 2007; Chambers et al., 2017; Wilson & Hollinshead, 2015). Through all of this is the central recognition of gender, not just as a category or field of study, but as an awareness and position that is taken throughout the entire research process, 'from the conception of the idea and the proposal of the objectives, to the choice of methodology, analysis and interpretation of the results and their publication' (Figueroa-Domecq & Segovia-Perez, 2020, p. 265).

In summary, this section has outlined six active and interlinking phases of gender scholarship in tourism. We recognize that such stages cannot necessarily be moved through or experienced in any neat, progressive or even chronological way. For example, some of what might be called the 'earlier' phases are still in effect in tourism research today (Pritchard et al, 2007; Pritchard & Morgan, 2017). Furthermore, we know the story of gender and tourism scholarship is ongoing, and there are other phases waiting to be added and voices to be heard. There is still work to do in moving towards a critical, gender-aware scholarship that recognizes the full plurality of gender in tourism. We hope this book contributes to this exploration, where scholars continue to research gender in tourism from multiple vantage points, contexts and perspectives.

4. About This Book

The following nine chapters reflect contemporary thinking on gender and tourism, with a lens on how gender will shape – and be shaped by – tourism now and into the future. In the call for submissions, we actively sought contributions and voices from Black, Indigenous, Latinx, Majority World and LGBTQI+ scholars, as well as from research students and those at early stages of their academic careers. While grounded in the context of tourism, we welcomed proposals from scholars outside of the tourism studies field, aiming for a book that genuinely reflects a collaboration of diverse and inclusive voices.

A diverse set of contributions by seventeen authors was received, reflecting key themes in the contemporary research agenda for gender and tourism.

This book is organized around these three core – but not exhaustive – areas of inquiry, namely:

- Part I: Gender and tourism: theory, analysis and review;
- Part II: Gender, tourism and work;
- Part III: Gendered tourism experiences;

Part I underscores the vital role of gendered analyses and review in any research agenda, and more specifically, how we might theorize and think differently about gender and tourism. In *Chapter 2*, Helene Pristed Nielsen critiques and explores the role of islands and 'islandness' in the tourism imaginary. Pristed Nielsen engages us in a critical chronology of islands as political, social, colonialized and gendered tourism spaces. Drawing on the somewhat disparate fields of island studies, feminist geography and island feminism, she takes a 'feminist-and-islandness' lens to link the literature on islands, gender and tourism. Here, she rejects strait-jacketed and overly exoticized notions of islands as 'separate', calling for new, intersectional analyses of gender, power, sexuality and race in our study of islands and tourism. Pristed Nielsen's chapter also exemplifies the methodological opportunities in studies of gender and tourism, and the importance of scholars in 'opening up' our assumptions about place and space.

Perhaps not surprisingly, COVID-19 features prominently in some of the chapters, revealing the very gendered impacts of the pandemic. In *Chapter 3*, Elaine Chiao Ling Yang shines much-needed light on the invisibility of migrant women in tourism work, advocating for a 'syndemic' agenda for gender and tourism research: that is, the synergies between social and cultural inequalities and the impacts of the pandemic. Yang specifically explores the gendered nature of hospitality during the pandemic, in an industry reliant on high numbers of casualized, migrant and often marginalized workers. Through a critical analysis of Australian newspaper articles, Yang exposes a gendered 'paper ceiling' in media representations, showing how the pandemic has merely exacerbated the precarious conditions of hospitality work. The analysis reveals that migrant women are 'framed' variously as victims, change agents, or threats. This chapter underscores the already existing inequalities of women in hospitality, and the significant power of news discourse in shaping public thought.

Jess Sanggyeong Je and Elaine Chiao Ling Yang conduct an analysis of gender equity reporting in *Chapter 4*. Specifically, they highlight the emergence of sustainability reporting (SR), beyond an environmental focus to include issues of society, culture, economy and gender. As Je and Yang demonstrate, little research has explored how tourism companies measure, disclose, and communicate gender equality performance. Their study investigates gender equality initiatives through an examination of SR based on the publicly available documents of 32 tourism companies. Despite women constituting more than half of the tourism workforce, their findings show that tourism corporations have substandard SR, suggesting that gender equality has not yet been reached or mainstreamed in tourism organizations.

In *Chapter 5*, Rafiah Almathami and Judith Mair use a systematic literature review (SLR) to outline the body of knowledge on women in the Saudi Arabian tourism and entertainment sector. At present, Saudi women make up a very small part of the Saudi tourism sector; the authors demonstrate how traditional, Muslim cultural values can work to limit Saudi women's ability to participate in the workforce. Their analysis reveals the challenges of conducting SLRs in areas with very little published research, showing only a handful of articles which assessed female participation in the Saudi tourism context. Almathami and Mair's ensuing discussion contributes to an enhanced cross-cultural understanding of gender issues for women in the Saudi Arabian workplace providing future research directions to aid empowerment of women in tourism.

Part II explores the enduring and ever-shifting intersections among gender, tourism and work. In *Chapter 6*, Seyedasaad Hosseini, Abolfazl Siyamiyan Gorji, Rafael Cortés Macías, and Fernando Almeida Garcíareturn to the themes of power and empowerment featuring in this volume, but this time from an Islamic perspective. Here, they discuss the role and agency of Iranian women in tourism, exploring the barriers for women in the country's tourism and hospitality industry. Hosseini and his colleagues outline some of the religious and cultural expectations for Muslim women in Iran, and how this has led to lower participation of many Muslim women in the tourism industry. The authors then discuss the findings of fifteen in-depth interviews with Iranian women working in tourism, which reveal a range of societal, attitudinal and organizational barriers to their career advancement. While these constraints are discussed, so too are the ways these women find empowerment and continue to challenge traditional, male-dominated norms in an Iranian context.

In *Chapter 7*, Sandeep Basnyat and Pau Ka (Carmen) Munstay with the research agenda of tourism employment and women, but this time in the context of hotel work in Macao, China. As in the previous chapter, we see the realities of an industry highly dependent on migrant workers, often precarious work conditions and 'round-the-clock' expectations, the brunt of which are felt increasingly by shift-working women. Basnyat and Mun look closely at the concept and developing nature of shift-work, and then present the stories of twenty-three qualitative interviews with female migrants working in Macao's luxury hotels. The social, physical and mental challenges of shift work are discussed, as the women undertake work away from home for long periods of time, while having to navigate the gendered responsibilities both at work and at home.

Further exploring the gendered impacts of COVID-19, *Chapter 8* presents a study of women's tourism work in the context of Colombia. Here, Claudia Becerra-Gualdrón, Karolina Doughty and Margreet van der Burg traverse the intersections among gender, tourism work and power in the city of San Gil, a region that has been highly dependent on adventure tourism income. Drawing on empowerment theory, Becerra-Gualdrón and her colleagues interview nineteen women working in the Colombian tourism industry, on how the pandemic has impacted their lives, and informed by their respective labour positions. While negative impacts such as loss of income were experienced, and existing gendered role expectations exacerbated, this chapter's research demonstrates how women can enact agency and power even in the face of an unfolding pandemic.

Part III focuses on specific gendered experiences of tourism, encompassing perspectives of gender-based violence for field researchers and women conference attendees. In *Chapter 9*, Heike Schänzel and Brooke Porter call for an agenda that draws attention to gender-based violence in the context of academic fieldwork – a largely overlooked and underdiscussed matter in many fields, but particularly so in tourism. Building on their previous work on 'femininities in the field', here the authors interview thirteen women academics about their fieldwork experiences. What is common across these stories is their encountering of unwanted attention, the male gaze, and sexual harassment. Speaking from a diverse range of perspectives and backgrounds, these women describe the emotional and physical impacts of gender-based violence and risk-taking in the (tourism) field. Schänzel and Porter offer a number of gendered strategies that can help support women's safety and wellbeing, and put these aspects at the forefront of tourism research discussions.

Elspeth Frew and Judith Mair delve into the experiences of female academics in *Chapter 10*, exemplifying the empowering role of friendship for women attending research conferences. Conferences can play a vital role in advancing academic careers, but little research has documented the gendered experience and impacts of such events. Drawing on a conceptual model centred on social capital, and taking a novel duoethnographic approach, Frew and Mair use their own dialogue to demonstrate how important their friendship – experienced through their interactions of attending academic tourism conferences over some fifteen years – has been in both their personal and professional lives. Their study reveals the critical, and largely undocumented, role of shared identity, solidarity and support offered by academic friendships, and how important these are to women's careers. Frew and Mair also advocate for further collaborative and gendered methodologies in tourism research.

5. Conclusion

In the final contribution to this book, Donna and Erica reflect in *Chapter 11* on what has been achieved so far in the study of gender and tourism, while looking forward to what can be further discussed, activated and celebrated. As critical, feminist researchers, and with the responsibility as editors of this book, we recognize the diversity, fluidity and complexity of 'gender'. We feel it important to keep moving beyond fixed notions of gender, woman, man, sexuality – and even 'tourism' and the 'tourist'. We hope to continually expand our own knowledge and understanding and to encourage others' expansion through books such as this, and in ongoing critiques of gender in the context of tourism.

These uncertain times also bring hope and opportunity for change, dialogue and greater understanding. In putting forward this research agenda for gender and tourism, we do so on the groundwork and great thinking of other scholars before us. We are alive to both the challenges and opportunities, and the roles and responsibilities, we have in imagining a different, better, more empowered, and more equitable (gendered) tourism world.

References

Aitchison, C. (1996). Patriarchal paradigms and the politics of pedagogy: A framework for a feminist analysis of leisure and tourism studies. *World Leisure and Recreation, 38*(4), 38–40.

Aitchison, C. (2001). Gender and leisure research: The 'codification of knowledge'. *Leisure Sciences, 23*(1), 1–19.

Aitchison, C. (2005). Feminist and gender perspectives in tourism studies: The social-cultural nexus of critical and cultural theories. *Tourist Studies, 5*(3), 207–24.

Alarcón, D.M. & Cole, S. (2019). No sustainability for tourism without gender equality. *Journal of Sustainable Tourism, 27*(7) 903–19.

Arday, J. & Mirza, H.S. (eds). (2018). *Dismantling race in higher education: Racism, whiteness and decolonising the academy*. London: Palgrave Macmillan.

Ateljevic, I., Harris, C., Wilson, E. & Leo Collins, F. (2005). Getting 'entangled': Reflexivity and the 'critical turn' in tourism studies. *Tourism Recreation Research, 30*(2), 9–21.

Ateljevic, I., Morgan, N. & Pritchard, A. (eds) (2007). *The critical turn in tourism studies: Innovative research methodologies*. Oxford and Amsterdam: Elsevier.

Bakas, F.E. (2017). A 'beautiful mess': Reciprocity and positionality in gender and tourism research. *Journal of Hospitality and Tourism Management, 33*, 126–33.

Bartos, R. (1989). *Marketing to women around the world*. Boston: Harvard Business School.

Bolles, A.L. (1997). Women as a category of analysis in scholarship on tourism: Jamaican women and tourism employment. In E. Chambers (ed.), *Tourism and culture: An applied perspective* (pp. 77–92). New York: State University of New York.

Byrne, A., & Lentin, R. (2000). *(Re)searching women: Feminist research methodologies in the social sciences in Ireland*. Dublin: Institute of Public Administration.

Chambers, D. (2007). Interrogating the 'critical' in critical approaches to tourism research. In I. Ateljevic, N. Morgan & A. Pritchard (eds), *The critical turn in tourism studies: Innovative research methodologies* (pp. 105–19). Oxford and Amsterdam: Elsevier.

Chambers, D. and Rakić, T. (2018). Critical considerations on gender and tourism: An introduction. *Tourism, Culture and Communication, 18*(1), 1–8.

Chambers, D., Munar, A.M., Khoo-Lattimore, C. & Biran, A. (2017). Interrogating gender and the tourism academy through an epistemological lens. *Anatolia, 28*(4), 501–13.

Cukier, J., Norris, J. & Wall, G. (1996). The involvement of women in the tourism industry of Bali, Indonesia. *Journal of Development Studies, 33*(2), 248–70.

Curthoys, A. (1994). Australian feminism since 1970. In N. Grieve & A. Burns (eds), *Australian women: Contemporary feminist thought* (pp. 14–28). Melbourne: Oxford University Press.

Dahles, H. (2002). Gigolos and rastamen: Tourism, sex, and changing gender identities. In M.B. Swain & J. Henshall Momsen (eds), *Gender/tourism/fun?* (pp. 180–94). New York: Cognizant Communication.

de Beauvoir, S. (1949/1989). *The second sex* (H.M. Parshley, trans.). New York: Vintage (Original work published in France, 1949).

Deem, R. (1995). Feminism and leisure studies. In C. Critcher, P. Bramham & A. Tomlinson (eds), *Sociology of leisure* (pp. 256–68). London: E & FN Spon.

Deem, R. (1999). How do we get out of the ghetto? Strategies for research on gender and leisure for the twenty-first century. *Leisure Studies, 18*(3), 161–77.

Devine, J. & Ojeda, D. (2017). Violence and dispossession in tourism development: A critical geographical approach. *Journal of Sustainable Tourism, 25*(5), 605–17.

Eger, C., Munar, A.M. & Hsu, C. (2022). Gender and tourism sustainability. *Journal of Sustainable Tourism, 30*(7), 1459–75.

Ferguson, L. (2011). Promoting gender equality and empowering women? Tourism and the third Millennium Development Goal. *Current Issues in Tourism, 14*(3), 235–49.

Figueroa-Domecq, C., Pritchard, A., Segovia-Perez, M., Morgan, N. & Villace-Molinero, T. (2015). Tourism gender research: A critical accounting. *Annals of Tourism Research, 52*, 87–103.

Figueroa-Domecq, C. & Segovia-Perez, M. (2020). Application of a gender perspective in tourism research: A theoretical and practical approach. *Journal of Tourism Analysis [Revista De Analisis Turistico], 27*(2), 251–70.

Figueroa-Domecq, C., de Jong, A. & Williams, A.M. (2020). Gender, tourism & entrepreneurship: A critical review. *Annals of Tourism Research, 84*, 1–13.

Fullagar, S. (2002). Narratives of travel: Desire and the movement of feminine subjectivity. *Leisure Studies, 21*(1), 57–74.

Gibson, H. & Jordan, F. (1998, 26–30 October). *Shirley Valentine lives! The experiences of solo women travellers.* Paper presented at the Fifth congress of the World Leisure and Recreation Association, Sao Paulo, Brazil.

Gregory, A. (2022). Covid has intensified gender inequalities, global study finds. *Guardian*, 2 March. https:// www .theguardian .com/ world/ 2022/ mar/ 02/ covid -intensified -existing -gender -inequalities -global -study -finds (accessed 30 April 2022).

Hall, D., Swain, M. & Kinnaird, V. (2003). Tourism and gender: An evolving agenda. *Tourism Recreation Research, 28*(2), 7–11.

Harris, C. & Ateljevic, I. (2003). Perpetuating the male gaze as the norm: Challenges for 'her' participation in business travel. *Tourism Recreation Research, 28*(2), 21–30.

Hawes, D. K. (1988). Travel-related lifestyle profiles of older women. *Journal of Travel Research, 28*(2), 22–31.

Henderson, K.A. (1994). Perspectives on analyzing gender, women and leisure. *Journal of Leisure Research, 26*(2), 119–37.

Khoo-Lattimore, C., Yang, C. & Je, S. (2019). Assessing gender representation in knowledge production: A critical analysis of UNWTO's planned events. *Journal of Sustainable Tourism,27*(7), 920–38.

Kinnaird,V. & Hall, D. (eds) (1994). *Tourism: A gender analysis.* Chichester: John Wiley and Sons.

Kinnaird, V. & Hall, D. (2000). Theorizing gender in tourism research. *Tourism Recreation Research, 25*(1), 71–84.

Krippendorf, J. (1997). The motives of the mobile leisureman: Travel between norm, promise and hope. In L. France (ed.), *The Earthscan reader in sustainable tourism* (pp. 38–53). London: Earthscan.

Lather, P. (1991). *Getting smart: Feminist research and pedagogy with/in the postmodern.* New York: Routledge.

McGehee, N.G., Loker-Murphy, L. & Uysal, M. (1996). The Australian international pleasure travel market: Motivations from a gendered perspective. *Journal of Tourism Studies, 7*(1), 45–57.

Momsen, J.H. (1994). Tourism, gender and development in the Caribbean. In V. Kinnaird & D. Hall (eds), *Tourism: A gender analysis* (pp. 106–20). Chichester: John Wiley and Sons.

Myers, P.B. & Moncrief, L.W. (1978). Differential leisure travel decision-making between spouses. *Annals of Tourism Research, 5*(1), 157–65.

Norris, J., & Wall, G. (1994). Gender and tourism. *Progress in Tourism, Recreation and Hospitality Management, 6*, 57-78.

Nunkoo, R., Thelwall, M., Ladsawut, J. & Goolaup, S. (2020). Three decades of tourism scholarship: Gender, collaboration and research methods. *Tourism Management, 78*, 1–11.

Oakley, A. (1972). *Sex, gender and society.* London: Maurice Temple Smith.

Ong, F., Vorobjovas-Pinta, O. & Lewis, C. (2020). LGBTIQ+ identities in tourism and leisure research: A systematic qualitative literature review. *Journal of Sustainable Tourism, 30*(7), 1476–99.
Pearce, P.L. (1988). *The Ulysses factor: Evaluating visitors in tourist settings.* New York: Springer-Verlag.
Pritchard, A. (2001). Tourism and representation: A scale for measuring gendered portrayals. *Leisure Studies, 20*(2), 79–94.
Pritchard, A. (2017). Predicting the next decade of tourism gender research. *Tourism Management Perspectives, 25,* 144–6.
Pritchard, A., & Morgan, N. (2017). Tourism's lost leaders: Analyzing gender and performance. *Annals of Tourism Research, 63 (March),* 34–47.
Pritchard, A., Morgan, N., Ateljevic, I. & Harris, C. (eds) (2007). *Tourism and gender: Embodiment, sensuality, and experience.* Oxfordshire: CABI.
Ryan, M., Henley, N. & Soutar, G. (1998). *Gender differences in tourism destination choice: Some implications for tourism marketers.* Paper presented at the Australia and New Zealand Marketing Academy Conference, Dunedin, New Zealand.
Scheyvens, R. (2000). Promoting women's empowerment through involvement in ecotourism: Experiences from the Third World. *Journal of Sustainable Tourism, 8*(3), 232–49.
Schneider, H. (2020). U.S. labor shock from pandemic hit women of color hardest; will it persist? Reuters, 5 October. https://www.reuters.com/article/us-great-reboot-data-idUSKBN26Q1LR (accessed 2 May 2022).
Small, J. (1999). Memory-work: A method for researching women's tourist experiences. *Tourism Management, 20*(1), 25–35.
Small, J., Harris, C. & Wilson, E. (2017). Gender on the agenda? The position of gender in tourism's high-ranking journals. *Journal of Hospitality and Tourism Management, 31,* 114–17.
Small, J., Harris, C. &Wilson, E.(2017),Gender in tourism's high ranking journals. *Journal of Hospitality and Tourism Management.* 31: 114–117.
Smith, V.L. (1979). Women: The taste-makers in tourism. *Annals of Tourism Research,* 6, 49–60.
Swain, M.B. (1989). Gender roles in indigenous tourism: Kuna Mola, Kuna Yala and cultural survival. In V.L. Smith (ed.), *Hosts and guests: The anthropology of tourism* (2nd edn, pp. 83–104). Philadelphia, PA: University of Pennsylvania Press.
Swain, M.B. (1995). Introduction: Gender in tourism. *Annals of Tourism Research, 22*(2), 247–66.
Thurnell-Read, T. & Casey, M. (eds) (2015). *Men, masculinities, travel and tourism.* London: Palgrave Macmillan.
Veijola, S. & Jokinen, E. (1994). The body in tourism. *Theory, Culture and Society, 11*(3), 125–51.
Vizcaino, P., Jeffrey, H. & Eger, C. (eds) (2020). *Tourism and gender-based violence: Challenging inequalities.* Oxfordshire: CABI.
Waitt, G. & Markwell, K. (2006). *Gay tourism: Culture and context.* Haworth Hospitality.
Warner-Smith, P. (2000). Travel, young women and 'The Weekly', 1956–1968. *Annals of Leisure Research, 3,* 33–46.
Westwood, S., Pritchard, A. & Morgan, N.J. (2000). Gender-blind marketing: Businesswomen's perceptions of airline services. *Tourism Management, 21,* 353–62.
Wilkinson, P.F. & Pratiwi, W. (1995). Gender and tourism in an Indonesian village. *Annals of Tourism Research, 22*(2), 283–99.

Wilson, E. & Hollinshead, K. (2015). Qualitative tourism research: Opportunities in the emergent soft sciences. *Annals of Tourism Research, 54*, 30–47.
Wilson, E. & Little, D.E. (2005). A 'relative escape'? The impact of constraints on women who travel solo. *Tourism Review International, 9*(2), 155–75.
Wilson, E., Harris, C. & Small, J. (2008). Furthering critical approaches in tourism and hospitality studies: Perspectives from Australia and New Zealand. *Journal of Hospitality and Tourism Management, 15*, 15–18.
Zalatan, A. (1998). Wives' involvement in tourism decision processes. *Annals of Tourism Research, 25*(4), 890–903.

PART I

Gender and tourism: theory, analysis and review

2 Theorising gender and tourism in island locations

Helene Pristed Nielsen

1. Introduction: The Lure of Islands

Islands have always fascinated the imagination (Gillis, 2007). An important aspect of this fascination has to do with the idea that 'islands suggest themselves as *tabulae rasae*: potential laboratories for any conceivable human project, in thought or in action. There is something about the insular that beckons specificity, greater malleability, less inhibition' (Baldacchino, 2006, pp. 5–6). For similar reasons, islands also seem to fascinate the tourist imagination. Thompson (2006) describes how already from the 1890s, the emerging British tourism industry engaged in a conscious effort to transform and visually promote the islands of the Caribbean 'into spaces of touristic desire for British and North American traveling publics' (p. 4).

Reviewing the very first paragraph above as first and foremost a gender researcher, my attention is drawn to descriptions such as 'malleable', 'uninhibited' and 'spaces of desire'. This suggests to me that islands as generic phenomena warrant further theorising as places of gendered encounters between tourists and residents. Thus, rather than focusing on empirical evidence of such encounters (although I will employ a few examples to illustrate some points), the focus of this chapter is on theorising the relationship between gender and tourism specifically *in island locations*. This does not mean that I propose we should not theorize the links between gender and tourism in other types of location, but simply that I propose that island locations (especially small island locations) throw up some particular aspects about gender, place and social encounters which warrant further theorising. Before proceeding, it is important to emphasize that I do not wish to offer a precise definition of smallness; indeed, 'there are no scientific dividing lines or thresholds defining the size of a small island' (Nimführ & Otto, 2021, p. 43). Islands worldwide represent an incredible geographic heterogeneity (Gaini & Pristed Nielsen, 2020; Royle, 2007), and Nimführ and Otto (2021) suggest that smallness should be considered something both produced and acted out, and as relating to both demography and geography, but also politics and social spaces.

I embark on my argument for the need to theorize gender and tourism specifically in island locations, because I fundamentally agree with Gillis (2007) that islands are 'good to think with' (p. 285). One reason being that they are defined as 'a piece of land completely surrounded by water' (*Oxford English Dictionary*, 2018). What is special about islands

> is that they are, as physical entities delimited by water, [which] may impose severe material constrains on local life while providing prospects for journeys abroad. At the same time, their territorial circumscription makes them distinguishable places of origin and, hence, possible sources of identification and belonging within wider contexts of life (Olwig, 2007, pp. 271–2).

This means that in most cases, it is possible to easily identify whether or not something is or is not on the island, whether something 'belongs' there. This makes parameters for empirical investigation easier to identify – at least in theory. However, as Eriksen (1993) argues, islands are not necessarily more isolated than other places, and all human societies are, to varying degrees, in contact with other societies (p. 144). Therefore, it would be misleading to consider links from islands to the outside world as 'extrasystemic links, as not forming part of the relevant social unit' (Eriksen, 1993, p. 134). On the contrary, as he demonstrates through the example of Mauritius, the fact of contact with the outside world is often – and has historically often been – a defining feature of island societies. Today, encounters with tourists arguably constitute one such defining feature of Mauritius, as the island's 1.265 million inhabitants welcomed just below 1.4 million tourists from abroad in 2018, prior to the pandemic (World Bank, 2021a, 2021b).

The aim of this chapter is to present some theoretical considerations about the relationship between gender and tourism, and why this relationship is particularly important to consider in the case of island tourism. I start with a generic discussion of the relationship between 'Tourism, gender and place', which is partly inspired by Swain's assertion that 'Tourism … is built of human relations, and thus impacts and is impacted by global and local gender relations' (1995, p. 247). This recognition is then coupled with traditions from feminist geography, where gendered analyses of global and local relations have been a stable element for some time. Yet, according to Karides (2017), gendered analyses of the importance of local places have largely been neglected in island studies literature. This is why the third section proceeds to discuss 'Tourism, gender and island places'. Here I draw on Karides (2017) in arguing for an intersectional approach to studying tourism in island locations, including aspects such as gender, sexuality, coloniality, tourist versus resident bodies, together with 'islandness' (Baldacchino, 2004). Having presented my theoretical argument, I proceed in the fourth section to sketch some 'Methodological implications' for how to approximate more holistic analyses of tourism in island places. By way of illustration, the chapter ends with a few 'Empirical considerations', where I – admittedly – cherrypick a few examples which may hopefully inspire tourism researchers undertaking empirical studies in island locations to co-consider both gender (and other intersecting social identities) and 'islandness' in their work.

2. Tourism, Gender and Place

The chapter builds from the premise that 'all parts of the tourism experience are grounded in, and influenced by, our collective understanding of the social construction of gender' (Kinnaird & Hall, 2000, p. 71). Kinnaird and Hall point to three implications of this insight: (1) all processes involved in tourism are constructed out of gendered societies; (2) it is important to consider gender relations as dynamic and able to be redefined over time; (3) power relations within processes of tourism are significant, and considering gender when analysing such power relations can provide important tools in understanding the nature and consequences of the relationships between tourism development and social processes (2000, p. 71). Xu (2018) echoes similar points, arguing that 'tourism itself is a product of gendered societies, and its processes are gendered in their construction, presentation, and consumption' (p. 721), furthermore adding that 'tourism development and gender equality are very much contextualized in social, economic, and political relationships' (p. 722). Therefore, a critical approach to contexts for tourism development, and the inherent power relations within the respective contexts, are important for several reasons, among these that 'the marketing of tourism-related activities has the potential to reinforce stereotypical roles for women and men' (Kinnaird & Hall, 2000, p. 75).

Overall, and as also witnessed through the publication of the present book, there is a growing recognition from tourism studies that gender constitutes an important analytic lens through which to view tourism and its effects on (interactions between) both residents and guests, as well as destinations. Fundamentally, tourism is about bodies moving from 'here' to 'there', from 'home' to 'away'. This is captured in what Leiper (1979, pp. 396–7) termed 'the geographical elements' in tourism, and which Saarinen and Varnajot

(2019) refer to as 'the spatial perspective on tourism'. Understanding tourism as involving spatial mobility entails that 'touristic behaviors cannot happen without public spaces, which include travel spaces and destinations. Public spaces are not innocuous and objectively defined, but rather, they are politicized, sexualized, subjective, and gendered' (Xu, 2018, p. 723). This point closely resembles key insights from feminist geography, where Massey has raised the point that we need to critically engage with 'the tendency to romanticise public space as an emptiness which enables free and equal speech [and] not take on board the need to theorize space as the product of social relations which are most likely conflicting and unequal' (Massey, 2005, p. 152). Feminist geographers have argued that gender relations both reflect and affect the spatial organization of society, and they have been particularly preoccupied with spatial constructions of femininity and masculinity, reaching the conclusion that 'spaces and places are experienced differently by different people, and come to be associated with presence or absence of different groups of people' (Nelson & Seager, 2005, p. 15). Such gendered analyses of spaces and places have been a stable element in feminist geography for some time, and Xu (2018) suggests it as being in its infancy within tourism studies.

Cresswell (1996) points out that there are different perceptions of what is considered socially acceptable in specific places and for specific bodies. Dominant ideas exist about what is acceptable (in place) and what is not acceptable (not in place) in a given place and in a given context and performed by a given body (Cresswell, 1996). Gender is a prominent dimension in these experiences, and the same applies to other socially differentiating factors such as age, class, bodily abilities, ethnicity, sexuality, etc. Futhermore, Cresswell points out how moving between different places can alter conditions for acceptability and perceptions of bodily performance, and hence alter the individual's social standing – a point which surely applies to tourism studies. Mills (1996, 2005) discusses gender and colonial space in a British context, arguing that colonial space troubled some of the binaries of imperial Britiain, allowing for new 'contact zones' to emerge. She points out how female British travellers in the colonies in particular were able to transgress spatial relations, in some cases travelling as 'honorary men' (Mills, 1996, p. 140). The overall argument is that we tend to have expectations about behaviour that relate a particular social position to actions in particular places, but movement through space can alter both social position and expectations about behaviour. This is related to Shields's ideas about space as being 'causative':

> Rather than 'a cause' the spatial is *causative*. Spatialization has a mediating effect because it represents the contingent juxtaposition of social and economic forces, forms of social organization, and constraints of the natural world and so on. But as

> 'a cause', in and of itself, it plays no role for it is not a locus of causal forces. Human agents have causal power (Shields, 1991, p. 57, emphasis in original).

As I proceed to argue, tourism (conceived of as a phenomenon whereby human agents move through space and hence contribute to new juxtapositions of social and economic forces) is a force which (when analysed with attention to forms of social organization and constraints of the natural world) may bring to attention the causative effects of space.

3. Tourism, Gender and Island Places

Emerging in the early 1990s (Grydehøj, 2017, p. 4), 'Island Studies' is a relatively recent academic field of interest, which is centred around 'the study of islands on their own terms' (McCall, 1996, p. 76). The relevance of island studies has been proposed along the argument that islands, small ones in particular, are distinct sites which often harbour extreme renditions of more general processes, hence warranting their relevance as subjects and objects of academic inquiry (Baldacchino, 2006, p. 9). Baldacchino uses the term 'islandness', which he proposes as 'an intervening variable that does not determine, but contours and conditions physical and social events in distinct, and distinctly relevant, ways' (Baldacchino, 2004, p. 278). Still undergoing rapid development and maturation, one recently emerging debate within island studies is how feminist approaches may contribute to deepen and refine analyses of social processes in island locations. Such social processes include those fuelled by tourism (whether by its presence, absence or the local characteristics of such tourism).

The clarion call for island studies to engage with feminism came from Karides. In her seminal article 'Why island feminism?', Karides (2017) presents the concept of 'island feminism' as a theoretical orientation that understands islands on their own terms while drawing from feminisms of intersectionality, geography, (post)coloniality and queer theory (p. 31). She argues for the relavance of this approach by pointing out that 'although places and spaces are gendered, oriented by sexuality regimes, class and racial hierarchies, and sculpted by coloniality and national status, Island Studies scholarship barely has considered how life and opportunities on islands and between islands are shaped by these factors' (Karides, 2017, p. 30). In response to this absence, 'Island feminism is offered as a synergistic perspective to enable critical analysis of the social inequalities and sexuality regimes within and across islands' (p. 30). Karides now speaks about 'island feminisms' in the plural, explaining that 'I have shifted from island feminism to the plural, island feminisms, to account for the range of feminisms as they are enacted across island regions' (p. 42).

Karides (2020) proposes that a feminist lens is particularly important when attempting to understand processes of social differentiation and emergence of new economic and social opportunities in island locations. Tying this in with the notion of the spatial as 'causative', we might argue that islands are causative spaces in particular ways, insofar as their boundaries are clearly marked by natural borders at the water's edge. In such locations, the arrival and departure of tourist bodies contribute to new juxtapositions of human agents, and therefore new constellations of social and economic forces. Obviously, any location and its attendant social relations will be marked by the arrival and departure of new human agents. But the argument about 'islandness' as an intervening variable which brings heightened attention to the geographic boundaries of the location in question may enhance attention to the causative effects of spatial co-constellation of human agents.

However, so far, I have yet to encounter any research explicitly engaging with tourism and gender while taking islandness as an intervening variable (a few examples which come close are discussed at the end of the chapter). Interestingly, Kinnaird and Hall (2000) include a discussion about 'rurality' in their article 'Theorizing gender in tourism research'. I would argue that some of the points they make could be relevant also for island locations. They refer to studies of tourist endeavours into the 'rural British idyll' which conclude that tourism in such places sometimes contributes to legitimize social hierarchies both at home and in the host community. This potential 'conservative' effect of tourism is related to another dynamic of tourism development described by Kinnaird and Hall (2000):

> global tourism derives its legitimation from the tourists' quest for cultural variation, which confirms the validity of local cultures and their differences. Globalization therefore requires emerging local particularisms to be legitimated in western terms. Places that become tourist destinations have to compare themselves to the tastes of their visitors. This may imply a cultural revival, the construction and accentuation of the 'authentic' and the invention of tradition (p. 75).

Such a quest for 'authenticity' more often than not tends to tightly script gender roles and expressions of sexuality, limiting them within confines of the imaginations of tourism developers and other powers that be. When such tight scripts develop, I argue, the fact of living in an already tightly scripted place (completely surrounded by water) may accentuate the conservative effects of any search for 'authenticity'.

Mills (2005) acknowledges the role of specific topographies in negotiating space, gender and colonial relations. She argues that spatial relations involve 'a complex negotiation between the physical setting itself – the architecture, topography, and the way they are coded in relation to power – and the types of behaviours that we image are appropriate to that context' (2005, p. 4). However, she is not preoccuped with spatial relations on islands in particular, but with colonial space more generally (quite of lot of which, of course, is exactly islands). Furthermore, while Mills (2005) does speak of contact zones 'where the colonised and colonising culture mutually influence each other's norms and values' (p. 29), her main empirical focus is on travel accounts (both autobiographical and fictional) by female British travellers in British colonies. The spatial negotiations she is thus able to document primarily relate to how these women were able to bend the rules of gendered spatial arrangements in the British colonies. This, however, did not necessarily entail greater room for negotiation of space among the local residents. Mills (2005) points out how the British women travellers by and large produced knowledge about the colonies which promoted 'a view of the world that saw European activities as essentially civilising' (p. 95), hence reaffirming or superimposing British norms.

One powerful medium through which processes of reaffirming or superimposing norms and 'authenticity' can happen is through photography. Thompson (2006) engages in a critical examination of what she terms 'the tropicalization' of the Caribbean: 'Tropicalization ... describes the complex visual systems through which the islands were imaged for tourist consumption and the social and political implications of these representations on actual physical space on the islands and their inhabitants' (p. 5). One actual physical change she mentions is the introduction of new plants considered more 'picturesque' by tourism developers. Such plants were literally introduced, for example, to Jamaica, for the sole purpose of being able to take pictures of local residents in 'picturesque' (in the British tourist imagination) surroundings (Thompson, 2006). Mills (2005) also remarks how British notions of 'the picturesque' involve 'a studied ignorance of the contexts of the objects described' (p. 92). As Thompson's example illustrates, any notion of 'authenticity' in visual media can be rendered an object of suspicion and hence warrant critical analysis. Thompson explains how 'These photographs of the islands, created and circulated by tourism promoters, generated what the sociologist Rob Shields (1991) defines as a "place-image", a set of core representations that form "a widely disseminated and commonly held set of images of a place or space"' (p. 69 in Thompson, 2006, p. 5).

Up against such 'commonly held sets of images' about places, feminist geographers call upon us to engage in critical examinations of why and how these images have become 'commonly held' and which power constellations have contributed to their (contemporary) solidification. In this vein, Massey (2005) calls on us to analyse places as constellations of processes rather than things (p. 141). This call is closely related to her point that 'what is special about place is precisely that throwntogetherness, the unavoidable challenge of negotiating a here-and-now' (p. 140). As she points out, 'Reconceptualising place in this way puts on the agenda a different set of political questions. There can be no assumptions of pre-given coherence, or of community or collective identity. Rather the throwntogetherness of place demands negotiation' (Massey, 2005, p. 141).

I shall return to this point below, when discussing a few empirical examples along with indications of how a feminist-and-islandsness lens can contribute to open up assumptions about pre-given coherence and further analyses of the 'throwntogetherness' of places.

4. Methodological Implications

Before discussing empirical examples, it is useful to dwell on how exactly the points raised above may give cause to new methodological considerations which could feed into future research on gender and tourism. As discussed above, Massey (2005) warns us against romanticising public space as 'an emptiness which enables free and equal speech' (p. 152). Similarly, although perhaps less starkly, Karides (2017) points out how 'Island feminism might facilitate a shift from an "island positive" to an "island critical" perspective within the consolidating field of Island Studies' (p. 31). I agree with Karides's indirect warning against conceptualising islands as *eo ipso* positive places, places which are prone to imaginations about exotic encounters. As pointed out by Tongan author Hau'ofa (1993[2008]), colonial renditions of the Pacific Islands have historically contributed to an exoticising Othering of Pacific Islanders, and as he further argues 'views held by those in dominant positions about their subordinates can have significant consequences for people's self-image and for the ways they cope with their situations' (p. 28). It is in this vein that Karides proposes island feminism(s) as a means to bring on a more critical perspective.

Established tourism researchers have for some time recognized the need for 'gender-aware research within tourism' (Figueroa-Domecq et al., 2015; Hall, Swain, & Kinnaird, 2003; Kinnaird & Hall, 1996 & 2000).

Importantly, I would add that such gender-awareness needs to go beyond binary conceptions of male/female and masculine/feminine. This is simply not sophisticated enough. As argued by Kinnaird and Hall, 'gender-aware conceptual frameworks in tourism research cannot afford to become dependent on assumptions of gender as a defined and uncontested category' (2000, p. 72), and consequently we need to invite debate over femininity and masculinity, as well as other contestable social categories.

Therefore, I propose that intersectional analyses, which take into account the various social identities of both tourists and resident populations (and the varying importance of such identities in social interactions), would be a fruitful avenue to pursue for academics working in tourism research. Such intersectional analyses seem rare in tourism research, although Swain (1995) already suggested their relevance in 1995, arguing that 'relationships within and between groups of hosts and guests can be analyzed by focusing on a number of characteristics including gender, class, age, ethnicity and race, and nationality. These distinctions intersect and affect each other' (p. 248). Nevertheless, writing almost 25 years later, Pritchard laments that 'thus far intersectionality has been too rarely discussed in tourism research' (2018, p. 145). A similar criticism is raised by Chambers and Rakić (2018), who argue that 'tourism gender research has also failed to take sufficient account of the complex intersectionalities between gender and a host of identifications including race, class, sexuality and age' (p. 5).

Karides's agenda (while not explicitly an agenda for tourism studies) is to call for more intersectional awareness in analysing island encounters. As she explains, 'Island feminism starts with the lived experiences, challenges, and opportunities of islanders, recognising that these are constantly formed and re-formed by changes in identities and the systems of gender and sexuality, race and ethnicity, or indigeneity' (Karides, 2017, p. 32). I therefore argue that it would be possible to follow Karides's (2017) proposal for an island feminist approach, and apply this directly to research on the role of tourism in island locations. The added emphasis on island locations entails that 'islandness' 'becomes a facet of intersectional analysis' (Karides, 2017, p. 34). This means that we need to pay specific attention to the fact of islands being 'completely surrounded by water' and therefore being clearly delimited. If we are able to accomplish an awareness of this fact as part of our analytic endeavours, we may be able to counteract what Karides terms a 'continental bias' (2017, p. 35).

Returning to the notion of promoting a more 'gender-aware' research agenda in tourism studies, I propose that Kinnaird and Hall's argument could be sharpened, and that they are missing what Karides (2017) identifies as 'an opportunity for a more provoking analysis' (p. 35). A more critical perspective could be achieved by expanding their directions for more gender-aware tourism research:

> Gender-aware research within tourism studies needs to be grounded in theoretical positions which not only allow robust interpretations of empirical data on, for example, tourism employment patterns or social and cultural change, but also create the space to actually redefine how researchers view tourism and tourism-related activity, and thus, how tourism is constructed as a product of *gendered* contemporary societies, *and contributes to further construct such gendered societies* (Kinnaird & Hall, 2000, p. 72, emphasis added).

In other words, I maintain that tourism cannot be studied as a phenomenon somehow floating above social relations of power and 'throwntogtherness'. I hold that tourism – as a phenomenon which brings human agents/human bodies into contact with each other in place – fundamentally alters the mixture of 'throwntogetherness', and therefore calls for new intersectional analyses of negotiations of power in place.

Such analyses are starting to appear within tourism research, but more systematic approaches are called for. I have for example come across the argument that 'by adding the components of place and space in discussions on gender and tourism, the social aspect of the gender and tourism issues can be disclosed clearly, and the underlying reasons for different consumer behaviors can be obtained' (Xu, 2018, p. 725). I do not, however, think that 'add place and space and stir' is a viable recipe in itself, nor one that will 'clearly' disclose any issues. However, as argued above, I certainly consider spatial analyses a required – albeit not sufficient – component in a sound methodological approach. I hold similar reservations about the claim that 'tourism is also a cross-cultural phenomenon, and in different cultures, the nature of the social construction of gender/sexuality can be easily revealed' (Xu, 2018, p. 725). The point about social constructions of gender is that one can only see them if actually looking for them. As much feminist theorising has taught us, the male norm usually goes unnoticed, and can only be brought into view through actual analytic engagement (de Beauvoir, 1949). The same applies to heteronormativity, which requires queering to be brought into the light (Ahmed, 2006; Karides, 2017).

The point has been raised that 'the overwhelmingly male voice of tourism's gatekeepers is less remarked upon, perhaps because as men, most senior figures do not even recognize that their experiences are gendered and the masculine remains the norm, the same, the self, hidden in full view, against which all others are measured' (Figueroa-Domecq et al., 2015, p. 89). A stable argument in feminist writing has long been that to bring such unspoken norms into the limelight requires attention also to one's own positionality (whether complicit or not) within these power relations. This entails attention to one's embodied positionality as researcher – both when entering field relations, but also when simply forming part of 'academia' (Chambers et al., 2017). Porter, Schänzel and Cheer's (2021) more recent edited volume, however, signifies an important remedy to the lacuna of acknowledging male norms in tourism research.

Hall, Swain and Kinnaird (2003) touch upon debates on power and the body, as well as embodied research. They argue for increased attention to the fact that the tourist has a body – and not just a 'gaze'. However, equally important, the researcher has a body, too. As pointed out by Swain (1995), 'Each scholar's experiences as a gendered person provide a rich basis to interpreting what one studies' (p. 252). In several senses, we therefore need to embody tourism research. Pioneers in this endeavour, Veijola and Jokinen (1994) provide an engaging account of the embodied presence of the researcher *cum* tourist in their critical appraisal of existing tourism scholarship. Although more than 25 years old, their points seem nonetheless topical in contemporary tourism research, for example when they ask 'Is the gaze really detachable from the eye, the eye from the body, the body from the situation?' (Veijola & Jokinen, 1994, p. 136).

One researcher who has been specifically preoccupied with how one's embodied positionality necessarily impacts on what and how we can know, is Haraway. She proposes 'a doctrine of embodied objectivity' (1988, p. 581). Haraway's central argument is that objective vision can only be made possible by acknowledging specific embodiment. Consequently, claims for disembodied objectivity 'fail to see that the subject of knowledge is always located somewhere and that its perspective is necessarily partial' (Prins, 1995, p. 353). Tying this argument in with Massey's entails that power positions are structured and negotiated by the different human agents or bodies involved in interaction in a particular location. As researchers, we therefore need to acknowledge our own roles in the 'throwntogetherness' of place.

Haraway describes feminist science as being 'about a critical vision consequent upon a critical positioning in an unhomogeneous gendered social space' (Haraway, 1988, p. 589). Adopting this stance therefore implies the existence of multiple interpreters and a rational posture towards knowledge where knowing becomes a conversation between multiple voices. Simultaneously, such a view also implies dispensing with what Haraway calls 'the god trick' of science, that is, the idea of 'seeing everything from nowhere' (1988, p. 581).

Such a notion of a disembodied and therefore disinterested view privileges male notions of disembodied knowledge. Although not referencing Haraway, Swain also problematizes how male experiences may erroneously be assumed to be universal if not questioned (1995, p. 253). This is precisely the problem addressed through Porter, Schänzel and Cheer's (2021) recent publication.

Haraway's points about what does or does not constitute legitimate knowledge relates not only to how we analyse objects of research, but also how we report on them, and how our research is received both within and outside academia. Haraway's ideas may be fruitfully applied in directing a reflexive gaze on the writing, collaboration and teaching practices of (tourism) academia (Chambers et al., 2017). Pritchard (2018) raises a related concern about 'struggling for legitimacy' when attempting to apply feminist approaches and methodologies in tourism research. Figueroa-Domecq et al.'s (2015) comprehensive bibliometric analysis of 'gender-aware' tourism research points out that 'if we are to build tourism knowledge that is holistic and inclusive, we must question hegemonic views of what are "legitimate" and "appropriate" methodologies and research topics' (p. 96). They also argue that there is a lack of 'a critical mass of standard bearers' in gender and tourism reasearch as a subfield (p. 96).

5. Empirical Considerations

Figueroa-Domecq et al. present the results of a bibliometric analysis of gender-aware tourism research published in indexed journals between 1985 and 2012. A striking fact is the absence of words such as 'male(s)', 'men' and 'masculinity' as well as 'femininity' from their Figure 2: 'the most popular words in titles of indexed tourism gender research papers, 1985–2012' (2015, p. 94). Swain (1995) also observes how 'the category "men" is not indexed' in *Annals of Tourism Research*(p. 254), pointing to how the male norm goes unnoticed, while only the 'different' are singled out for indexing. Figueroa-Domecq et al (2015) conclude that 'tourism analyses of masculinities are sadly lacking' (p. 98). The same point is echoed in Chambers and Rakić (2018), who state that 'issues of masculinity are often elided in tourism studies on gender' (p.3). More attention is due to the male gender and performative aspects of gender expressions in tourism research, yet, there are important contributions also in this field, including a couple of edited volumes (Porter, Schänzel & Cheer, 2021; Thurnell-Read & Casey, 2014) and articles by Heldt Cassell and Pashkevich (2018), for example. But more studies of men and masculinity in tourism studies are important for advancing an agenda for gender-aware tourism research.

Malam's (2008) analysis of how in-migrating male Thai bar workers on one of the southern islands of Thailand negotiate their position both vis-à-vis female and male tourists, local island residents and transgender sex workers in the neighbouring bar, is exemplary in undertaking the kind of analysis I am calling for. Further recommendable is Persson, Zampoukos and Ljunggren (2021), who analyse women's empowerment through tourism development processes in Samoa. However, although they *do* address intersections of gender, class/social hierarchy and indirectly 'islandness' (through references to the significance of overseas experience and access to coastline locations), they do not engage with the embodied presence of either tourists or researchers in their analysis. Hence, they do not dig as deep into the 'throwntogetherness' of place as I argue Malam manages to do.

Relatedly, Waitt and Markwell (2014) co-consider gender, sexuality, age, ethnicity, class/social hiearachy and embodied (both their own and their interviewees') negotiations of 'throwntogetherness', but although their empirical study is situated on the island of Bali, they do not relate their findings to 'islandness', only to the space of nightclubs. Although never making any reference to island studies literature nor to feminist literature on intersectionality, Malam precisely manages to execute an intersectional analysis which takes account of diverse social and spatial identities such as gender, sexuality, class, islander/non-islander, migrant and tourist. Through doing so, she manages to showcase the different positionalities of the bartenders both in terms of the social space inside and outside the bar, and in terms of the geographic space of 'islandness'. Although not explicating it herself, I would argue that 'islandness' becomes an intersecting variable in Malam's analysis at the point where she explains how access to a boat and the possibility of taking female tourists off to other nearby secluded islands becomes a power position for the barmen.

> Bar workers could also mobilize resources outside of the bar space in order to seduce potential girlfriends or support existing ones. Some examples of this in-kind support include taking women on free trips to nearby deserted beaches in boats belonging to their employers ... Mastery of space for bar workers was an expression of their creativity in applying strategic knowledge about the kinds of resources they could covertly acquire and the best times to do this (Malam, 2008, p. 588).

Malam argues about the site of her field work (Pha-ngan Island in Thailand) that it is 'a site of intense encounters which can bring boundaries between identity categories into sharp focus' (Malam, 2008, p. 584). Although she limits herself to making claims about this particular island, I argue that due to their geographically clearly demarcated boundaries ('completely suroundeded by water'), many islands may be conceptualized as 'sites of intense encounters', perhaps especially for the resident population, certainly if they face material restraints in being able to leave. Furthermore, if the site is sufficiently small and the number of residents relatively limited, the chance (risk if you will) of meeting someone again is all the greater. Anonymity may be hard to achieve in small island societies (Nimführ & Otto, 2021), and may be a boon more sought for among residents than visitors.

The question of anonymity – maybe even a perceived need for concealment – also arises, I would argue, in relation to issues of sexuality. While sex and sexuality do appear among the 'most popular words in titles' among the corpus of research analysed by Figueroa-Domecq et al. (2015), I suspect more refined empirical analyses could be undertaken also in this field. As described by Kinnaird and Hall, 'Significant attention has been devoted to the emergence of sex tourism and the gender relationships which characterise the activity' (2000, p. 72). Yet, most analyses of sex tourism seem to take place into account only insofar as the destination is imagined as a 'place away' for the travellers, and therefore potentially a place of 'greater malleability, less inhibition' as suggested by Baldacchino (2006, p. 6). Even Veijola and Jokinen's otherwise critical account suggests as much, when debating how bodily consciousness seems to change in tourist destinations, where one may wear 'a practically transparent gala dress' and actually dance rather than simply gaze at others dancing (1994, p. 133). While sympathetic to their call for greater attention to embodiment in tourism research, I would argue that even their account neglects the fact of the destination being a 'place of home' for the residents. I propose that an intersectional analysis which takes into account place, and specifically 'islandness', could bring to the fore power relations and islands as spaces of (im)possibility for variously positioned bodies.

One case in point would be bodily expressions (whether intentionally sexual or not) in public space in Puerto Rico. According to Puerto Rico's official tourism agency, the island is particularly welcoming towards LGBTQ travellers (Discover Puerto Rico). Browsing through the colourful pictures of women holding hands and men kissing seems paradoxical given research about restraints on bodily expressions in public space (for residents), even expressions that are not intentionally sexual (La Fountain-Stokes, 2008, 2011; Rodriguez-Coss, 2020). Rodriguez-Coss (2020) analyses a feminist public happening in Puerto Rico in 2009, where activists appeared barebreasted, but covered in body paint expressing various political statements about the embodied impossibilities of female experience in Puerto Rico. Based on interviews with key activists, Rodriguez-Coss recounts the schisms experienced by the activists in living in a country where female tourists routinely walk the beaches more or less naked, while local women's bodies are subjected to scrutiny and moralising gazes.

It is clear that different scripts apply for how to occupy space vis-à-vis 'islandness' – similar to points made by Mills (2005) vis-à-vis coloniality. If one 'belongs' on the island, one cannot walk barebreasted in public space, whereas according to the tourist agency, 'Everyone is welcome here! We say *bienvenidos* to inclusivity, equality, and – above all else, love! As one of the most LGBTQ-friendly islands in the Caribbean, you'll find that Puerto Rico is the perfect setting to let your rainbow flag fly high and proud' (Discover Puerto Rico). In this case, Veijola and Jokinen's critical engagement with Rojek's work on the body in tourism could be expanded. They quote his statement that 'the shedding of clothing, within the licensed limits of public nudity, is seen as a right of everyone' (Rojek, 1993, p.189 in Veijola & Jokinen, 1994, p. 137). Well, perhaps if 'everyone' happens to be a tourist, I suggest.

By way of contrast, La Fountain-Stokes (2008 & 2011) describes how dominant notions of Puerto Ricanness do not accept homosexuality or other marginalized sexualities (2008, 2011). This suggests that it is possible to be an American homosexual in Puerto Rico, but not a Puerto Rican homosexual in Puerto Rico. In this way, Puerto Rico becomes a space of impossibility for homosexuality or transvestism among the locally born population. Those Puerto Rican born individuals who do self-identify as homosexual or transgender persons, La Fountain-Stokes (2011) argues, become 'translocas', who belong neither here nor there, and are seen as too *loca* to fit in. Waitt and Markwell (2014) describe how one of their locally born interviewees experienced only being able to sustain his homosexuality after 'his migration to the tourism spaces of Bali' (p. 111). However, they do not address whether it is possible to live a complete life in these 'tourism spaces' – there must be places in Bali outside of nightclubbing which require other negotiations of 'throwntogetherness' if living permanently on the island as openly homosexual.

Representations of islands as 'exotic, otherworldly, *the* place to "get away from it all" [...] attractive for their perceived isolation and pared-down lifestyle' (Brinklow, 2013, p. 39, emphasis in original), neglect to analyse the power relations inherent in local settings and position islanders as 'Other' by categorising their bodies as exotic. Such categorizations may conceal struggles against imposed perceptions (even prescriptions) of islands as 'destinations' for tourism, as 'possibilities' for transnational investors, or as potential 'laboratories', for example, for birth control pills or sterilization experiments (Pristed Nielsen & Rodriguez-Coss, 2020).

Imagining research as complicit in such political projects may be a tall order for some researchers. Are these really relevant considerations for tourism academics? Let me end by returning to my opening example of Thompson's analysis of early British endeavours to turn the Caribbean into a place suitable for tourist consumption. As she documents, such endeavours started as early as the 1890s through production of 'picturesque' renditions of the islands. She points out how the intended effect on the potential tourists also had side-effects on locals:

> Not only were tourist images seen in the colonies, but locals paid acute attention to how these representations were in turn seen by 'others', the outside world. In short, images created to project an image to the outside world also shaped how local communities learned to see themselves and their environments. (Thompson, 2006, p.12)

While this may seem a matter-of-fact observation, Thompson in later parts of her book goes on to discuss how local governments are currently trying to instill a sense of duty to behave well towards tourists, for example in Jamaica, Dominica and Barbados. She describes such initiatives as aiming to 'instill a civic sense of the importance of tourism in all sectors of society' (Thompson, 2006, p. 302), with governments urging residents to behave in ways that facilitate the tourism industry, for example, by smiling and behaving like 'a walking tourist attraction' (Pattullo, 1996, p.62 in Thompson, 2006, p. 302).

6. Conclusion

The call to smile and behave like a walking tourist attraction may be hard to ignore if living on an island where tourism is a crucial part of the local economy. Especially if the island is small and inhabited by relatively few people, anyone not performing may be easily singled out for unwanted attention from fellow islanders. Therefore, I hold that theorising gender relations in tourism is important in all contexts, but maybe even more so in small island contexts.

Figueroa-Domecq et al. (2015) argue that 'the extent to which any field addresses gender is a useful indicator of its epistemological maturity' (p. 88). As a gender researcher, I agree with this claim, and above I have pointed out how Island Studies is yet another academic (sub)field which is currently starting to address gender among its concerns (Gaini & Pristed Nielsen, 2020; Karides, 2017, 2020). Thinking across these two research fields, I suggest that theorising gender and tourism development specifically in small island locations opens up new avenues of inquiry which may lead to cross-pollination and enhanced attention to the social and cultural forces which are played out across space in encounters between embodied human agents. Overall, I argue that island spaces have a mediating effect on tourist and resident encounters because such spaces represent – paraphrasing Shields (1991) – the contingent juxtaposition of social and economic forces, forms of social organization, and constraints of the natural world which are clearly demarcated at the water's edge.

Hopefully, the present chapter has provided inspiration for tourism researchers contemplating research in island locations, providing suggestions for how a feminist-and-islandness lens can contribute to open up assumptions about pre-given coherence, to encourage more nuanced analyses of the 'throwntogetherness' of places and their inherent power constellations. It has thus been my aim to inspire tourism researchers undertaking empirical studies in island locations to co-consider both gender (together with other intersecting social identities) and 'islandness' in their work. To paraphrase Figueroa-Domecq et al. (2015), we should strive towards achieving a greater number of critical standard bearers, as this may be more important than numbers in themselves. Feminist theorists of political representation have argued that critical *acts* are more important than critical *mass* (Dahlerup, 1988), because critical acts are likely to lead to further changes in the position of the minority. Tourism studies in island locations which take account of gendered, classed, ethnic and other social identities together with intersections with place or 'islandness', I suggest, is a field ripe for critical acts of producing insightful research on the 'throwntogetherness' of places.

References

Ahmed, S. (2006). *Queer phenomenology. Orientations, objects, others.* Durham, NC: Duke University Press.

Baldacchino, G. (2004). The coming of age of island studies. *Tijdschrift voor Economische en Sociale Geografie, 95*(3), 272–83.

Baldacchino, G. (2006). Editorial: Islands, island studies. *Island Studies Journal, 1*(1), 3–18.

Brinklow, L. (2013). Stepping-stones to the edge: Artistic expressions of islandness in an ocean of Islands. *Island Studies Journal, 8*(1), 39–54.

Chambers, D. & Rakic, T. (2018). Critical considerations on gender and tourism: An introduction. *Tourism, Culture and Communication, 18*(1), 1–18.

Chambers, D., Munar, A.M., Khoo-Lattimore, C. & Biran, A. (2017). Interrogating gender and the tourism academy through epistemological lens. *Anatolia, 28*(4), 501–13.

Cresswell, T. (1996). *In place/out of place: Geography, ideology and transgression.* Minneapolis, MN: University of Minnesota Press.

Dahlerup, D. (1988). From a small to a large minority: Women in Scandinavian politics. *Scandinavian Political Studies, 11*(4), 275–98.

De Beauvoir, S. (1949). *Le deuxième sexe* [*The second sex*]. Paris: Gaillimard.

Discover Puerto Rico. https://www.discoverpuertorico.com/things-to-do/lgbtq-travel (accessed February 1, 2021).
Eriksen, T.H. (1993). In which sense do cultural islands exist? *Social Anthropology*, 1993(1), 133–47.
Figueroa-Domecq, C., Pritchard, A., Segovia-Perez, M., Morgan, N. & Villace-Molinero, T. (2015). Tourism gender research: A critical accounting. *Annals of Tourism Research*, *52*, 87–103.
Gaini, F. & Pristed Nielsen, H. (eds) (2020). *Gender and island communities*. Abingdon: Routledge.
Gillis, J.R. (2007). Island sojourns. *The Geographical Review*, *97*(2), 274–87.
Grydehøj, A. (2017). A future of island studies. *Island Studies Journal*, *12*(1), 3–16.
Hall, D., Swain, M. & Kinnaird, V. (2003). Tourism and gender: An evolving agenda. *Tourism Recreation Research*, *28*(2), 7–11.
Haraway, D. (1988). Situated knowledges: The science question in feminism. *Feminist Studies*, *14*(3), 575–99.
Hau'ofa, E. (1993/2008). Our sea of islands. In *We are the ocean: Selected works*, pp. 27–40. Honolulu: University of Hawaii Press.
Heldt Cassel, S. & Pashkevich, A. (2018). Tourism development in the Russian Arctic: Reproducing or challenging the hegemonic masculinities of the frontier. *Tourism, Culture & Communication*, *18*(1), 67–80.
Karides, M. (2017). Why island feminism? *Shima*, *11*(1), 30–9.
Karides, M. (2020). An island feminist approach to scholar-activism. In F. Gaini & H. Pristed Nielsen (eds), *Gender and island communities*, pp. 21–45. Abingdon: Routledge.
Kinnaird, V. & Hall, D. (1996). Understanding tourism processes: A gender-aware framework. *Tourism Management*, *17*(2), 95–102.
Kinnaird, V. & Hall, D. (2000). Theorizing gender in tourism research. *Tourism Recreation Research*, *25*(1), 71–84.
La Fountain-Stokes, L. (2008). Queer diasporas, Boricua lives: A meditation on sexile. *Review: Literature and Arts of the Americas*, *41*(2), 294–301.
La Fountain-Stokes, L. (2011). Translocas: Migration, homosexuality, and transvestism in recent Puerto Rican performance. *E-misférica*, 8(1). https://hemisphericinstitute.org/en/emisferica-81/8-1-essays/translocas.html (accessed 27 September 2021).
Leiper, N. (1979). The framework of tourism: Towards a definition of tourism, tourist, and the tourist industry. *Annals of Tourism Research*, *6*(4), 390–407.
Malam, L. (2008). Bodies, beaches and bars: Negotiating heterosexual masculinity in southern Thailand's tourism industry. *Gender, Place & Culture*, *15*(6), 581–94.
Massey, D. (2005). *For space*. London: Sage.
McCall, G. (1994). Nissology: A proposal for consideration. *Journal of the Pacific Society*, *63–64*(17), 93–106.
McCall, G. (1996). Clearing confusion in a disembedded world: The case for Nissology. *Geographische Zeitschrift*, *84*(2), 74–85.
Mills, S. (1996). Gender and colonial space. *Gender, Place and Culture: A Journal of Feminist Geography*, *3*(2), 125–48.
Mills, S. (2005). *Gender and colonial space*. Manchester: Manchester University Press.
Nelson, L. & Seager, J. (2005). *A companion to feminist geography*. Oxford: Blackwell.
Nimführ, S. & Otto, L. (2021). (Un)Making smallness: Islands, spatial ascription processes and (im)mobility. *Island Studies Journal*,16(2), 39–58.
Olwig, K.F. (2007). Islands as places of being and belonging. *The Geographical Review*, *97*(2), 260–73.

Oxford University Press (2018). *Oxford English Dictionary*. https:// www .oed .com/ (accessed 7 March 2018).
Persson, K., Zampoukos, K. & Ljunggren, I. (2021). No (wo)man is an island: Socio-cultural context and women's empowerment in Samoa. *Gender, Place & Culture, 29*(4), 482–501.
Porter, B.A., Schänzel, H.A. & Cheer, J.M. (eds) (2021). *Masculinities in the field: Tourism and transdisciplinary research*. Bristol: Channel View.
Prins, B. (1995). The ethics of hybrid subjects: Feminist constructivism according to Donna Haraway. *Technology & Human Values*, 20 (3), 352–67.
Pristed Nielsen, H. & Rodriguez-Coss, N. (2020). Island studies through love and affection to power and politics. In F. Gaini & H. Pristed Nielsen (eds), *Gender and island communities*, pp.158–73. Abingdon: Routledge.
Pritchard, A. (2018). Predicting the next decade of tourism gender research. *Tourism Management Perspectives, 25*, 144–6.
Rodriguez-Coss, N. (2020). An intersectional analysis of island feminist praxis in Puerto Rico. In F. Gaini & H. Pristed Nielsen (eds), *Gender and island communities*, pp. 82–99. Abingdon: Routledge.
Rojek, C. (1993). *Ways of escape: Modern transformations in leisure and travel*. London: Palgrave Macmillan.
Royle, S.A. (2007). Definitions and typologies. In G. Baldacchino (ed.), *A world of islands. An island studies reader*, pp. 33–56. Malta: Agenda Academic.
Saarinen, J. & Varnajot, A. (2019). The Arctic in tourism: Complementing and contesting perspectives on tourism in the Arctic. *Polar Geography, 42*(1), 1–16.
Shields, R. (1991). *Places on the margin. Alternative geographies of modernity*. London: Routledge.
Swain, M.B. (1995). Introduction: Gender in tourism. *Annals of Tourism Research, 22*(2), 247–66.
Thompson, K. (2006). *An eye for the tropics: Tourism, photography, and framing the Caribbean picturesque*. Durham, NC: Duke University Press.
Thurnell-Read, T. & Casey, M. (eds) (2014). *Men, masculinities, travel and tourism*. Basingstoke: Palgrave Macmillan.
Veijola, S. & Jokinen, E. (1994). The body in tourism. *Theory, Culture and Society, 11*, 125–51.
Waitt, G. & Markwell, K (2014). 'I don't want to think I am a prostitute': Embodied geographies of men, masculinities and clubbing in Seminyak, Bali, Indonesia. In T. Thurnell-Read & M. Casey (eds), *Men, masculinities, travel and tourism*, pp. 104–19. Basingstoke: Palgrave Macmillan.
World Bank (2021a). Mauritius. https://data.worldbank.org/country/MU (accessed 15 February 2021).
World Bank (2021b). International arrivals in Mauritius, 2018. https://data.worldbank .org/indicator/ST.INT.ARVL(accessed 15 February 2021).
Xu, H. (2018). Moving toward gender and tourism geographies studies. *Tourism Geographies, 20*(4), 721–7.

3 Migrant women in hospitality: a critical analysis of Australian newspapers during COVID-19

Elaine Chiao Ling Yang

1. Introduction

The hospitality sector globally is infamously characterized by a low-paid, low-skilled, and casualized workforce, which relies heavily on marginalized workers (Baum, 2012; Janta et al., 2011; Rydzik et al., 2017). A large proportion of the hospitality workforce comprises women migrants, refugees, and international students (Baum et al., 2020). These marginalized female hospitality workers are employed in precarious and, for some, exploitative conditions and are exposed to significant health and safety risks. The gendered nature of hospitality work has further exposed marginalized female workers to the risk of sexual harassment, which has been more broadly highlighted by the global #MeToo movement (Ram, 2018). The racial identity of workers and their visa conditions add extra layers of inequality to the already parlous work. Despite the significance of the issue, the matter of female hospitality workers' conditions has received inadequate research and policy attention. The employment experience of migrant women in hospitality is so far anecdotal. Their voices remain inaudible despite their increasing visibility in the hospitality workplace.

The health and economic crises resulting from the COVID-19 pandemic have aggravated and exposed the precarious and unsafe work conditions of hospitality workers at large, and of migrant and female hospitality workers in particular, by foregrounding pre-existing inequalities (Baum et al., 2020). Hospitality venues such as restaurants and cafés have been identified as locations with high risk of COVID-19 spread (Chang et al., 2021). Hospitality workers who continue to provide essential services, such as food preparation and delivery for the general public, and catering, cleaning, and security services in quarantine hotels should be considered frontline workers, but many have not received adequate health and safety training and protection. In Australia, infected quarantine hotel workers, including security guards and cleaners, sparked a COVID-19 outbreak in Victoria (Schneiders, 2020) and have been responsible for lockdowns in Brisbane (Gramenz, 2021) and Western Australia (Laschon, 2021). The Victorian government's COVID-19 Hotel Quarantine Inquiry report identified workers from culturally and linguistically diverse backgrounds (i.e., migrant workers) as a concern, especially those who are underpaid and have insecure work and thus are likely to work multiple jobs and be less likely to take leave while sick, thereby increasing the risk of infection and transmission (Coate, 2020).

Using the COVID-19 pandemic as a prism, this chapter consolidates and provides a critical analysis of news reporting on migrant women in hospitality. Australia is used as a case study due to its high reliance on migrant workers. Migrants contributed 64 per cent of the population growth in Australia in 2017 (Simon-Davies, 2018) and continue to provide an important workforce, which is particularly valuable to Australia's hospitality sector which, before the pandemic, had been projected to face a shortage of nearly 30,000 workers in 2020 (Austrade, 2015). While gender-segregated data are not available, it has been estimated that migrants account for 39 per cent of the Australian hospitality workforce (Treuren et al., 2019; Unions NSW, 2020). Approximately 70 per cent of migrants in Australia consist of temporary visa holders, 40 per cent of whom are student visa holders (Simon-Davies, 2018). A large population of international students work part-time during their study and stay in Australia. Due to their unfamiliarity with the language and regulations in the new environment, international student-workers are vulnerable to wage theft and exploitation (Nyland et al., 2009). In 2020, reports warned of the looming pandemic-induced humanitarian crisis in Australia among temporary migrant workers who have little financial and social protection and limited access to sick leave allowances and affordable medical care (Berg & Farbenblum, 2020).

Through the analysis of news articles, this chapter throws light on the work conditions and intersectional inequalities experienced by migrant female hospitality workers, and the impact of the pandemic on this group of workers in Australia. Based on the findings, an agenda is proposed to inform future research on gender in hospitality, with a focus on transforming the hospitality workplace into one that is just and safe.

2. Migrant Women in Hospitality

United Nations World Tourism Organization (UNWTO) reports and scholarly research have consistently highlighted the persistent gender inequality encountered by women workers in tourism and hospitality (Mooney, 2018; UNWTO, 2019; UNWTO & UN Women, 2010). Women make up 60–70 per cent of the global hospitality workforce (UNWTO, 2019). Hospitality work exemplifies gendered labour division where the lower level and front-facing jobs rely heavily on aesthetic, affective, and emotional labour, which is traditionally deemed feminine (Coffey et al., 2018). In addition to gender pay gaps and barriers to career progression (Mooney, 2018), female workers are also at risk of the gender-based violence and sexual harassment pervasive in the hospitality sector (Ram, 2018; UNWTO, 2019).

The low barriers to working in the hospitality industry suggest it is 'refuge employment' (Treuren et al., 2019, p. 20) for female migrants who are double-marginalized by their gender and migrant status within the labour market (Janta et al., 2011). Migrant workers are commonly engaged in informal hospitality employment (Baum et al., 2020) and are most likely to experience discrimination, exploitation, and inadequate health and safety protection (Janta et al., 2011). Research shows that migrant women are twice as likely to be paid below the legal minimum wage as men (Jayaweera & Anderson, 2008). In Australia, female room attendants from minority ethnic backgrounds have been reported as facing a greater risk of sexual harassment than others (Kensbock et al., 2015). However, migrant female workers are less likely to challenge exploitative practices due to time, cost, and risk of dismissal (Boucher, 2018; Janta et al., 2011).

Prior research has indicated that gender intersecting with migrant and racial identities renders some groups more vulnerable to exploitation than others (Alberti et al., 2013; Janta et al., 2011). Nonetheless, existing research on hospitality work has often assumed a gender-blind approach (Duncan et al., 2013; Morgan & Pritchard, 2019). While this is changing with a growing stream of hospitality literature taking up a gender perspective (Mooney, 2018; Segovia-Pérez et al., 2019), few have investigated different subgroups among women and the intersection of gender with other social identities in shaping women's work experience (Adib & Guerrier, 2003). The works of Rydzik and colleagues (Rydzik, Pritchard, Morgan, & Sedgley, 2012, 2013, 2017) are the few exceptions that have explicitly investigated migrant female workers in hospitality. While addressing an important knowledge gap, these publications were based on a small-scale qualitative study and investigated a specific group of migrants in a unique mobility context (i.e., Poles in the UK under the European Union agreement). In addition, Rydzik's works focused on mobilities instead of employment experience. Apart from this, migrant female hospitality workers have received less scholarly attention than they justifiably deserve in both migrant and hospitality scholarships.

3. Impact of COVID-19 on Women and Migrant Hospitality workers

The impact of COVID-19 on women has been widely related in government reports and the media. The Workplace Gender Equality Agency (WGEA, 2020) in Australia underlines the fact that women are disproportionately affected by pandemic-induced unemployment due to gender segregation in certain sectors and are over-represented in casual employment, both of which facts are pertinent to the hospitality sector. Data released by the Australian Bureau of Statistics (ABS, 2020) show that jobs in accommodation and food services have been the most impacted. Data from the United States record a similar pattern but further highlight the intersection of gender and racial disparity in the fallout from the impact of COVID-19 (Institute for Women's Policy Research, 2020). Specifically, female casual workers from culturally and linguistically diverse backgrounds in the service sector, including restaurants, cafés, and hotels have been the hardest hit by the pandemic (Institute for Women's Policy Research, 2020). Within this group, those with temporary or undocumented migrant status and informal employment are the most vulnerable of all (Baum et al., 2020). Pre-existing gender inequalities further exacerbate the circumstances of migrant female workers who have to deal with the strain of childcare responsibility expected of them and the alarming rate of domestic violence reported worldwide as the pandemic unfolds (Baum et al., 2020; Taub, 2020).

Sönmez et al. (2020) made an astute observation on the lack of attention to the impact of the pandemic on migrant workers in the plethora of tourism and COVID-19 research published in 2020. Similarly, Baum et al. (2020) assessed the impact of the pandemic on the hospitality workforce and underlined the plight of migrant workers, who are concentrated in casual, low-level, and informal work with little job security or protection from unfair or non-existent work contracts. The precarious work conditions have been amplified during the COVID-19 pandemic (Baum et al., 2020), with migrant hospitality workers experiencing greater adverse effects than non-migrant workers (Sönmez et al., 2020). Using Australia as an example, temporary migrants and short-term casual workers are not eligible for the federal government wage subsidy package. While non-migrant hospitality workers are experiencing job loss during lockdowns, they are in a less dire financial position than temporary migrants.

Some scholars have advocated for a *syndemic* framework to appropriately account for the synergy of the contextual factors and social inequalities that render some groups more vulnerable than others in the face of COVID-19 (Mendenhall, 2020; Sönmez et al., 2020). Sönmez et al. (2020) elucidated the social, economic, and structural factors and industry practices that contribute to the health and safety risk of migrant hotel and food service workers under normal circumstances, and how these pre-existing work-induced health conditions could render this group of workers more vulnerable in the face of COVID-19. In the same vein, Baum et al. (2020) sharply pointed out the limitations of the regulatory system in protecting precarious hospitality workers and their compounding vulnerability, precipitated by social disparities (e.g., gender, race, migrant status, etc.). Crowded living quarters and working multiple jobs have been identified as two factors that make migrant communities from lower socio-economic backgrounds more susceptible to a COVID-19 outbreak, as evidenced in Singapore and Melbourne (Kerr, 2020; Koh, 2020).

With the easing of lockdown restrictions, hospitality jobs are slowly returning but this may foreshadow a public health risk. Migrant workers in front-facing hospitality jobs are exposed to the risk of COVID-19, but their precarious work and living conditions and limited access to financial support, social security, and healthcare due to their visa conditions suggest that this group of workers are more vulnerable to the risk of exposure at the workplace and of community transmission. Apart from a handful of viewpoint articles, there has been little empirical research on the impact of the COVID-19 pandemic on migrant female hospitality workers. As such, this book chapter serves as a starting point for collating the empirical accounts of this group of workers, specifically of how they experienced the impact of the COVID-19 pandemic, as reported in the newspapers.

4. Agenda Setting and Framing Through News Media

The agenda-setting theory elucidates the power of the news discourse in raising, shaping, and changing public opinion on trending social and political issues, which can have an effect on policy making and social movements (Scheufele, 2000). Agenda setting consists of three building blocks: objects, attributes of the objects, and frames (McCombs & Shaw, 2006). The selection and coverage of the objects, such as the COVID-19 pandemic or an election in the news, prompt the audience as to *what* they should think about these matters through salience and priming (McCombs & Shaw, 2006). Real-world events and issues compete to be the news objects, but the initial selection and subsequent reporting that keeps the issues prominent are determined by political actors, elites, and interest groups (Scheufele, 2000).

The frames, on the other hand, shape *how* the audience thinks about the objects by invoking interpretive schemas (Scheufele, 2000). The framing theory provides a triadic framework to examine the mechanisms of news stories in shaping public interpretations (de Vreese, 2005; Scheufele, 2000). *Frame-building* concerns the internal (e.g., editorial policies, news values) and external (e.g., prevailing political and cultural ideologies) factors that determine the selection (or omission) of news and the ways the news stories are portrayed (de Vreese, 2005). *Frame-setting* refers to the process where the audience interacts with the framed news content in setting their interpretation of the issues presented in the news (de Vreese, 2005). The interpretations are subject to individuals' preconceived knowledge and predispositions. The *consequences* of this process are manifested in the effect on attitude, opinion, and behaviour at an individual level, and political outcomes at the societal level (de Vreese, 2005).

The impact of news media on public opinion is well documented (McCombs & Shaw, 2006; Scheufele, 2000). The extant literature has examined the news reporting about women, highlighting the notion of the paper ceiling, a term indicative of women's underrepresentation in the news media (Shor et al., 2015). Other studies have also investigated the framing of violence against women (Sutherland et al., 2019) and specifically of Muslim women (Terman, 2017), underlining the dominant social inequalities such as sexism and racism that underpin and continue to propagate in the news media. Recent studies have examined the framing of migrants in the news media (Horsti & Nikunen, 2013; Lawlor & Tolley, 2017; Liu, 2019). In particular, Liu (2019) conducted a cross-regional comparison of the framing of migrants in newspapers in the United States, the United Kingdom, Taiwan, and Hong Kong. While concluding the dominance of negative frames in the representation of migrants as economic and cultural threats, the study observed a shift towards cultural integration and humanistic narratives.

However, these portrayals are often embedded in the hero frames where migrants are depicted as victims who lack agentic power. Liu (2019) further substantiated the external and contextual factors contributing to regional differences, with the finding that Western countries focus overwhelmingly more on immigration threats than do other countries. In their critique of the agenda setting of the anti-immigration movement on the media, Horsti and Nikunen (2013) proposed the *ethics ofhospitality*, drawn from Jacques Derrida's (2001) work on hospitality that explores the ethical treatment of strangers to provide a guiding framework to fair and responsible news reporting that would account for diverse and, in particular, marginalized voices.

Past studies have investigated the impact of news media in shaping public perception of issues pertinent to the tourism and hospitality industry, including terrorism and travel safety (Hall, 2002), tourism in protected areas (Schweinsberg et al., 2017), and overtourism (Phi, 2020). Limited attention, however, has been given to the representation of migrant hospitality workers in general on the news, much less from a gender perspective. This book chapter addresses the gap by investigating the agenda setting and framing of migrant women in hospitality as portrayed in the Australian newspapers.

5. Method

This study is guided by the critical realist paradigm, which posits a three-level ontology where reality is stratified into the empirical, actual, and real levels (Bhaskar, 2008; Fletcher, 2017). The empirical reality can be experienced through our senses, generating what is known as transitive knowledge. The actual reality or intransitive knowledge refers to events that exist independently of our experience. The real reality, however, is mostly unobservable and is generated by social relations and mechanisms. Critical realism offers an instrumental perspective for feminist studies, as it recognizes gender inequalities within and beyond individual experiences and gives emphasis to the investigation of the underpinning social mechanisms in order to instigate social transformations (Clegg, 2006; Gunnarsson et al., 2016). The social inequality practised against migrant female workers is an actual reality, which is examined in this study through: the empirical evidence as reported and framed on the news; the mechanisms that underpinned the experience of this group of workers during the COVID-19 pandemic; and if and how their experiences were reported.

This study aims to provide a critical qualitative analysis of newspapers relating to migrant women in the Australian hospitality sector. Newspapers were selected over televised and radio news, because the text-based format permits systematic search and retrieval using online news databases, which ensures the comprehensibility and reliability of the data (Delahunt-Smoleniec & Smith-Merry, 2020). The news articles were primarily identified from ProQuest Australia and New Zealand Newsstream database (https://search.proquest.com/anznews/index), which is a specialized regional database that covers more than 400 national and local newspaper titles from major news companies, including the Australian Broadcasting Corporation (ABC), News limited, and Fairfax. Some examples of titles include *The Sydney Morning Herald, The Australian, The Age, The Courier-Mail, The Daily Telegraph*,and *The Herald-Sun*. The effectiveness of the database has been established in prior research that examined the representation of young people in Australian news (Delahunt-Smoleniec & Smith-Merry, 2020). The search was conducted using a combination of the following keywords: 'migrant', 'women', and 'hospitality/hotel/restaurant/café'. The search was conducted on 4 February 2021 and was limited to news articles published after 1 January 2020. The initial search returned 471 titles. After removing articles published in New Zealand and duplicate titles, 171 articles were included in the analysis. The full articles were read and ranked based on their relevance to migrant women in the Australian hospitality sector. A majority of the articles referred to 'hotel' in the context of hotel quarantine, and 'café' and 'restaurant' as a place where a meeting or event took place. As a result of the sifting process, only eight articles were identified as highly relevant, directly addressing migrant female workers in hospitality. Another 26 articles were ranked as somewhat relevant for featuring 'migrant' and 'women' separately, or 'migrant women' but not related to the hospitality sector.

To triangulate the search outcomes and ensure all relevant articles were captured, supplementary searches using the same keywords were conducted on Dow Jones Factiva (www.factiva.com), a global news database collecting more than 30 000 titles. Factiva is a commonly used database for news analysis because of its wide coverage (Lawlor & Tolley, 2017; Nolan et al., 2011). In this study, Factiva was used for triangulation purposes because, unlike the primary database, it does not have an Australian focus. A total of 683 articles were identified using Factiva. After removing duplicate titles within the search outcomes and cross-checking with the articles identified from Proquest, the remaining articles were filtered for relevance. Only five articles were found to be somewhat relevant to the subject of investigation and included in further analysis.

A qualitative content analysis was utilized to analyse the 39 news articles. The analysis was conducted by the sole author, who is a migrant woman of Malaysian Chinese descent in Australia. The analysis and interpretation of the findings were inevitably shaped by the author's personal, professional, and cultural background. Detailed memos were recorded to reflect on the influence of the author's subjectivity on the analysis process. The articles were coded according to the types of articles (e.g., news story, commentary, original text of a speech, etc.), relevance to the COVID-19 pandemic, key issues reported in relation to migrant women in hospitality, and the reporting frames. The frames were analysed according to the journalists' position (i.e., positive or negative representation) and how the issues were reported. To enhance the credibility of the interpretations, the key issues were coded inductively based on the data, while the frames were coded abductively where a coding scheme was adapted from Liu's (2019) study on the news framing of immigration. The frames from Liu (2019) were 'migrant as victim', 'migrant as criminal', 'economic threat', and 'cultural integration'. Informed by the data, new frames such as 'migrant as change agent', 'hospitality business as hero', 'COVID-19 threat', and 'social threat' were identified. The coding was performed using MAXQDA, a qualitative research piece of software, to organize and retrieve the codes and coded texts.

6. Findings

The main purpose of this study was to consolidate and provide a critical analysis of the anecdotal evidence of migrant female hospitality workers as reported in Australian newspapers during the COVID-19 pandemic. This section will first analyse the coverage of this group of workers on the news, then analyse the news frames. The impact of the pandemic will then be examined, with attention to the underlying social and political factors that constitute the workers' circumstances.

6.1 Marginalized Workers, Marginalized Agenda

One stark observation from the analysis was the nearly non-existent newspaper coverage of migrant female hospitality workers. As mentioned in the previous section, only eight news articles directly addressed this group of workers. The minimal coverage indicates the marginalization of migrant women in hospitality in the news agenda, which is determined by dominant actors and groups in power (Scheufele, 2000). The lack of interest and reporting relegates the salience of migrant female workers to nothingness in public discourse, as the audience is not primed to think about their existence and experience. The remaining 31 articles that were deemed somewhat relevant predominantly reported the impact of COVID-19 on migrants, women, and hospitality workers separately. Some articles pointed out that women and migrants are more likely to be engaged in the hospitality sector and therefore, would experience more calamity during the pandemic. However, migrant female hospitality workers were not examined as an independent group in these articles.

6.2 Framing: Victims, Change Agents and Threats

Frame analysis (de Vreese, 2005) revealed *how* migrant women in hospitality were portrayed on the news, which subsequently influenced public interpretations and perceptions. Two competing frames were observed – 'migrant women as victims' and 'migrant women as change agents'. A majority of the articles portrayed migrant women as the victims of exploitation, wage theft, and systemic inequalities. For instance, a migrant woman was exploited on the promise of a permanent visa sponsorship ('Worker enslaved at North East restaurants without pay', 2020). The woman was enslaved to unpaid work at an ethnic restaurant where the owner threatened to both assault and deport her. At the time of writing this book chapter, a female migrant worker was violently assaulted in a bubble tea café where she worked (Sulda, 2021). The incident was allegedly instigated by a wage dispute[1]. Many of these 'migrant women as victims' were either current international students or had arrived in Australia on a student visa.

However, a quarter of the articles also presented migrant women as change agents with the agentic power to empower other migrant women and to instigate change in their circumstances. Several articles featured not-for-profit hospitality businesses operated by migrant women with a goal to empower other migrant women through employment opportunity and integration into the community (Kirkham, 2020a; Lewis, 2020). For instance, A Pot of Courage café is a social enterprise in Ballarat that was formed by a group of migrant women (Kirkham, 2020a). The café moved online when the COVID-19 pandemic hit, and the women continued running the kitchen and providing work opportunities for migrant women who were struggling with unemployment. The café received support from the community and the state government at a time when many hospitality businesses were unable to survive the pandemic. Underpinning these stories is the 'hospitality' extended by hospitality businesses via the spaces with low entry barriers that they provide for migrant women to gain 'refuge employment' (Treuren et al., 2019, p. 20), spaces for workers from diverse linguistic backgrounds to practise English, and spaces to promote cross-cultural understanding between the workers and

---

1 There was more news coverage of this incident weeks after the search was concluded; these news articles were not included in the content analysis but were referred to in order to gain a fuller picture of the incident.

the community (Kirkham, 2020a; Lewis, 2020). A related frame was identified that portrayed hospitality businesses as heroes for providing migrant women with work opportunities that would otherwise not be available. For instance, one article reported on how a migrant woman received a job offer from a large hospitality organization after her experience with unemployment was featured on the local news (Toxward & Mortimer, 2020). The organization's remark on 'fair go' and 'equality' was underscored in the article.

Two news articles referred to the frame of economic threat where migrant workers in general were described as competitors for local jobs (Elliot, 2020; Rilley, 2020). In both cases, however, the threat was presented as a contested frame rather than the central narrative. The framing of migrants as COVID-19 threats was discerned in one article where migrant communities were explicitly blamed for community transmission (Bolt, 2020). Several articles addressed this frame by critically examining the social disparities that have been brought to light by the pandemic (Bachelard, 2020; Hope, 2020; Penberthy, 2020).

6.3 Impact of COVID-19 on Migrants, Women, and Hospitality Workers

The impact of the COVID-19 pandemic on migrants and women respectively was mentioned in nearly half of the news articles. Statements such as 'recent migrants and women are among those hardest hit' (Kirkham, 2020b, p. 6) were seen in numerous articles. The analysis reveals that most weight was given to the impact on women in general. The news articles consistently reported on women experiencing greater unemployment than men and on domestic violence during the pandemic, highlighting pre-existing gender inequalities (see, e.g., Bachelard, 2020; Gavin, 2020; McIlwain, 2020). Women were more likely to take up care work, both paid and unpaid, and casual employment in pandemic-stricken sectors such as hotels, restaurants, and cafés than men (McIlwain, 2020). Migrant workers were identified as another vulnerable group predisposed to precarious employment and often in the hospitality sector (Gavin, 2020; McIlwain, 2020). While statements such as 'women, frequently migrant workers, too often numbered among the working poor and the insecure' (Gavin, 2020) were noted in several news articles, few authors discerned the complex intersections of social inequalities that render migrant female hospitality workers most susceptible to the impact of COVID-19.

One exception to the criticism above was Tullis (2020), who reported on the topic of racism and featured the story of a skilled migrant female hospitality worker who lost her job during lockdown and was unable to find another due to systematic inequality, as she was not eligible for JobKeeper, a wage subsidy scheme introduced in Australia in response to the pandemic. Even before the pandemic, her experience working as an assistant manager in a five-star hotel in her home country was not recognized in Australia, where she was deskilled and received an exploitative wage, lower than AUD10 per hour. The lack of universal access to social security and welfare benefits such that temporary migrant workers in Australia were left destitute was noted in several articles (Barns, 2020; Fitzsimmons, 2020). Charity assistance provided to migrants and women was also reported (Kirkham, 2020b). In another article, the race discrimination commissioner at the Australian Human Rights Commission commented that migrant workers face more systematic challenges and sometimes outright racism in regaining employment, although they have equivalent skills to those of the job winners and good English proficiency (Woods, 2020). The Commissioner also noted that for many migrants, language can be an additional barrier to overcome (Woods, 2020). Albeit not addressing the pandemic, one article provided anecdotal evidence of the double employment disadvantages experienced by migrant women new to Australia because of their caring responsibilities and language levels (Lewis, 2020).

Several news articles highlighted further social disparities from the impact of COVID-19 in light of the discovery that areas with higher migrant populations experience the worst outbreaks (Schneider, 2020a, 2020b). One article explicitly presented migrant workers' dilemma of having to weigh up between health risks and economic circumstances (Schneider, 2020a). As victims of social and systemic inequalities, many migrants work in low-paid, casual, and labouring jobs such as those in the hospitality sector where working-from-home and social distancing are not an option (Hope, 2020). Moreover, to make ends meet, migrant workers in precarious employment often work multiple jobs, increasing their risk of infection and community transmission, such as that which precipitated the COVID-19 outbreak in Melbourne (Mendenhall, 2020). One article also reported the findings of a trade union's study, which suggested marginalized workers might go to work despite developing minor symptoms due to economic pressure, as these are 'not all equal choices' (Schneider, 2020b, p. 23). Although these articles did not focus on migrant female hospitality workers per se, they delineated the wider social context in which this group of workers is situated.

7. Discussion

This chapter addresses a critical gap in the growing gender scholarship in tourism. An increasing body of literature has addressed gender inequality in tourism from the perspectives of women as travellers (Yanget al., 2019) and workers (Coffey et al., 2018). For the latter, many studies have examined barriers to women's career advancement in large tourism and hospitality organizations (Calinaud et al., 2020; Mooney, 2018). To consider career progression, one must at least have a secure job. As indicated in many reports and studies, migrant women are often employed in the hospitality sector as casual workers in low-skilled and low-paid positions (Baum, 2012; Baum et al., 2020). The parlous work conditions of migrant female hospitality workers have been alluded to in the extant literature (Baum et al., 2020; Janta et al., 2011), but only a handful of studies has investigated the experiences of this group of workers (Rydzik et al., 2012, 2013, 2017). Inadequacy of data has hindered wider discussion and action to address the issue. The COVID-19 pandemic has severely affected the hospitality sector, which in turn has further disadvantaged precarious hospitality workers. The plight of these workers, as cautioned by Baum et al. (2020), provided the impetus for this chapter. News reporting on migrant female hospitality workers in Australia from January 2020 to February 2021 was analysed, with a focus on agenda setting, framing, and the impact of the pandemic on this group of workers. Specific attention was also given to the social inequalities and contextual factors that engendered the circumstances of these workers.

Overall, migrant female hospitality workers have received minimal coverage in mainstream newspapers, despite their considerable contribution to Australia's hospitality workforce (Treuren et al., 2019). What is included and prioritized in the news agenda is framed by the broader social discourse, and reflects the society in which the news is reported (de Vreese, 2005). This study expands the notion of the paper ceiling (Shor et al., 2015) by revealing a double bias against women of colour in the news. The dearth of reporting reinforces the marginalization of migrant women in the public and political agenda and perpetuates the lack of empirical accounts of the actual reality of migrant female hospitality workers. The frame analysis concerns how migrant women in hospitality were portrayed on the news in 2020. Differing from the findings in the extant literature where migrants were often framed as economic and cultural threats (Liu, 2019), the findings in this study show that only a handful of news articles have used the threat framing. Rather, migrant female hospitality workers were found to be predominantly framed as victims of exploitation and precarious work. It is worth noting that an agentic frame was also observed, albeit to a lesser extent. In contrast to the dominant exploitation narratives, hospitality spaces, especially restaurants and cafés run by migrant communities, were cited as meeting places for migrant women and places that provide these women job opportunities that would otherwise not be available.

Reporting of the impact of COVID-19 primarily referred to women and migrant workers in hospitality as two distinctive groups, overlooking the interlocking inequalities arising from the intersections of gender, race, and migrant identities. Intersectional statistics were absent, and most accounts about the situation of these workers came from experts, union secretaries, and charity workers rather than from the workers' perspectives. The deafening silence of the lived experience of migrant female hospitality workers is observed, reinforcing the framing of migrants as victims who lack power (Liu, 2019) and in this study, voice. In spite of the fragmented accounts, the systemic discrimination against temporary migrant workers in Australia is evident. Reflecting on the *ethics of hospitality* in general (Derrida, 2001) and in the context of news reporting (Horsti & Nikunen, 2013), the findings of this study point to the unethical treatment of migrant female hospitality workers and their unheard voices. While the overall sentiment in the reporting shows empathy over blame towards migrant workers, and there were some attempts to inform the public of the social disparities in the impact of COVID-19, considering the overall lack of coverage, the salience of this news agenda is questionable.

8. Conclusion

The hospitality sector has been hit hard by the COVID-19 pandemic due to lockdowns and social distancing. In response to the hit, hospitality businesses have understandably prioritized mitigation of the financial impact and staying afloat. However, the casualization of the workforce predicated on the neoliberal profit-driven business model is flawed, as brought to light by the pandemic. Casual hospitality positions are most likely to be filled by women and migrants as a result of the gender and race segregation of hospitality work and broader social inequalities (Baum et al., 2020; Mooney, 2018; Sönmez et al., 2020). The already precarious livelihood of these casual hospitality workers has been further aggravated by the pandemic. Borrowing the words from Sönmez et al. (2020), 'If there is any type of silver lining to the COVID-19 pandemic, it is the exposure of what needs to change at national and corporate levels to protect the millions of workers ...' (p. 4).

Notwithstanding the small sample, the insights gleaned from the news analysis serve to initiate a dialogue for change. In this spirit, three recommendations are provided to inform future research on gender in hospitality, with a focus on migrant women in hospitality and in light of the COVID-19 pandemic.

8.1 An Intersectional Lens

The lack of attention to their entwined identities has hindered a meaningful understanding and thereby improvement of the work conditions of marginalized female hospitality workers. To illustrate, gendered barriers experienced by a non-migrant, female hotel manager are different from those of a migrant, female housekeeper. The apparent knowledge gap about migrant female hospitality workers necessitates further research to collect empirical data on the lived experience of these women in their own voices and it should employ an intersectional lens to examine the interlocking inequalities that they have experienced. Given the small sample size of this study, future research is encouraged to explore different keywords (e.g., female, accommodation, bar, pub, etc.) and to examine a wider range of media representations (e.g., television media and social media) of this group of workers.

8.2 Context Matters

Adding to the intersectional lens, researchers studying migrant women in hospitality are advised to situate the study in social, political, and regulatory contexts and examine the underlying social mechanisms that contribute to their circumstances. A syndemic framework may be valuable for investigating the impact of COVID-19 on this group of workers, as the framework considers the interaction of contextual factors and social inequalities that render them vulnerable to facing more adverse health and economic risks than others. Such situated insights are crucial for informing social policy changes within the context.

8.3 Participatory Planning for Recovery

As the COVID-19 vaccine programme launches, the hospitality sector is on the road to recovery. To ensure the sector does not simply revert to the pre-COVID employment practices that have left many migrant workers in destitution, participatory research that engages women and migrant workers in the planning for recovery is critically warranted in order to envision and transform hospitality work into such that reflects the ethics of hospitality.

References

ABS. (2020). *160.0.55.001 – Weekly payroll jobs and wages in Australia, week ending 8 August 2020*. Retrieved from https://www.abs.gov.au (accessed 10 December 2020).

Adib, A., & Guerrier, Y. (2003). The interlocking of gender with nationality, race, ethnicity and class: The narratives of women in hotel work. *Gender, Work & Organization, 10*(4), 413–32.

Alberti, G., Holgate, J., & Tapia, M. (2013). Organising migrants as workers or as migrant workers? Intersectionality, trade unions and precarious work. *The International Journal of Human Resource Management, 24*(22), 4132–48. https://doi.org/10.1080/09585192.2013.845429

Austrade. (2015). *Australian tourism labour force report: 2015–2020.* Retrieved from https://www.austrade.gov.au/Australian/Tourism/Policy-and-Strategy/labour-and-skills (accessed 10 January 2021).

Bachelard, M. (2020, 11 July. Feeling the heat. *The Age,* p. 21 (accessed 24 February 2021).

Barns, G. (2020, 6 April). When the chips are down, Australia's compassion dries up. *The Mercury,* p. 22.

Baum, T. (2012). *Migrant workers in the international hotel industry.* Geneva: International Labour Organization.

Baum, T., Mooney Shelagh, K.K., Robinson Richard, N.S., & Solnet, D. (2020). COVID-19's impact on the hospitality workforce: New crisis or amplification of the norm? *International Journal of Contemporary Hospitality Management, 32*(9), 2813–29. https://doi.org/10.1108/IJCHM-04-2020-0314

Berg, L., & Farbenblum, B. (2020, 17 August). 'I will never come to Australia again': New research reveals the suffering of temporary migrants during the COVID-19 crisis. *The Conversation.* Retrieved from https://theconversation.com/i-will-never-come-to-australia-again-new-research-reveals-the-suffering-of-temporary-migrants-during-the-covid-19-crisis-143351 (accessed 10 September 2020).

Bhaskar, R. (2008). *A realist theory of science.* London: Routledge.

Bolt, A. (2020, 21 September). Dan's reward plan. *The Daily Telegraph,* p. 21.

Boucher, A. (2018). Measuring migrant worker rights violations in practice: The example of temporary skilled visas in Australia. *Journal of Industrial Relations, 61*(2), 277–301. https://doi.org/10.1177/0022185618783001

Calinaud, V., Kokkranikal, J., & Gebbels, M. (2020). Career advancement for women in the British hospitality industry: The enabling factors. *Work, Employment and Society, 35*(4), 677–95. https://doi.org/10.1177/0950017020967208

Chang, S., Pierson, E., Koh, P.W., Gerardin, J., Redbird, B., Grusky, D., & Leskovec, J. (2021). Mobility network models of COVID-19 explain inequities and inform reopening. *Nature, 589*(7840), 82–7. https://doi.org/10.1038/s41586-020-2923-3

Clegg, S. (2006). The problem of agency in feminism: A critical realist approach. *Gender and Education, 18*(3), 309–24. https://doi.org/10.1080/09540250600667892

Coate, J. (2020). *COVID-19 hotel quarantine inquiry, final report and recommendations* (Vol. 1). Victorian Government.

Coffey, J., Farrugia, D., Adkins, L., & Threadgold, S. (2018). Gender, sexuality, and risk in the practice of affective labour for young women in bar work. *Sociological Research Online, 23*(4), 728–43. https://doi.org/10.1177/1360780418780059

de Vreese, C.H. (2005). News framing: Theory and typology. *Information Design Journal & Document Design, 13*(1), 51–62.

Delahunt-Smoleniec, N., & Smith-Merry, J. (2020). A qualitative analysis of the portrayal of young people and psychosis in Australian news reports. *Journalism Practice, 14*(7), 847–62. https://doi/org/10.1080/17512786.2019.1640071

Derrida, J. (2001). *On cosmopolitanism and forgiveness.* London: Routledge.

Duncan, T., Scott, D.G., & Baum, T. (2013). The mobilities of hospitality work: An exploration of issues and debates. *Annals of Tourism Research, 41*, 1–19. https://doi.org/10.1016/j.annals.2012.10.004

Elliot, T. (2020, 31 March). It's life (and death) but not as we know it. *Sydney Morning Herald*, p. 12.

Fitzsimmons, C. (2020, 17 May). The uneven pain of the pandemic. *Sun Herald*, p. 22.

Fletcher, A.J. (2017). Applying critical realism in qualitative research: Methodology meets method. *International Journal of Social Research Methodology, 20*(2), 181–94. https://doi.org/10.1080/13645579.2016.1144401

Gavin, M. (2020, September). Pandemic highlights inequalities women suffer. *Sydney Morning Herald*. Retrieved from https:// www .smh .com .au/ business/ workplace/ pandemic-highlights-inequalities-women-suffer-20200817-p55miy.html (accessed 24 February 2021).

Gramenz, E. (2021, 7 January). Quarantine hotel worker tests positive for coronavirus in Brisbane, Queensland records two new cases. *ABC News*. Retrieved from https:// www .abc .net .au/ news/ 2021 -01 -07/ coronavirus -queensland -quarantine -hotel -worker-tests-positive/13034046 (accessed 24 February 2021).

Gunnarsson, L., Martinez Dy, A., & van Ingen, M. (2016). Critical realism, gender and feminism: Exchanges, challenges, synergies. *Journal of Critical Realism, 15*(5), 433–9. https://doi.org/10.1080/14767430.2016.1211442

Hall, C.M. (2002). Travel safety, terrorism and the media: The significance of the issue-attention cycle. *Current Issues in Tourism, 5*(5), 458–66. https:// doi .org/ 10 .1080/13683500208667935

Hope, Z. (2020, 5 July). New times same blame. *Sunday Age*, p. 9.

Horsti, K., & Nikunen, K. (2013). The ethics of hospitality in changing journalism: A response to the rise of the anti-immigrant movement in Finnish media publicity. *European Journal of Cultural Studies, 16*(4), 489–504. https:// doi.org/ 10.1177/ 1367549413491718

Institute for Women's Policy Research. (2020). *Women lost more jobs than men in almost all sectors of the economy*. Retrieved from http:// iwpr .org/ wp -content/ uploads/2020/07/QF-Jobs-Day-April-FINAL.pdf (accessed 10 January 2021).

Janta, H., Ladkin, A., Brown, L., & Lugosi, P. (2011). Employment experiences of Polish migrant workers in the UK hospitality sector. *Tourism Management, 32*(5), 1006–19. https://doi.org/10.1016/j.tourman.2010.08.013

Jayaweera, H., & Anderson, B. (2008). *Migrant workers and vulnerable employment: A review of existing data*. Retrieved from https:// www .compas .ox .ac .uk/ 2008/ pr -2008-migrants_vulnerable_employment/ (accessed 15 February 2021).

Kensbock, S., Bailey, J., Jennings, G., & Patiar, A. (2015). Sexual harassment of women working as room attendants within 5-star hotels. *Gender, Work & Organization, 22*(1), 36–50. https://doi.org/10.1111/gwao.12064

Kerr, J. (2020, 29 July). Expert's hotspot warning as fever clinics swamped. *The Courier Mail*. Retrieved from https://www.couriermail.com.au/ (accessed February 24, 2021)

Kirkham, R. (2020a, 19 September). A pot of courage expands flavour. *The Courier*, p. 20.

Kirkham, R. (2020b, 14 August). Study reveals who has been most affected by COVID-19. *The Courier*, p. 6.

Koh, D. (2020). Migrant workers and COVID-19. *Occupational and Environmental Medicine, 77*(9), 634–6. https://doi.org/10.1136/oemed-2020-106626

Laschon, E. (2021, 31 January). Coronavirus lockdown announced for Perth and South West after quarantine hotel worker tests positive. *ABC News*. Retrieved from https://

www.abc.net.au/news/2021-01-31/covid-quarantine-hotel-worker-tests-positive-in-perth-wa/13106968 (accessed 25 February 2021).
Lawlor, A., & Tolley, E. (2017). Deciding who's legitimate: News media framing of immigrants and refugees. *International Journal of Communication, 11*(25), 967–91.
Lewis, K. (2020, 9 September). From Cartagena to Canberra: New cafe supports city's most vulnerable. *The Canberra Times*, p. 4.
Liu, S.-J.S. (2019). Framing immigration: A content analysis of newspapers in Hong Kong, Taiwan, the United Kingdom, and the United States. *Politics, Groups, and Identities, 9*(4), 759–783. https://doi.org/10.1080/21565503.2019.1674162
McCombs, M.E., & Shaw, D.L. (2006). The evolution of agenda-setting research: Twenty-five years in the marketplace of ideas. *Journal of Communication, 43*(2), 58–67. https://doi.org/10.1111/j.1460-2466.1993.tb01262.x
McIlwain, K. (2020, 25 May). Working women hit hard by virus. *Illawarra Mercury*, p. 10.
Mendenhall, E. (2020). The COVID-19 syndemic is not global: Context matters. *Lancet (London, England), 396*(10264), 1731. https://doi.org/10.1016/S0140-6736(20)32218-2
Mooney, S. (2018). Jobs for the girls? Women's employment and career progression in the hospitality industry. In R. Burke & J.M.C. Hughes (eds), *Handbook of human resource management in the tourism and hospitality industries* (pp. 184–215). Cheltenham, UK and Northampton, MA, USA: Edward Elgar.
Morgan, N., & Pritchard, A. (2019). Gender matters in hospitality. *International Journal of Hospitality Management, 76*, 38–44. https://doi.org/10.1016/j.ijhm.2018.06.008
Nolan, D., Farquharson, K., Politoff, V., & Marjoribanks, T. (2011). Mediated multiculturalism: Newspaper representations of Sudanese migrants in Australia. *Journal of Intercultural Studies, 32*(6), 655–71. https://doi.org/10.1080/07256868.2011.618109
Nyland, C., Forbes-Mewett, H., Marginson, S., Ramia, G., Sawir, E., & Smith, S. (2009). International student-workers in Australia: A new vulnerable workforce. *Journal of Education and Work, 22*(1), 1–14. https://doi.org/10.1080/13639080802709653
Penberthy, D. (2020, 31 July). Failures that led Vics down dangerous path. *The Advertiser*, p. 13.
Phi, G.T. (2020). Framing overtourism: A critical news media analysis. *Current Issues in Tourism, 23*(17), 2093–7. https://doi.org/10.1080/13683500.2019.1618249
Ram, Y. (2018). Hostility or hospitality? A review on violence, bullying and sexual harassment in the tourism and hospitality industry. *Current Issues in Tourism, 21*(7), 760–74. https://doi.org/10.1080/13683500.2015.1064364
Rilley, A. (2020, 4 May). Yes, it is time to rethink our immigration intake – to put more focus on families. *The Conversation*. Retrieved from https://theconversation.com/yes-it-is-time-to-rethink-our-immigration-intake-to-put-more-focus-on-families-137783 (accessed 17 August 2020).
Rydzik, A., Pritchard, A., Morgan, N., & Sedgley, D. (2012). Mobility, migration and hospitality employment: Voices of Central and Eastern European women. *Hospitality & Society, 2*(2), 137–57. https://doi.org/10.1386/hosp.2.2.137_1
Rydzik, A., Pritchard, A., Morgan, N., & Sedgley, D. (2013). The potential of arts-based transformative research. *Annals of Tourism Research, 40*(0), 283–305. http://dx.doi.org/10.1016/j.annals.2012.09.006
Rydzik, A., Pritchard, A., Morgan, N., & Sedgley, D. (2017). Humanising migrant women's work. *Annals of Tourism Research, 64*, 13–23.

Scheufele, D.A. (2000). Agenda-setting, priming, and framing revisited: Another look at cognitive effects of political communication. *Mass Communication and Society, 3*(2–3), 297–316.

Schneider, B. (2020a, 9 August). A city divided on COVID-19 class lines. *Sunday Age*, p. 1.

Schneider, B. (2020b, 9 August). In sickness and in wealth: Why a pandemic prefers poor people. *Sun Herald*, p. 23.

Schneiders, B. (2020, 3 July). How hotel quarantine let COVID-19 out of the bag in Victoria. *The Age*. Retrieved from https://www.theage.com.au/national/victoria/how-hotel-quarantine-let-covid-19-out-of-the-bag-in-victoria-20200703-p558og.html (accessed 24 February 2021).

Schweinsberg, S., Darcy, S., & Cheng, M. (2017). The agenda setting power of news media in framing the future role of tourism in protected areas. *Tourism Management, 62*, 241–52.

Segovia-Pérez, M., Figueroa-Domecq, C., Fuentes-Moraleda, L., & Muñoz-Mazón, A. (2019). Incorporating a gender approach in the hospitality industry: Female executives' perceptions. *International Journal of Hospitality Management, 76*, 184–93.

Shor, E., van de Rijt, A., Miltsov, A., Kulkarni, V., & Skiena, S. (2015). A paper ceiling: Explaining the persistent underrepresentation of women in printed news. *American Sociological Review, 80*(5), 960–84. https://doi.org/10.1177/0003122415596999

Simon-Davies, J. (2018). *Population and migration statistics in Australia*. Retrieved from https:// www .aph .gov .au/ About _Parliament/ Parliamentary _Departments/ Parliamentary _Library/ pubs/ rp/ rp1819/ Quick _Guides/ PopulationStatistics (accessed 19 January 2021).

Sönmez, S., Apostolopoulos, Y., Lemke, M.K., & Hsieh, Y.-C. (2020). Understanding the effects of COVID-19 on the health and safety of immigrant hospitality workers in the United States. *Tourism Management Perspectives, 35*, 100717. https://doi.org/10.1016/j.tmp.2020.100717

Sulda, D. (2021, 3 February). Woman slapped, kicked in bubble tea brawl. *The Advertiser*, p. 11.

Sutherland, G., Easteal, P., Holland, K., & Vaughan, C. (2019). Mediated representations of violence against women in the mainstream news in Australia. *BMC Public Health, 19*(1), 502. https://doi.org.10.1186/s12889-019-6793-2

Taub, A. (2020, 6 April). A new Covid-19 crisis: Domestic abuse rises worldwide. *The New York Times*. Retrieved from https://www.nytimes.com/2020/04/06/world/coronavirus-domestic-violence.html (accessed 15 December 2020).

Terman, R. (2017). Islamophobia and media portrayals of Muslim women: A computational text analysis of US news coverage. *International Studies Quarterly, 61*(3), 489–502.

Toxward, E., & Mortimer, L. (2020, 24 December). Labrador's Nancy Heron offered job as usher with The Star Gold Coast after desperate plea for work in the Gold Coast Bulletin. *The Gold Coast Bulletin*. Retrieved from https:// www .goldcoastbulletin .com .au/ news/ gold -coast/ labrador -local -nancy -heron -has -submitted -51 -job -applications-and-heard-nothing-she-is-desperate-for-any-job-on-the-gold-coast/news-story/347bb9a167cbc116ee1ef618070bfdf0 (accessed 24 February 2021).

Treuren, G.J.M., Manoharan, A., & Vishnu, V. (2019). The hospitality sector as an employer of skill discounted migrants. Evidence from Australia. *Journal of Policy Research in Tourism, Leisure and Events, 13*(1), 20–35.

Tullis, A. (2020, 15 June). People of colour speak out about casual racism in Illawarra. *Illawarra Mercury*, p. 3.

Unions NSW. (2020). *No worker left behind survey results*. Retrieved from https://www.unionsnsw.org.au/wp-content/uploads/2020/08/NWLB_survey_results_aug_2020.pdf (accessed 19 January 2021).

UNWTO. (2019). *Global report on women in tourism – Second edition*. Madrid: UNWTO.

UNWTO, & UN Women. (2010). *Global report on women in tourism 2010*. Madrid: UNWTO and UN Women. (accessed May 11, 2018)

WGEA. (2020). *Gendered impact of COVID-19*. Retrieved from https://www.wgea.gov.au/topics/gendered-impact-of-covid-19 (accessed 17 January 2021).

Woods, C. (2020, 16 September). Australian Human Rights Commissioners outline the challenges and solutions for marginalized workers post-COVID. *The Mandarin*. Retrieved from https://www.themandarin.com.au/139832-australian-human-rights-commissioners-outline-the-challenges-and-solutions-for-marginalized-workers-post-covid/ (accessed 16 January 2021).

Worker enslaved at North East restaurants without pay. (2020, 30 July). *The Border Mail*, p. 3.

Yang, E.C.L., Yang, M.J.H., & Khoo-Lattimore, C. (2019). The meanings of solo travel for Asian women. *Tourism Review, 74*(5), 1047–57. https://doi.org/10.1108/TR-10-2018-0150

4 Gender equality reporting in tourism

Jess Sanggyeong Je and Elaine Chiao Ling Yang

1. Introduction

The United Nations (UN) has urged for an end to inequality and injustice in the 2030 Agenda for Sustainable Development (UN, 2021). The 2030 Agenda is built on the United Nations' 17 Sustainable Development Goals (SDGs) where 'decent work' and 'gender equality' are included as Goals No. 8 and No. 5, respectively (UN, 2021). Accordingly, the International Labour Organization (ILO) integrated the 2030 Agenda in its Decent Work programme to establish a more sustainable workplace for all (Winchenbach et al., 2019). The ILO, a specialized agency of the UN, has brought governments, employers, and workers together and set labour standards so as to promote decent workplaces and build promising futures (ILO, 2021). The Decent Work agenda strives for fair income, job security, and employees' freedom to participate in decision-making processes that affect equality of employment opportunities and treatment for both women and men (ILO, 2021).

A growing coalition of international non-governmental organizations (NGOs) has also recognized the need for corporations to promote gender equality globally (Roberts, 2015). With their increasing power and resources in neo-liberal economies, corporations have the potential to advance gender equality (Grosser & McCarthy, 2019). This is especially relevant to tourism, one of the largest and fastest growing economic sectors in the world (Țîțu, et al., 2016). Tourism accounts for one in every ten jobs, and women hold 54 per cent of those positions (UNWTO & UN Women, 2019; WTTC, 2021).

While tourism has been hit hard by the COVID-19 pandemic (Qiu et al., 2020), at the same time, the pandemic has revealed many pre-existing gender inequalities inherent in the sector. Since women are more susceptible to informal and casual jobs in tourism than men, they have faced greater chances of losing their income while yet providing extraordinary care for their families (Equality in Tourism, 2021; UN, 2020). Therefore, it is imperative to examine tourism corporations' approaches to the gender equality goal. However, as yet, existing tourism research has predominantly focused on the environmental aspects of sustainable development, neglecting the social issues of sustainable workplaces and in particular, of gendered employment (Baum, 2016).

The increasing pressure on businesses to act sustainably has given rise to concepts such as corporate social responsibility (CSR) (Dupire & M'Zali, 2018; Perez-Batres et al., 2012). The principle of CSR stipulates that businesses have economic and legal responsibilities as well as ethical and philanthropic responsibilities (Stankeviciute & Savaneviciene, 2013). It requires businesses to assess the impact of organizational activities on stakeholders including employees (Stankeviciute & Savaneviciene, 2013). Thus not only profitability, but also sustainable human resource management, are viewed as central to organizational performance (Herrera & de las Heras-Rosas, 2020).

To be socially responsible, corporations are using sustainability reporting (SR) as a tool to measure and communicate CSR performance in relation to sustainability (Singh et al., 2009). SR refers to a non-financial report that conveys companies' economic, social, and environmental performance (Burhan & Rahmanti, 2012). By disclosing the organization's measurement and implementation progress, SR provides useful information for examining how corporations implement their CSR commitments to stakeholders (Burhan & Rahmanti, 2012). Prior research underlines that information about target (goal), process, and recipients of policies and strategies is crucial to evaluate corporate approaches to gender equality (Armstrong et al., 2009). However, little research has examined how tourism corporations measure, disclose, and communicate gender equality performance let alone how they include target (goal), process and recipients through SR. Therefore, this chapter aims to investigate how tourism corporations measure and disclose gender equality initiatives through an examination of SR based on the publicly available documents of 32 tourism companies. Specifically, this study seeks to examine if and how tourism corporations have disclosed information about the target (goal), process and recipients of gender equality initiatives.

The next section provides a brief review of the literature on the development of gender equality initiatives for sustainable tourism workplaces, gender research in tourism, and the status of gender in SR. The method of conducting a document analysis is outlined, followed by findings related to the target (goal), procedure, and recipients of gender equality initiatives. The research questions are addressed in the Discussion section, along with the practical implications and suggestions for future research.

2. Gender Equality for Sustainable Tourism Workplaces

Women comprise more than half of the tourism workforce globally (UNWTO & UN Women, 2019). Hence, it is imperative to make equitable and decent workplaces for women in tourism. Although there have been attempts to promote gender equality in tourism development, gender equality remains neglected in the theory and practice of sustainable tourism (Equality in Tourism, 2021). The *Global Report on Women in Tourism* (UNWTO & UN Women, 2019) indicated that women earn 10–15 per cent less than their male counterparts and predominantly work as informal, seasonal, sub-contracting and casual workers. A large sector of travel and tourism, such as hotels, could be in the vanguard of an uptake in gender equality practices since it encompasses numerous establishments and employs a large number of workers in multiple countries (Baum, 2013). Moreover, corporations like global hotels have significant resources for human resource development such as training, compared to small to medium-sized companies (Baum, 2013). Still, women earn less than men due to the significant gender segregation of positions although in hotels, they occupy more jobs than men (Baum, 2013).

Considering that a sustainable workplace should provide a fair income, security and opportunities for female employees in decision-making processes (ILO, 2021), the persistence of gendered tourism employment issues shows that gender equality may not have been sufficiently understood, or translated into core practice in tourism. Alarcón and Cole (2019) highlighted that advocating gender equality (Goal No. 5 of the SDGs) can contribute to achieving other SDGs in tourism. For example, in terms of ensuring inclusive quality education for all (Goal No. 4 of the SDGs), it is important to acknowledge that in some cases still, women have frequently received only limited opportunities to progress from primary to professional education due to cultural factors and reproductive roles (Alarcón & Cole, 2019). Therefore, gender equality needs to be considered as a core element of their business by tourism corporations which claim to uphold the SDGs and make equitable workplaces for all.

2.1 Gender Research in Tourism

Gender research in tourism is shaped by major waves of feminism, including liberal feminism, standpoint feminism and post-structural feminism (Pritchard, 2014). Examining how gender roles are socially constructed has been the core work of tourism researchers (Baum, 2013). Liberal feminists focus on women's legal and labour rights, and this movement started from the late nineteenth century liberal politics (Figueroa-Domecq et al., 2015). Liberal feminists mainly emphasize female participation in decision-making processes (Munar, 2017) call for change within existing social structures and place a great emphasis on laws, rules, and regulations (Ackerly, 2001), including corporate policies, to promote women to senior positions and include women in board membership. Tourism scholars have scrutinized employment patterns and management structures that perpetuate gender inequalities (Heimtun & Morgan, 2012) by identifying the representation of women in managerial positions (Perkov, Primorac, & Perkov et al., 2016) and identifying gendered career obstacles such as being young women, pregnancies, and high demand for being present at work (Carvalho et al., 2018).

Standpoint feminism, or so-called socialist feminism, sprang from the minority groups in the 1960s and 1970s. It embraces different positionalities such as class (Marxist feminism), sexuality (socialist feminism), and race (Black feminism) to address structural and material disadvantages in societies (Aitchison, 2005; Figueroa-Domecq et al., 2015). Standpoint feminists highlight that women need to have equal access to education, fundamental reproductive rights, and economic opportunities (Munar, 2017). The cause of women's oppression has been disputed by Marxist and socialist feminism in standpoint feminism. While Marxist perspectives emphasize economic relations over patriarchy as the cause of gendered oppression, socialist feminism sees both patriarchy and capitalism as dual oppression. Nonetheless, both Marxist and socialist feminism commonly highlight material or tangible resources which can emancipate women from financial subordination (Duffy et al., 2015). Post-structural or post-modern feminism puts the subjectivity of women at the centre of discussion (Munar, 2017). Post-modern feminism has focused on the deconstruction of masculinized language and practice to identify the cultural workings of gendered power relations (Heimtun & Morgan, 2012). This may relate to cultural practices such as diversity training in organizations, which impacts the attitude and belief of people towards equality (Madera, 2018).

The contemporary capitalist society is underpinned by neo-liberalization (Thorsen & Lie, 2006), where corporations are powerful enough to influence regulations, business practices, and gender relations (Grosser & McCarthy, 2019). The neo-liberalization of feminism has been driven by the increased power of changed governance of corporations, international organizations, NGOs, and other regulatory bodies. (Grosser & McCarthy, 2019; Prügl, 2015). The neo-liberalization of feminism takes the form of the 'business case for gender equality' (Prügl, 2015, p. 618). It suggests that private companies and individuals may generate economic growth and social welfare more than governments (Bockman, 2013). Corporations can challenge wider societal issues such as gender inequalities using their power and resources (Acker, 2006). With more than half of the workforce being women (UNWTO & UN Women, 2019), tourism corporations have formed various diversity management initiatives such as diversity councils, diversity training programs, employee networking programmes and women's leadership programmes (Madera, 2013). Business feminism is a brand of feminism in which corporations prioritize women's advancement (Fodor et al., 2019). In the same vein, transnational business feminism, a product of the neo-liberalization of feminism, indicates that corporations invest in women to expand the talent pool and consumers, which increases corporate competitiveness and profits (Roberts, 2015). Under the label of corporate social responsibility (CSR), corporations are often criticized for claiming to invest in or empower women (Prügl, 2015) where women's empowerment becomes 'selling points' for business (Grosser & McCarthy, 2019).

The neo-liberalization of feminism is of concern because it may ignore the historical and structural causes of gender-based inequalities (Roberts, 2015). Companies can be conceived of as inequality regimes where the exploitation of women still occurs in terms of stereotyping, low pay, and unpaid care work (Acker, 2006). Previous tourism research noted *statement culture*, where equality or diversity is only practised as a rhetoric rather than practice (Chambers et al., 2017). It exemplifies *femwashing*where the masculine is privileged as the authoritative norm despite the organization's claim of gender equality (Khoo-Lattimore et al., 2019). Therefore, an examination of the corporate approach is necessary to investigate how a gender-sensitive approach is considered significant in the decision-making process and practice under the name of CSR. However, few studies have examined how corporations integrate gender perspectives in CSR policy and practice in tourism, which may hinder the removal of inequalities with organizational change. Further, it is necessary to acknowledge the oversimplified classification of various forms of feminism into different 'waves'. The waves are instrumental to the identification and differentiation of distinctive feminist goals at different points in history. Therefore, the classification is not an objective form of measurement and remains a theoretical dispute among academics (Burris, 2012; Laughlin et al., 2010). Therefore, the authors view how liberal, standpoint or post-modern feminism might have evolved within gender equality initiatives by tourism corporations in the era of neo-liberalization.

3. Sustainability Reporting and Gender

SR is a tool where companies demonstrate their CSR commitment (Font & Lynes, 2018) and inform their implementation progress towards sustainability goals (Burhan & Rahmanti, 2012). Companies engage in SR to balance the conflicting demands of various stakeholders and maintain good relationships with them (Uyar et al., 2020). Although it is disputed whether SR accurately portrays the social and environmental impacts of business activities (Adams & Frost, 2008), many organizations use SR to monitor their performance in the course of preparing their reports and to inform their planning across the different departments (Singh et al., 2009). Therefore, it is necessary to pay attention to how and what companies disclose and how they do so, regarding the sustainability performance (Uyar et al., 2020; Van Der Ploeg & Vanclay, 2013).

SR in tourism is based on internal guidelines or indicators from external bodies such as inter-governmental organizations (Medrado & Jackson, 2016). The indicators or monitoring tools are essential to track the progress toward sustainability goals (White et al., 2006) and inform decision-makers about the appropriateness of certain tourism activities (Torres-Delgado & Saarinen, 2014). The voluntary act of reporting on sustainability performance has become a norm at the international level (Delbard, 2008). Many international and inter-governmental organizations, including the UN, the Global Reporting Initiative (GRI), International Integrated Reporting Council, and Social and Governance Reporting by the London Stock Exchange Group have proposed SR about the human and labour rights of female and male employees, including non-discrimination based on social status (Franzoni & Avellino, 2019). In particular, the GRI reporting standards are predominantly used by corporations in tourism (Medrado & Jackson, 2016). These tools enable corporations to demonstrate and benchmark CSR performance by measuring goals, progress, activities, and outcomes (Siew, 2015). The achievement of social responsibility including gender equality needs technical processes such as measuring and reporting the performance in SR (Grosser & Moon, 2005). Therefore, an evaluation of SR allows researchers to analyse whether gender equality initiatives are 'mainstreamed' in the CSR agenda (Grosser & Moon, 2005).

In tourism, SR has predominantly focused on environmental sustainability and the attainment of sustainable certifications sometimes has substituted some degree of SR (Buckley, 2012). Medrado and Jackson (2016) conducted a review of SR in lodging, cruise lines, and food and beverage firms in the United States. Their SR shows that most firms repeatedly disclosed information on environmental concerns: water usage, energy conservation, and waste generation (Medrado & Jackson, 2016). Meanwhile, the information about employee compensation, benefits, stress level, or feedback about well-being programmes, was not explicitly presented in SR by hospitality corporations (Medrado & Jackson, 2016). Moreover, while their equal promotion policy was frequently highlighted by most tourism firms, less than half of the sample companies addressed the percentage of women in management positions, and only 14.3 per cent provided background information for those who hold managerial positions (Medrado & Jackson, 2016). Little information was found on work–life balance including childcare support and maternity leave options for male and female employees (Medrado & Jackson, 2016). However, the research conducted by Medrado and Jackson (2016) did not include an investigation of how systematically tourism corporations measure, review, and disclose gender equality performance in terms of target (goal), progress, and outcome. Considering little sustainable tourism research has examined gender equality in SR, this study focuses on the disclosure of information such as target (goal), progress, and outcome of gender equality initiatives and investigates whether tourism corporations over-state their commitment to gender equality for sustainable workplaces.

3.1 Examining Sustainability Reporting: A Gender-Sensitive Approach

This study has a gender-sensitive approach to examine SR because it identifies the necessary information to mainstream gender equality as well as the behaviour of organizations through SR. SR requires corporations to demonstrate their CSR commitments and report performance by measuring targets (goals), progress, and outcome (Siew, 2015). Having a target or goal is imperative because a goal is a form of internal normative pressure guiding in which way the company should behave (Amran & Haniffa, 2011). Any plan must have a specific goal if it is to become operational (Allen et al., 2004). The evaluation of implementing gender equality policies and strategies needs the clear adoption of targets (Rubery, 2002). Particularly, the planning for an organization's diversity involves the examination of a company's current diversity status, the development of a route for achieving the goal and the determination of where those organizations want to be in the future (Allen et al., 2004). The target (goal) is an important indicator to examine progress in sustainable development (Holden et al., 2014; Moyer & Hedden, 2020). The global goals like SDGs translate social norms often with a time-bound target with members and interest groups to achieve sustainability (Fukuda-Parr & McNeill, 2019). Therefore, this study examines how clearly tourism corporations set up a target or goal to achieve gender equality in workplaces.

The process of implementing policies and strategies is also important to analyse how those initiatives have evolved over time (Runhaar et al., 2006). In terms of gender equality, keeping mind of 'What was the length of parental leave?' and 'Was the leave paid?' is important to evaluate the direction of policies and strategies (Armstrong et al., 2009). In relation to SR, how the organizations influence, or are influenced by, the expectation for sustainability needs to be documented (Lozano et al., 2016). The outcome of gender equality initiatives also needs to be demonstrated in SR, which refers to the consequence of the sustainability initiatives (Barkemeyer et al., 2015). Since gender equality has been a part of corporate governance, it is necessary to investigate how feminism has been translated into practice through performance indicators such as SR (Marx, 2019). For this research, the recipients of gender equality initiatives have received specific attention as the outcome of gender equality initiatives is important to see who is involved and who has received benefits from organizations. It is critical to examine the inclusiveness of recipients since a large number of women occupy informal or casual positions with limited access to benefits and policies (UN, 2020).

4. Methodology

Document analysis was conducted to investigate how large public companies address their performance regarding gender equality. Document analysis is a systematic approach to review and evaluate institutional documents and enables the researcher to track changes or development of an issue, project, or programme (Bowen, 2009). In the discourse of sustainable governance and public policy processes, document analysis is often used to conceptualize ideas and categorizations in order to get a basic idea of an issue (Runhaar et al., 2006). Therefore, it is a suitable method for this study which aims to gain an understanding of to what extent tourism corporations disclose information about gender equality initiatives through reports.

Forbes Global 2000: The World's Largest Public Companies (Forbes, 2019) was used to identify tourism corporations. The extensive list included various tourism-related sectors, such as food and beverage services, railways, airlines, and accommodation. While the demand for service products (including food and beverage and railway) includes a large number of local consumers, the demand for airlines and accommodation substantially comes from visitors (UNWTO and ILO, 2014). Therefore, this study focused on airlines and accommodation providers, and a total of 10 global hotels and 22 airlines were identified from the Forbes' list (See Table 4.1).

Table 4.1 World's largest public hotels and airlines: Forbes (2019)

Name of company	Industry	Country	Rank No.
Carnival	Hotels & Motels	United States	312
Marriott International	Hotels & Motels	United States	411
Royal Caribbean Cruises	Hotels & Motels	United States	573
Shenzhen Overseas Chinese Town Co., Ltd	Hotels & Motels	China	808
Hilton Worldwide	Hotels & Motels	United States	857
Accor Hotels	Hotels & Motels	France	1041
Norwegian Cruise Line Holdings	Hotels & Motels	United States	1075
Oriental Land Co., Ltd	Hotels & Motels	Japan	1174
Great Eagle Holdings	Hotels & Motels	Hong Kong	1707
Hyatt Hotels	Hotels & Motels	United States	1787
Delta Air Lines	Airlines	United States	203
United Continental Holdings	Airlines	United States	306
American Airlines Group	Airlines	United States	373
Southwest Airlines	Airlines	United States	398
Deutsche Lufthansa	Airlines	Germany	413
International Airlines	Airlines	United Kingdom	428
All Nippon Airways	Airlines	Japan	702
China Southern Airlines	Airlines	China	713
China Eastern Airlines	Airlines	China	768
Japan Airlines	Airlines	Japan	776
Ryanair Holdings	Airlines	Ireland	841
Air France-KLM	Airlines	France	950
Turkish Airlines	Airlines	Turkey	1034
Singapore Airlines	Airlines	Singapore	1078
Qantas Airways	Airlines	Australia	1282
Cathay Pacific Airways	Airlines	Hong Kong	1285
Hainan Airlines	Airlines	China	1393

Name of company	Industry	Country	Rank No.
Korean Air	Airlines	South Korea	1446
Air Canada	Airlines	Canada	1578
Latam Airlines	Airlines	Chile	1622
Alaska Air Group	Airlines	United States	1672
EasyJet	Airlines	United Kingdom	1912

A total of 67 of the most recent corporate documents was identified from the websites of the companies in the sample. Since sustainability reporting is a central instrument to show accountability of companies who adopt sustainability codes of conduct (Brown et al., 2009), additional documents such as codes of conduct were also included for the analysis. Annual reports were also examined since they often demonstrate the representation of women as executive or board members. The authors manually searched gender-related information on sustainability reporting using keywords such as 'social', 'woman', 'women', 'gender', 'equality', and 'empower'. A total of 15 codes of conduct, 12 gender pay gap reports, 14 annual reports, 19 CSR reports, two sexual harassment retaliation policy documents, two women empowerment initiatives, and three diversity policy documents were available with gender-related information.

Content analysis is useful to identify key patterns and themes based on the frequency of words (Vaismoradi, Turunen, & Bondas, 2013). With content analysis, the authors could identify what types of policies and strategies were adopted by tourism corporations. Then, each policy and strategy was manually searched to identify any information regarding what has been achieved (target or goal), how it had been achieved (process), and who received benefits from gender equality initiatives (recipients). Table 4.2 shows examples of the coding process. The coding was conducted by the first author and was triangulated by the second author. The authors met regularly to discuss the coding process and cross-check emerging themes.

5. Findings

This chapter investigates how tourism corporations disclose information of target (goal), process, and recipients for gender equality initiatives. Table 4.3 provides a summary of gender equality policies and strategies documented in SR which were published by tourism corporations. According to the table,

Table 4.2 Examples of the Coding Process

Main theme	Definition	Sub-themes	No. of references in corporate documents	Examples of excerpts extracted from the selected document	Target (goal)	Process	Recipients
Structural	Promote gender equality through corporate rules and regulations	Provide leadership development programmes for women	19	**Accor Hotels**, *CSR report (2018)* 'The strategic Leaders Development Program, facilitated by AccorHotels Academia is the group's high potential female leadership programme designed to accelerate the development of female department managers.'	Unknown	Unknown	Unknown
Structural	Promote gender equality through corporate rules and regulations	Ensure diversity in recruitment	9	**Accor Hotels**, *CSR report (2018)* 'In order to support the access of women to senior positions, we strongly recommend the drawing up of short lists made up of an equal number of female and male candidates.'	Known '35% of hotels' General Managers are women by 2017; the Australian target is 50% by 2018'	Unknown	Unknown

Main theme	Definition	Sub-themes	No. of references in corporate documents	Examples of excerpts extracted from the selected document	Target (goal)	Process	Recipients
Material	Improve women's access to material resources	Support families through childcare service reimbursement and more	13	**Turkish Airline**,*CSR report (2017)* 'Kindergarten and birth allowance for the female employees with dependent children.'	Unknown	Unknown	Unknown
Cultural	Foster organizational culture that supports gender equality	Provide diversity & awareness training about gender equality and unconscious bias	7	**Royal Caribbean Cruise**, *Gender pay gap report (2018)* 'Changing the culture including face-to-face mandatory "unconscious bias" training for all employees.'	Unknown	Unknown	Unknown

gender equality policies and strategies were identified as structural, material, and cultural, which signifies the influence of major feminism approaches in tourism organizations. The analysis of SR showed that most tourism corporations claim structural policies and strategies to achieve gender equality compared to material and cultural policies. Overall, most corporations did not provide information regarding target (goal), process, or recipients of gender equality policies and strategies.

5.1 Target (Goal) of Gender Equality Initiatives

Table 4.3 shows that leadership development programmes for women were the most frequently claimed policy for gender equality. Some corporations provided process-related information such as online platforms that many women can access flexibly. Several companies documented professional development programmes, including for business management, marketing, customer service and foreign language for development. However, there was missing information about the number of programmes that have been offered or will be provided; and about how many women participated, or how many will be encouraged to participate in those programmes. About half of the corporations highlighted promoting women to leadership and executive positions. Doing this is regarded as an imperative step for achieving gender equality and it results in various styles of management (Perkov et al., 2016), which improves the organizational performance and decision-making (Isidro & Sobral, 2015). However, only a few companies set a specific target for having a certain percentage of women's representation at senior or executive positions and indicated whether the target was met for the year.

As indicated, 12 out of 32 tourism corporations highlighted equal wages or reported a gender pay gap. The disclosures encompass hourly pay difference, bonus gap, and the proportion of men and women receiving a bonus. Meanwhile, few companies set a target to close the pay gap between men and women. The reports originated in certain countries such as the United Kingdom and Australia where there are national requirements for large companies to report on the gender pay gap (GOV.UK, 2019; WGEA, 2019).

In terms of cultural initiatives, some companies highlighted diversity training to achieve equitable workplaces for both women and men. Diversity training could enhance employee empathy for diverse colleagues, guests, and customers (Reynolds et al., 2014). According to the analysis, diversity training was conducted for all employees from front-line to managers by tourism corporations. For instance, Royal Caribbean Cruise claimed to offer face-to-face mandatory training about unconscious bias for every employee. Nevertheless, it is unclear as to how often the training was conducted, will be conducted, and what was delivered in the training content regarding gender equality.

5.2 Implementing Gender Equality Initiatives

According to Table 4.3, tourism corporations commonly underlined the involvement of employees in diversity management initiatives to create an inclusive organizational culture. Involving employees when formulating diversity initiatives is an important step to achieve tactical diversity management initiatives (Riccò & Guerci, 2014). Delta Airlines (2018) run a business resource group with diverse types of employees to promote a culture of inclusion. Nevertheless, it is not known who manages the group, who is encouraged to participate, when they participate, and what kind of work they do to promote inclusive organizational culture. About a quarter of tourism corporations stated they provide networking opportunities for women. Networking has also been a critical reason for the career advancement of women who often have fewer informal and formal networks than men (Powell, 2018). Meanwhile, little is known of what kind of networking opportunities were created by whom, how often networking opportunities were given, and how many women employees participated.

Without providing further information, several companies claimed that they provided flexible parental and maternity leave. For instance, Korean Air did not specify how long the paid parental leave was or how many women and men took parental leave. Meanwhile, this company offered other critical information to show the active involvement of female and male employees in taking leave including the rate of return to work after taking leave (100 per cent), the rate of retention (88.9 per cent), and the increasing number of male employees who take parental leave over time (8 per cent) (Korean Air, 2018). The information about the post-maternity period is particularly important because women experience extra stress compared to men by being 'thrown in' the system in tourism (Ma et al., 2021, p. 6). The information about the participation of men in parental leave is also important for analysing the redistribution of care responsibilities and un-paid domestic work between women and men (Haas, 2003). While most companies focused on material policies regarding caring responsibilities, the International Airlines Group claimed to provide sponsorship for women senior managers (Figure 4.1). Nevertheless, the International Airlines Group did not specify how many women senior managers were involved and what kind of sponsorship the company provided them.

Workforce diversity

The progression of women into leadership roles is vitally important and we have set a target to reach 33% women across our senior executive levels (top 200) by 2025. We will monitor and report on our progress, including the management pipeline across the Group. We have put in place an extensive programme of action to help deliver this, some of these achievements in 2018 included:

- A series of roadshows across the Group to engage leadership teams and raise awareness.
- A diagnostic questionnaire for approximately 2000 managers across the Group in June, which identified their experiences around gender inclusion. Key actions are being developed in the individual Operating Company diversity plans.
- British Airway & Avios reported their Gender Pay Gap figures in April.
- International Women's Day was marked with British Airways and Aer Lingus flights crewed and operated by women colleagues in March.
- IAG partnered with Rocking Ur Teens, a social enterprise, hosting a teen STEM conference in November for 250 school girls aged 13 to 15. This was to help motivate and inspire the next generation of young women into the airline industry.
- Established mentoring and sponsorship programmes across the Group for senior managers.

Figure 4.1 Annual report by International Airlines Group (excerpt)

Partnerships with third parties such as universities, NGOs, and governments to promote gender equality were noted in eight companies. For example, Marriott International had numerous partnerships with the Women's Business Enterprise National Council where its partnership certification has been a marketing tool to promote more visibility (Marriott International, 2018). Accor Hotels joined UN Women's HeForShe programme to actively increase gender equality in the workforce (Accor Hotels, 2017). Carnival Corporation established a partnership with local schools and colleges in the United

Kingdom (Carnival UK, 2018). The purpose of that partnership was to encourage more women and girls to start their career as cadets in shipping and cruise lines. Nonetheless, the analysis shows that few corporations elaborated on how these partnerships worked and what was included and what improved through these partnerships in SR. In terms of Carnival Cruise, little is known of what kind of jobs were taken by local women and girls or of how their initiatives impacted the recruitment of local women and girls.

5.3 Recipients of Gender Equality Initiatives

As shown in Table 4.3, eight of 32 tourism corporations set up career events for women, which included a series of inspirational talks, panel debates and workshops designed to inspire women employees career-wise. According to Khoo-Lattimore et al. (2019), the inclusive representation of speakers in terms of gender and race is important in events where gendered expertise and knowledge are materialized and (re)produced. However, it is not clear who organized those events and who was invited as keynote speakers. Considering Hilton invited 3000 out of 405,000 team members to Women@Hilton events in 2019 (see Figure 4.2), further information (e.g., positions) is needed about the employees who were included and how many women and men were invited to those events.

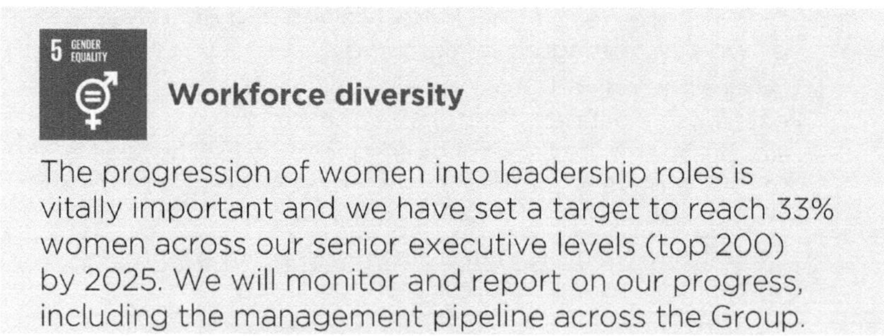
5 GENDER EQUALITY

Workforce diversity

The progression of women into leadership roles is vitally important and we have set a target to reach 33% women across our senior executive levels (top 200) by 2025. We will monitor and report on our progress, including the management pipeline across the Group.

Figure 4.2 Women@Hilton Conference

Material policies and strategies were mostly designed for employees with caring responsibilities. For employees who have caring responsibilities, reimbursement for childcare services or provision of an on-site childcare service has been highlighted by many companies. However, little is known as to how much has been allocated to support women and men employees with caring responsibilities. For example, Marriott International (2018) highlighted the financial benefits it offered to support families including eight weeks of fully paid leave for birth and adoptive parents in the United States. Considering that the United States is the only country without the national entitlement for paid parental leave among Organisation for Economic Co-operation and Development countries (OECD, 2019), the provision of paid leave seems to be a crucial incentive for women who do most of the caring work (UNWTO & UN Women, 2019). However, Marriott's other support for women including lactation support, on-site childcare service, and childcare reimbursements was missing information about how much they provided and how the support was distributed between men and women.

Four tourism corporations were promoting gender equality campaigns to increase awareness of gender equality. For example, Air France conducted an internal campaign #Osonsledire (#Let'ssayit) to encourage employees to speak up and share their experiences about exploitation and harassment. This type of campaign is an important strategy to investigate harassment incidents and hold offenders accountable for their actions (Nimri et al., 2021). However, company documents were missing information such as the rate of incidents and retaliation, as well as how the campaign impacted men and women's perception of gender-based discrimination and harassment. In the same vein, it was not clear how companies cultivated a supportive culture through equality advocates and who was nominated as advocates for gender equality; nor was it clear whether men were involved as advocates as well.

6. Discussion

This study closely examined SR, determining to what extent tourism corporations measure and disclose their performance regarding gender equality, which contributes to making sustainable and equitable workplaces in tourism. In the domain of sustainable development, the target (goal) is an important dimension for examining the progress toward a goal (Holden et al., 2014; Moyer & Hedden, 2020) including gender equality. The implementation process is as important as the recipient to examine how the policies and strategies have evolved over time (Runhaar et al., 2006). Unfortunately, the analysis of SR shows that tourism corporate reports have limited information on target (goal), process, and recipients for gender equality initiatives. The poor quality of SR regarding gender equality is of concern because simple adopting of policy is not sufficient to ensure sustainability becomes a reality (White et al., 2006). Medrado and Jackson (2016) provided plausible explanations for little disclosure on wages, benefits, and work–life balance by tourism companies: they might not want to make the information publicly available and do not see those areas as competitive advantages.

Table 4.3 Gender equality initiatives claimed by tourism corporations in SR

Policies and strategies for gender equality	*No. of references	Target (goal)	Process	Recipients
Structural *Promote gender equality through corporate rules and regulations*	144			
Provide leadership development programmes for women	19	Unknown	Known	Unknown
Abide by the law of no discrimination and equal opportunity	18	Unknown	Unknown	Unknown
Involve employees in formulating diversity initiatives	18	Unknown	Unknown	Unknown
Promote women to middle management and executive positions	15	A few known	Unknown	Unknown
Ensure board member diversity	10	Unknown	Unknown	A few known
Establish a partnership with government and NGOs to promote gender equality	9	Unknown	Unknown	Unknown
Ensure diversity in recruitment	9	Unknown	Unknown	Unknown
Set up conferences or events for women	8	Unknown	Unknown	Unknown
Provide networking opportunity for women	7	Unknown	Unknown	Unknown
Address women's health, safety issues and following guidelines	7	Unknown	A few known	A few known

Policies and strategies for gender equality	*No. of references	Target (goal)	Process	Recipients
Structural *Promote gender equality through corporate rules and regulations*	144			
Ensure employees' awareness of policy against sexual harassment, discrimination, and retaliation.	5	Unknown	Unknown	Unknown
Hire gender & diversity specialist	5	Unknown	Unknown	Unknown
Offer mentorship for women employees	5	Unknown	Unknown	Unknown
Provide flexible working hours	4	Unknown	Unknown	Unknown
Encourage full-time women workers	3	Unknown	Unknown	Unknown
Provide minimum wages for women	1	Unknown	Unknown	Unknown
Abide by the law of maximum working hours	1	Unknown	Unknown	Unknown
Material *Improve women's access to material resources*	32			
Provide equal wages and report gender pay gap	12	Unknown	Known	Known
Support families through childcare service reimbursement and more	13	Unknown	Unknown	Unknown
Provide flexible parental and maternity leave	6	Unknown	Unknown	A few known
Provide sponsorship for women employees	1	Unknown	Unknown	Unknown

Policies and strategies for gender equality	*No. of references	Target (goal)	Process	Recipients
Structural *Promote gender equality through corporate rules and regulations*	144			
Cultural *Foster organizational culture that supports gender equality*	23			
Establish partnership with educational institution to encourage more women to work in technology or engineering jobs	8	Unknown	Unknown	Unknown
Provide diversity & awareness training about gender equality and unconscious bias	7	Unknown	Unknown	Unknown
Run campaigns to increase awareness about gender equality	4	Unknown	Unknown	Unknown
Create supportive organizational culture	2	Unknown	Unknown	Unknown
Have equality & diversity advocates including men	2	Unknown	Unknown	Unknown

Note: *No. of references indicates the reference to initiatives in each company document.

To measure the performance of gender equality initiatives, tourism corporations should clearly disclose the information on target (goal), process and recipients. Such disclosure can also lead to their competitive advantage to attract the best talent (Medrado & Jackson, 2016). Sincere efforts in SR may eradicate statement culture or the 'femwashing' practice of tourism corporations in the era of neo-liberalism.

The fragmented or missing information can be problematic for benchmarking and generating an integrated review of sustainability performance (Franzoni & Avellino, 2019), including gender equality/sustainable workplace performance. This substandard SR could be attributed to the absence of standardized reporting guidelines to assess and present performance for gender equality initiatives (Van Der Ploeg & Vanclay, 2013). For instance, Global Reporting Initiative (GRI) is a universal framework for organizations to produce sustainability reporting in a consistent and credible way (GRI, 2020). In terms of social assessment, GRI only emphasizes the demographic ratio of the workforce in terms of gender, race, and age. Likewise, the Ten Principles of the UN Global Compact engage companies to uphold the elimination of discrimination and establish a culture of integrity (UN Global Compact, 2020). These principles provide some examples that companies can adopt such as the establishment of unconscious bias training and skill development for employees (UN Global Compact, 2020). However, the principles do not provide detailed information such as how companies can make unconscious bias training effective and how companies evaluate and/or report training results. The UN also provides a Women's Empowerment Principles Gender Gap Analysis Tool (WEPs Tool). This tool particularly helps organizations to identify strengths and gaps with concrete targets regarding gender equality (UN Global Compact, 2019). Nevertheless, it is only a learning platform which does not serve as a regulatory reporting mechanism for gender equality. The absence of standardization with clear criteria or methodology is of concern because it is difficult for organizations to review and benchmark gender equality/sustainable workplace performance (Siew, 2015). Table 4.4 recommends some example questions that tourism corporations can consider and elaborate upon in SR to mainstream gender equality in CSR agendas.

To reflect the findings of this study, and on gaps and the potential improvements of gender equality reporting by elaborating critical information, a framework is proposed for tourism organizations to systematically measure and disclose gender equality performance and promote equitable workplaces in tourism. Figure 4.3 shows that major waves of liberal, standpoint, and post-structural feminism have influenced the formation of structural, material, and cultural gender equality initiatives in tourism organizations.

Table 4.4 Recommended questions in SR regarding gender equality

Target (goal)	What is the goal of gender equality policies and strategies? What is the numeric value to close the disparity? What is the target number of participants for the following year? How often will the programmes or events be conducted? What is the target number of women to become full-time workers? What is the target value for job flexibility?
Process	Who was involved to formulate initiatives? Who invited the recipients? What opportunities or programmes were provided for women? How often were opportunities or programmes given?
Recipients	How many were women and men as recipients? Who are they (e.g., gender, ethnicity, age, and sexuality)? How were the recipients or participants chosen? What were the job positions of recipients?

Nonetheless, little is known as to whether gender equality was mainstreamed and if a gender-sensitive approach is incorporated into the implementation and evaluation of initiatives by corporations (Davids et al., 2014). The lack of information on target (goal), process, and recipients in SR indicates that tourism corporations may over-claim their commitments to gender equality. The notion of statement culture is of concern because corporations can be conceived as inequality regimes where neo-liberalization of feminism ignores the structural causes of gender inequalities. Therefore, the framework suggests that clear and concrete measurement and reporting of the information on target (goal), process, and recipients trigger the mainstreaming of gender equality. The systematic measurement and disclosure of gender equality performance can end the practice of femwashing and create decent, equitable, and sustainable workplaces in tourism.

7. Conclusion

Although women constitute more than half of the tourism workforce (UNWTO & UN Women, 2019), sustainable tourism research has neglected gender equality as well as corporations' approaches to make decent workplaces for both women and men. In addition, few studies have explored SR to investigate to what extent tourism corporations develop, measure, and review gender equality performance. In response to these gaps, this chapter set out to investigate how tourism corporations measure and disclose the target (goal), process, and recipients of gender equality initiatives through an examination of SR.

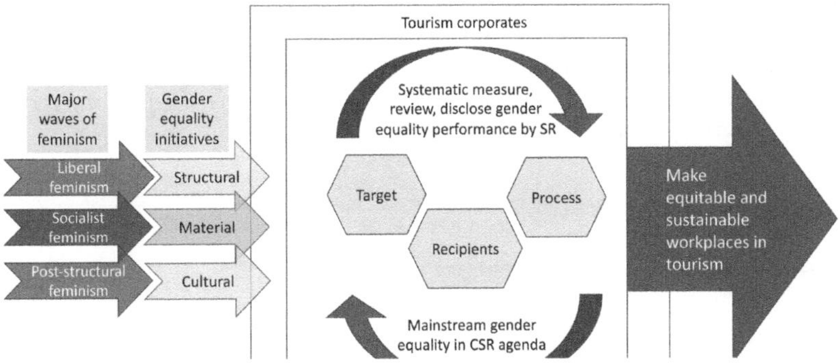

Figure 4.3 Sustainability reporting framework for gender equality initiatives

The findings show that tourism corporations have substandard SR on target (goal), process, and recipients and they might not have made sincere efforts to measure and disclose gender equality performance. The poor SR may relate to the absence of a standardized reporting mechanism for gender equality. This is of concern because the inadequate SR regarding gender equality performance indicates that gender equality has not yet mainstreamed in tourism organizations. This study argues that information on target (goal), process, and recipients of gender equality initiatives can indicate proactive and sustainable human resource management by tourism corporations. This study has its value in the investigation of corporate approaches for achieving gender equality (Goal No. 5 of the UNSDGs). This critical reflection can help corporations to remove potential femwashing practice and mainstream gender equality through sincere SR.

This study only considered publicly available documents through corporate websites. Future research is encouraged to investigate company internal documents to measure their mechanisms and performance regarding the implementation of gender equality initiatives. This could be facilitated through partnership with tourism corporations. Furthermore, this study focuses on women employees because gender inequality has been a persistent issue manifested in the gender pay gap, and in gender segregation in power and job categories in tourism (UNWTO & UN Women, 2019).

Further research is warranted to examine tourism corporations' gender equality initiatives extended to other women such as consumers, suppliers, and members of local communities. Although this study has not given simultaneous recognition to multiple identities such as gender and ethnicity (Budgeon, 2011), it suggests that in SR, corporations should consider the intersectional identities of the recipients, including gender, ethnicity, age, and sexuality. Despite these limitations, this study provides a major contribution by investigating the approaches of tourism corporations to gender equality by integrating SR with a gender-sensitive approach.

References

Accor Hotels. (2017). *Corporate responsibility report.* Retrieved 10 March 2020 from https://group.accor.com/en/commitment

Acker, J. (2006). Inequality regimes: Gender, class, and race in organizations. *Gender & Society, 20*(4), 441–64.

Ackerly, B.A. (2001). Feminist theory: Liberal. In N.J. Smelser & P.B. Baltes (eds), *International encyclopedia of the social and behavioral sciences* (pp. 5499–502). Oxford: Pergamon.

Adams, C.A., & Frost, G.R. (2008). *Integrating sustainability reporting into management practices.* Paper presented at the Accounting Forum.

Aitchison, C.C. (2005). Feminist and gender perspectives in tourism studies: The social-cultural nexus of critical and cultural theories. *Tourist Studies, 5*(3), 207–24.

Alarcón, D.M., & Cole, S. (2019). No sustainability for tourism without gender equality. *Journal of Sustainable Tourism, 27*(7), 903–19.

Allen, R., Dawson, G., Wheatley, K., & White, C.S. (2004). Diversity practices: Learning responses for modern organizations. *Development and Learning in Organizations: An International Journal, 18*(6), 13–15. https://doi.org/10.1108/14777280410564185

Amran, A., & Haniffa, R. (2011). Evidence in development of sustainability reporting: A case of a developing country. *Business Strategy and the Environment, 20*(3), 141–56.

Armstrong, J., Walby, S., & Strid, S. (2009). The gendered division of labour: How can we assess the quality of employment and care policy from a gender equality perspective? *Benefits, 17*(3), 263–75.

Barkemeyer, R., Preuss, L., & Lee, L. (2015). On the effectiveness of private transnational governance regimes – evaluating corporate sustainability reporting according to the Global Reporting Initiative. *Journal of World Business, 50*(2), 312–25.

Baum, T. (2013). *International perspectives on women and work in hotels, catering and tourism.* Working Paper 1/2013. ILO. Geneva, Switzerland.

Baum, T. (2016). *Human resource issues in international tourism* (2nd ed.). Elsevier. https://doi.org/10.1016/0261-5177(94)90013-2

Bockman, J. (2013). Neoliberalism. *Contexts, 12*(3), 14–15.

Bowen, G.A. (2009). Document analysis as a qualitative research method. *Qualitative Research Journal, 9*(2), 27.

Brown, H.S., de Jong, M., & Levy, D.L. (2009). Building institutions based on information disclosure: Lessons from GRI's sustainability reporting. *Journal of Cleaner Production, 17*(6), 571–80.

Buckley, R. (2012). Sustainability reporting and certification in tourism. *Tourism Recreation Research, 37*(1), 85–90.
Budgeon, S. (2011). The contradictions of successful femininity: Third-wave feminism, postfeminism and 'new' femininities. In R. Gill & C. Scharff (eds), *New femininities* (pp. 279–92). London: Palgrave Macmillan.
Burhan, A.H.N., & Rahmanti, W. (2012). The impact of sustainability reporting on company performance. *Journal of Economics, Business, & Accountancy Ventura, 15*(2), 257–72.
Burris, J.M. (2012). *Finding feminism in American political discourse: A discourse analysis of post-feminist language.* University of North Florida. UNF Graduate Theses and Dissertations. Retrieved from https://digitalcommons.unf.edu/etd/395
Carnival UK. (2018). *Gender pay report fleet.* Retrieved 15 March 2020 from https://www.carnivalcorp.com/governance/business-conduct-ethics
Carvalho, I., Costa, C., Lykke, N., & Torres, A. (2018). *Agency, structures and women managers' views of their careers in tourism.* Paper presented at the Women's Studies International Forum.
Chambers, D., Munar, A.M., Khoo-Lattimore, C., & Biran, A. (2017). Interrogating gender and the tourism academy through epistemological lens. *Anatolia, 28*(4), 501–13.
Davids, T., Van Driel, F., & Parren, F. (2014). Feminist change revisited: Gender mainstreaming as slow revolution. *Journal of International Development, 26*(3), 396–408.
Delbard, O. (2008). CSR legislation in France and the European regulatory paradox: An analysis of EU CSR policy and sustainability reporting practice. *Corporate Governance (Bradford), 8*(4), 397–405.
Delta Airlines. (2018). *Corporate social responsibility report.* Retrieved 17 March 2020 from https://www.delta.com
Duffy, L.N., Kline, C.S., Mowatt, R.A., & Chancellor, H.C. (2015). Women in tourism: Shifting gender ideology in the DR. *Annals of Tourism Research, 52*, 72–86.
Dupire, M., & M'Zali, B. (2018). CSR strategies in response to competitive pressures. *Journal of Business Ethics, 148*(3), 603–23.
Equality in Tourism. (2021). *Why gender matters.* Retrieved 5 April 2021 from https://www.equalityintourism.org/about-us/our-vision/
Figueroa-Domecq, C., Pritchard, A., Segovia-Pérez, M., Morgan, N., & Villacé-Molinero, T. (2015). Tourism gender research: A critical accounting. *Annals of Tourism Research, 52*, 87–103.
Fodor, É., Glass, C., & Nagy, B. (2019). Transnational business feminism: Exporting feminism in the global economy. *Gender, Work & Organization, 26*(8), 1117–37.
Font, X., & Lynes, J. (2018). Corporate social responsibility in tourism and hospitality. *Journal of Sustainable Tourism, 26*(7), 1027–42.
Forbes. (2019). Global 2000: The world's largest public companies. Retrieved 25 November 2019 from https://www.forbes.com/global2000/#647ac9b5335d
Franzoni, S., & Avellino, M. (2019). Sustainability reporting in international hotel chains. *SYMPHONYA Emerging Issues in Management, 1*, 96–107.
Fukuda-Parr, S., & McNeill, D. (2019). Knowledge and power in setting and measuring SDGs. *Global Policy, 10*(1), 5–15.
GOV.UK. (2019). *Gender pay gap service.* Retrieved 27 November 2019 from https://gender-pay-gap.service.gov.uk/Employer/WDQu77k5/2017
GRI. (2020). The global standards for sustainability reporting. Retrieved 15 February 2020 from https://www.globalreporting.org/standards/

Grosser, K., & McCarthy, L. (2019). Imagining new feminist futures: How feminist social movements contest the neoliberalization of feminism in an increasingly corporate-dominated world. *Gender, Work & Organization, 26*(8), 1100–16.
Grosser, K., & Moon, J. (2005). Gender mainstreaming and corporate social responsibility: Reporting workplace issues. *Journal of Business Ethics, 62*(4), 327–40.
Haas, L. (2003). Parental leave and gender equality: Lessons from the European Union. *Review of Policy Research, 20*(1), 89–114.
Heimtun, B., & Morgan, N. (2012). Proposing paradigm peace: Mixed methods in feminist tourism research. *Tourist Studies, 12*(3), 287–304.
Herrera, J., & de las Heras-Rosas, C. (2020). Corporate social responsibility and human resource management: Towards sustainable business organizations. *Sustainability, 12*(3), 841.
Holden, E., Linnerud, K., & Banister, D. (2014). Sustainable development: Our common future revisited. *Global Environmental Change, 26*, 130–9.
ILO. (2021). Decent work. Retrieved 4 January 2021 from https://www.ilo.org/global/topics/decent-work/lang--en/index.htm
Isidro, H., & Sobral, M. (2015). The effects of women on corporate boards on firm value, financial performance, and ethical and social compliance. *Journal of Business Ethics, 132*(1), 1–19.
Khoo-Lattimore, C., Yang, E.C.L., & Je, J.S. (2019). Assessing gender representation in knowledge production: A critical analysis of UNWTO's planned events. *Journal of Sustainable Tourism, 27*(7), 920–38.
Korean Air. (2018). Sustainability report. Korean Air. Retrieved 20 December 2019 from www.koreanair.com
Laughlin, K.A., Gallagher, J., Cobble, D.S., Boris, E., Nadasen, P., Gilmore, S., & Zarnow, L. (2010). Is it time to jump ship? Historians rethink the waves metaphor. *Feminist Formations, 22*(1) 76–135.
Lozano, R., Nummert, B., & Ceulemans, K. (2016). Elucidating the relationship between sustainability reporting and organizational change management for sustainability. *Journal of Cleaner Production, 125*, 168–88.
Ma, E., Wu, L., Yang, W., & Xu, S.T. (2021). Hotel work-family support policies and employees' needs, concerns and challenges: The case of working mothers' maternity leave experience. *Tourism Management, 83*, 104216.
Madera, J.M. (2013). Best practices in diversity management in customer service organizations: An investigation of top companies cited by Diversity Inc. *Cornell Hospitality Quarterly, 54*(2), 124–35.
Madera, J.M. (2018). What's in it for me? Perspective taking as an intervention for improving attitudes toward diversity management. *Cornell Hospitality Quarterly, 59*(2), 100–11.
Marriott International. (2018). *Serve 360 report*. Retrieved 1 November 2019 from https:// serve360 .marriott .com/ wp -content/ uploads/ 2018/ 10/ 2018 _Serve _360 _Report.pdf
Marx, U. (2019). Accounting for equality: Gender budgeting and moderate feminism. *Gender, Work & Organization, 26*(8), 1176–90.
Medrado, L., & Jackson, L. A. (2016). Corporate nonfinancial disclosures: An illuminating look at the corporate social responsibility and sustainability reporting practices of hospitality and tourism firms. *Tourism and Hospitality Research, 16*(2), 116–32.
Moyer, J.D., & Hedden, S. (2020). Are we on the right path to achieve the sustainable development goals? *World Development, 127*, 104749.
Munar, A.M. (2017). To be a feminist in (tourism) academia. *Anatolia, 28*(4), 514–29.

Nimri, R., Kensbock, S., Bailey, J., & Patiar, A. (2021). Management perceptions of sexual harassment of hotel room attendants. *Current Issues in Tourism, 24*(3), 354–66.

OECD. (2019). *OECD family database*. Retrieved 22 November 2019 from http://www.oecd.org/els/family/database.htm

Perez-Batres, L.A., Doh, J.P., Miller, V.V., & Pisani, M.J. (2012). Stakeholder pressures as determinants of CSR strategic choice: Why do firms choose symbolic versus substantive self-regulatory codes of conduct? *Journal of Business Ethics, 110*(2), 157–72.

Perkov, D., Primorac, D., & Perkov, M. (2016). Position of female managers in Croatian tourism. *International Journal of Economic Perspectives, 10*(1), 62–70.

Powell, G.N. (2018). *Women and men in management*. Thousand Oaks, CA: Sage.

Pritchard, A. (2014). Gender and feminist perspectives in tourism research. In C.M. Hall, A. Lew, & A.M. Williams (eds), *The Wiley Blackwell companion to tourism* (1st edn, pp. 314–24). London: John Wiley & Sons.

Prügl, E. (2015). Neoliberalizing feminism. *New Political Economy, 20*(4), 614–31.

Qiu, R.T., Park, J., Li, S., & Song, H. (2020). Social costs of tourism during the COVID-19 pandemic. *Annals of Tourism Research, 84*, 102994.

Reynolds, D., Rahman, I., & Bradetich, S. (2014). Hotel managers' perceptions of the value of diversity training: An empirical investigation. *International Journal of Contemporary Hospitality Management, 26*(3), 426–46.

Riccò, R., & Guerci, M. (2014). Diversity challenge: An integrated process to bridge the 'implementation gap'. *Business Horizons, 57*(2), 235–45.

Roberts, A. (2015). The political economy of 'transnational business feminism' problematizing the corporate-led gender equality agenda. *International Feminist Journal of Politics, 17*(2), 209–31.

Rubery, J. (2002). Gender mainstreaming and gender equality in the EU: The impact of the EU employment strategy. *Industrial Relations Journal, 33*(5), 500–22.

Runhaar, H., Dieperink, C., & Driessen, P. (2006). Policy analysis for sustainable development. *International Journal of Sustainability in Higher Education, 7*(1), 34–56. https://doi.org/10.1108/14676370610639236

Siew, R.Y.J. (2015). A review of corporate sustainability reporting tools (SRTs). *Journal of Environmental Management, 164*, 180–95.

Singh, R.K., Murty, H.R., Gupta, S.K., & Dikshit, A.K. (2009). An overview of sustainability assessment methodologies. *Ecological Indicators, 9*(2), 189–212.

Stankeviciute, Z., & Savaneviciene, A. (2013). Sustainability as a concept for human resource management. *Economics and Management, 18*(4), 837–46.

Thorsen, D.E., & Lie, A. (2006). What is neoliberalism? Oslo, University of Oslo, Department of Political Science, Manuscript, 1–21.

Țîțu, M.A., Răulea, A.S., & Țîțu, Ș. (2016). Measuring service quality in tourism industry. *Procedia-Social and Behavioral Sciences, 221*, 294–301.

Torres-Delgado, A., & Saarinen, J. (2014). Using indicators to assess sustainable tourism development: A review. *Tourism Geographies, 16*(1), 31–47.

UN. (2020). *Policy brief: COVID-19 and transforming tourism*. Retrieved from https://www.un.org/sites/un2.un.org/files/sg_policy_brief_covid-19_tourism_august_2020.pdf

UN. (2021). *The 17 goals: History*. Retrieved 5 January 2021 from https://sdgs.un.org/goals

UN Global Compact. (2019). *Empower women in the workplace, marketplace and community*. Retrieved 27 November 2019 from https://www.unglobalcompact.org/what-is-gc/our-work/social/gender-equality

UN Global Compact. (2020). *The ten principles of the UN Global Compact.* Retrieved 14 January 2020 from https://www.unglobalcompact.org/what-is-gc/mission/principles

UNWTO & ILO. (2014). *Measuring employment in the tourism industries – guide with best practices.* Retrieved from https://www.e-unwto.org/doi/book/10.18111/9789284416158

UNWTO & UN Women. (2019). *Global report on women in tourism – second edition.* Retrieved from Madrid, Spain: https://www.e-unwto.org/doi/pdf/10.18111/9789284420384

Uyar, A., Koseoglu, M.A., Kılıç, M., & Mehraliyev, F. (2020). Thematic structure of sustainability reports of the hospitality and tourism sector: A periodical, regional, and format-based analysis. *Current Issues in Tourism*, 24*(18)*, 1–26.

Vaismoradi, M., Turunen, H., & Bondas, T. (2013). Content analysis and thematic analysis: Implications for conducting a qualitative descriptive study. *Nursing & Health Sciences, 15*(3), 398–405.

Van Der Ploeg, L., & Vanclay, F. (2013). Credible claim or corporate spin?: A checklist to evaluate corporate sustainability reports. *Journal of Environmental Assessment Policy and Management, 15*(03), 1350012.

WGEA. (2019). Australia's Gender Pay Gap Statistics. Retrieved 14 December 2019 from https://www.wgea.gov.au/data/fact-sheets/australias-gender-pay-gap-statistics

White, V., McCrum, G., Blackstock, K., & Scott, A. (2006). Indicators and sustainable tourism: Literature review. The Macaulay Institute,Aberdeen.

Winchenbach, A., Hanna, P., & Miller, G. (2019). Rethinking decent work: The value of dignity in tourism employment. *Journal of Sustainable Tourism, 27*(7), 1026–43.

WTTC. (2021). Economic impact reports. Retrieved 20 March 2021 from https://wttc.org/Research/Economic-Impact

5 Socio-cultural barriers to Saudi women's participation in the tourism industry: a systematic literature review

Rafiah Almathami and Judith Mair

1. Introduction

Gender diversity in any workplace not only increases productivity but can also foster creativity, effectiveness, marketing opportunities, recruitment and maximization of the industry image (Green et al., 2002; Pattnaik & Tripathy, 2014). Indeed, some studies show that organizations with women in leadership roles are more profitable (Bierema, 2016; Kotiranta et al., 2010; Loeffen, 2016; Thompson, 2015). Female leadership plays a significant role in inspiring other women to seek employment, to succeed and to improve their future (Bear et al., 2017; Chan & Drasgow, 2001; London et al., 2019; Paglis & Green, 2002; Thompson, 2015). Furthermore, there are positive effects on the economies of countries with women participating in all sectors and across different levels of seniority (Ritter-Hayashi et al., 2016). Thus, gender diversity in the workplace offers both social and economic benefits.

In many countries, the tourism industry has been identified as a significant source of economic growth and sustainable development (Khan et al., 2017; Petrevska, 2013; Richardson, 2010), thus rendering it an appropriate context for study. Studies of gender participation in tourism suggest that the more diverse the industry becomes, the more productive it also becomes (Cole, 2018; Figueroa-Domecq et al., 2020). Therefore, it is argued that countries that empower women and support their participation in the tourism industry will reap benefits that are not limited to women only, but that extend to both the industry sector and the national economy as well, contributing to a reduction in poverty and unemployment (Zhang & Zhang, 2020). Gender parity in these industries cannot be ignored for its potential in increasing the overall creativity of the organizations, leading to innovative solutions and ideas (Green et al., 2002; Pattnaik & Tripathy, 2014). In addition to these immediate benefits, with women acting as role models in these industries, the effects could be exponential for future generations, leading to diversification of girls' future career options in the long term.

In the Kingdom of Saudi Arabia's (KSA) tourism industry, women are dramatically underrepresented, making up only 1.2 per cent of the workforce, according to the General Authority for Statistics of Saudi Arabia (2018). This underrepresentation creates a number of issues that affect the national economy, the status of women and workforce diversity. In 2000, the United Nations World Tourism Organization (UNWTO) developed the Millennium Development Goals, which articulated the importance of supporting gender equality and the empowerment of women (UNSDG, 2018). Recognising this, Saudi Arabia is working to empower women and increase female participation in the labour market by addressing workplace culture to make the working environment more suitable for women.

The initiatives implemented by Crown Prince Mohammed bin Salman to enhance women's empowerment, such as increasing job opportunities for women in fields that were previously limited to men only, allowing women to drive and the rescinding of the male-guardianship law, are notable recent changes that enable women to work more equitably with men (Eloubeidi, 2020). These changes are also helping to shift public perception of women's work and are beginning to transform society to become more supportive of gender equality. As a result of eliminating these long-standing obstacles, female participation in the overall labour market has increased from 10.3 per cent to 14.2 per cent during 2005–2009 (Alfarran, 2016).

One key initiative has been Saudi Vision 2030, which aims to actively encourage the few current Saudi female leaders to positively influence young women to increase the proportion of women in leadership positions. Additionally, the National Transformation Program (NTP), a programme within Saudi Vision 2030, aims to improve the conditions of women's working lives in all sectors (Alturki & Alsharif, 2018). As Saudi Arabia is considered a tourist destination regionally and globally, the tourism and entertainment sectors are a key focus of the Saudi Vision 2030 programme's efforts to improve women's participation in the workforce (Alturki & Alsharif, 2018; Saudi Arabia Vision 2030, 2016a).

The tourism and entertainment sectors in Saudi Arabia have been identified as priority areas of the economy and a valuable income source (Sherbini et al., 2016). The creation of diverse job opportunities in the tourism and entertainment sectors is intended to enable the Saudi Arabian government to increase the contribution of the tourism and entertainment sectors to the national economy (Alturki & Alsharif, 2018; Saudi Arabia Vision 2030, 2016b). Although many countries use the term 'tourism and events sector', in the Saudi Arabian context, the term 'tourism and entertainment sector' is more readily used and more widely understood. The General Entertainment Authority (GEA) in Saudi Arabia was established in 2016 to contribute to the economy and supplement the tourism industry. The GEA states that entertainment should be available to all, regardless of income or social status and must meet global standards in order to enhance social cohesion (General Entertainment Authority, 2020).

Despite these relatively rapid changes in the economic and business environment for women in Saudi Arabia, and the accompanying government initiatives, research has not kept pace with these developments. Thus, research is needed to explore and understand the opportunities and challenges for women working in the tourism and entertainment industries and the role of the government in empowering Saudi women in these sectors.

2. Women in the Workforce: A Global Context

The twentieth century witnessed a significant change in the workforce as women stepped in during the First and Second World Wars (Toossi, 2002). This was accompanied by women asserting their rights, beginning with the suffrage movement and then the first wave of feminism, which focused on property, access to education, professional careers and the right to vote through political and social lobbying (Wellman, 1991). The second and third waves of feminism secured further rights for women in family and workplace domains and was global in its impact (Burkett, 2015; Jenny, 2012). We are arguably now in a fourth wave, which involves leveraging social media to seek justice for women, particularly in respect to sexual harassment and violence (Chamberlain, 2017), as evidenced in the #metoo movement.

Nevertheless, there continues to be inequity between the genders with respect to domestic responsibilities, with women continuing to bear the load (Morello et al., 2018), and in the workplace. For example, only 24 of the Fortune 500 organizations have female CEOs (Atkins, 2018). Women's underrepresentation in leadership positions is often attributed to the cultural perception that valued leadership traits are masculine, while women are viewed as not having the authority and strength to lead (Hymowitz, 2011; Michailidis et al., 2012). Often, women are expected to masculinize their behaviour, lower their ambitions and/or change their career path (Dainty et al., 2000) when confronted with these barriers. These gendered barriers have been exacerbated by COVID-19, with women also being more vulnerable to losing their jobs and returning to unpaid domestic responsibilities, including childcare (Women UN, 2020; Workplace Gender Equality Agency, 2020). The notable rise in gender-based violence correlates with these changes (Women UN, 2020). Equality cannot truly be achieved for women unless the equity issues associated with paid and unpaid care are addressed (Women UN, 2020).

The extent of these differences varies significantly across cultures and nationalities. Culture intersects with gender, education level, generation, religion, organization, or department in shaping the glass ceiling or barrier that impedes women's progression in the workplace. There are strategies for overcoming barriers and managing diversity and intercultural competence through developing 'knowledge, skills and attitude that result in effective communication' (Wilson, 2014). Cultural awareness programmes, for example, enhance employee engagement and reduce harassment complaints in the workplace (Distelhorst, 2007). A detailed discussion of intersectionality is beyond the scope of this chapter, but it is important to recognize that although research has taught us much about the generic and global challenges and barriers that face women in the workplace, there are specific cultural issues that relate to contexts those faced by women in Islamic countries like Saudi Arabia.

3. The Saudi Arabian Context

In 2019, only 22.12 per cent of the workforce was female in Saudi Arabia (World Bank, 2020) and while a worsening gender pay gap is considered to be one of the most significant challenges for working women in the Western world, in the KSA, female graduates simply are unable to access employment is seen as a greater challenge (Elmulthum & Elsayed, 2017). In order to understand some of the drivers of this situation, two key areas – educational and employment opportunities – merit further investigation.

3.1 Educational Opportunities

Women's education and work status in Saudi Arabia have been restricted by the interlinking nature of culture and traditions (Al Alhareth et al., 2015; Sabbagh, 1996). However, changes have slowly commenced. In the 1960s, profits from oil production, along with gender-focused socio-economic changes, promoted the advancement of women, leading to an increase in female school enrolment.

For example, in 1960, only 15 educational institutions allowed Saudi females to attend, but by the early 1970s this had increased to 155 institutions (Almohsen, 2001; Hamdan, 2005). Saudi Arabia currently has 29 public universities and 14 private universities, most of which now accept both genders; however, campuses are gender-segregated (Allahmorad and Zreik, 2020). Furthermore, most of the government universities have several campuses, as well as community colleges or junior colleges in rural areas, which not only allows women to study but also encourages them to diversify their fields of studies (Allahmorad & Zreik, 2020). Every year, the Saudi government approves a monthly monetary incentive for both male and female students to encourage tertiary education and pursuing higher degrees (El-Sanabary, 1994). Because of this initiative, the number of female students enrolled in higher education has grown exponentially from 182 187 in the 1960 to 1970s to 3 142 640 in 2017 (El-Sanabary, 1994; Saudi Census, 2018). This 15-fold increase over four decades is predicted to continue (First Voluntary National Review, 2018).

In 2005, the King Abdullah Sponsorship Program was launched in an effort to encourage Saudi students, irrespective of gender, to study abroad, gain higher education degrees and international experience (Kim & Alghamdi, 2019; Taylor & Albasri, 2014). In the last two years, the national 'Your Job-Your Scholarship' scheme has been offered by different ministries to fill their required positions with young Saudis and to increase female representation (Ministry of Education, 2018). According to Wilcke (2010):

> Central to King Abdullah's reform project have been four areas directly tied to the human rights of Saudi citizens: women's rights, freedom of expression, judicial fairness, and religious tolerance. Today, Saudis are freer than they were five years ago—Saudi women are less subject to rigid sex segregation in public places, citizens have greater latitude to criticize their government, and reform in the justice system may bring more transparency and fairness in judicial procedures. (n.p.)

The Saudi government goal to raise the number of Saudi women workers to 28 per cent by 2020 (Gazette, 2015; Naseem & Dhruva, 2017) was exceeded, with female workforce numbers reaching 31.3 per cent that year (Darasha, 2021). Nevertheless, there is still significant opportunity for further increase considering that 54 per cent of Saudi university graduates are female, and they remain mostly unemployed due to the lack of jobs offered to women (Gazette, 2015). Measures are being taken to make the working environment more suitable for women, such as increasing women's representation in managerial positions through training and leadership orientation for women, and creating supportive employment programmes to help create a more suitable workplace environment for women (National Transformation Program, 2018).

Tourism organizations in Saudi Arabia work to enhance productivity by providing training courses in tourism institutes or providing scholarships for studying abroad (SCTA, n.d.). Ibraheem Al-Sini, Dean of the Tourism and Hospitality College at King Abdul Aziz University (KAU), points out that on a global average, 75 per cent of the employees and students in the tourism sector were female. Thus, decision makers at KAU have recognized its importance and decided to create an events management department for women – previously the programmes were only available to males. The goal is to provide a targeted degree for females and will form one of the specialties in the Department of Tourism and Hospitality at KAU (Hameed, 2018, p. 121). Moreover, the Saudi government is working towards significant reform in relation to women's empowerment and rights with the Ministry of Tourism and the entertainment sector offering their own scholarships to potential workers, (Gazette, 2020) especially females (Saudi Arabia Vision 2030, 2016b).

3.2 Employment Opportunities

Women's employment rate into the future in the KSA is likely to be positively impacted by government plans to decrease the overall unemployment rate of Saudis from 11.5 per cent to be 9 per cent (Naseem & Dhruva, 2017). More specifically, The Vision 2030 agenda aims to provide more than 50 000 employment opportunities for Saudi women (Business Line, 2017). Furthermore, new labour laws and regulations which govern family relations, particularly marriage, divorce and custody of children (Aldosari, 2016; An-Na'im, 2002), have been initiated with the goal of increasing the participation of women in the workplace (Thompson, 2015).

Current initiatives are designed to help diversify and expand female participation beyond the education and health sectors where they have been traditionally employed (Alzaeem, 2016). Saudi women occupied around 35 per cent of positions in the Ministry of Education and 18 per cent in the Ministry of Health (Alzaeem, 2016). Overall, the aim (pre-Covid-19) was to increase the number of women in the labour force from 17.8 per cent in 2015 to 30 per cent by 2020 (Alturki & Alsharif, 2018). Saudi Vision 2030 is specifically committed to encouraging women to work in diverse fields such as the tourism and entertainment industry and this is seen as a way to make a significant contribution to this increase in female employment; however, with only 1.2 per cent of the tourism workforce being Saudi women (General Authority for Statistics Kingdom of Saudi Arabia, 2018), there is still some way to go.

The Saudi Arabian government seeks to enhance gender equality in the tourism sector to raise tourism productivity, as well as to promote, grow and support the creation of job and leadership opportunities for Saudi women (First Voluntary National Review, 2018). For example, a small number of programmes exist to support and encourage women to learn traditional crafts, start their own small business and commercialize their craft (SCTA, n.d.). The outcomes of these initiatives are evidenced in the proportion of female employees and wage growth in tourism (Saudi Arabian Business Council, 2017).

Women remain a marginalized component of tourism research despite governments working towards encouraging, supporting and empowering women, particularly in the context of their employment in the tourism industry (Gentry, 2007; Hammond, 2003). Furthermore, given the cultural context of the KSA, it is important not to assume that generic global barriers and challenges to women's employment apply. Therefore, this chapter will now identify, using a systematic literature review as a basis, the cultural factors affecting women in employment and the workplace, and its application to Saudi Arabia.

4. Methodology

This study employed a systematic literature review (SLR) approach. SLRs involve collecting and evaluating a wide range of journal articles over a specific period of time (Williams & Plouffe, 2007) in order to help the researcher to position their research within what is known in their chosen field of study (Creswell & Creswell, 2017). There are three broad approaches to a SLR: a meta-analysis, traditional narrative review or systematic quantitative review (Pickering et al., 2015). The meta-analysis approach uses statistical analysis of all the research findings over a given period of time based on a set of inclusion and exclusion criteria. Patterns and differences are identified (Mays et al., 2005). The traditional narrative review is suited to more broad research questions, and was not used as the approach lacks a study protocol, has no specific search strategy, is prone to selection bias, does not result in evidence-based conclusions, does not produce a critical appraisal and is subject to personal bias in the conclusions (Allen, 2017; Pae, 2015). The systematic quantitative review adopts a systematic approach that is captured in a flowchart that presents the number of research articles captured and excluded (see Figure 5.1). This approach is effective in mapping the boundaries of knowledge and capturing the complexity of research undertaken (Pickering et al., 2015). It is this methodology that has been adopted as it is important to map a diverse landscape of research.

4.1 The Systematic Review Process

The systematic review process involves the development of a research protocol that contains the search terms and screening criteria. Five steps are involved – (1) defining the research question; (2) formulating the review protocol; (3) searching the literature; (4) extracting the literature; and (5) synthesizing the findings (Yang et al., 2017). As a first stage, the research question underpinning the review was determined to be: What factors influence the employment of women in the tourism and entertainment industries?

Based on the traditional systematic literature review process, a set of guidelines and criteria were selected to analyse the existing literature. This approach identifies the gaps in existing knowledge on the gender issues in the tourism and entertainment industries. This study used the Preferred Reporting Items for Systematic Reviews and Meta-Analyses (PRISMA) methodology requiring the researcher to document the steps that are used in collecting and evaluating the articles in a transparent manner (Moher et al., 2009) (Figure 5.1).

Systematic reviews have been used in comparable contexts such as gender in tourism (Figueroa-Domecq et al., 2020; Yang et al., 2017); gender perspectives on entertainment (Reich, 2021); leisure studies (Henderson & Gibson, 2013); and in the context of gender in events and festivals (Almathami et al., 2020). The aim here in this chapter's study is to provide an objective assessment of the research in the field (in this case socio-cultural barriers to Saudi women's participation in the tourism and entertainment industry), and that may be readily be duplicated by others (Pickering et al., 2015)

There were six inclusion criteria for the systematic review. The article had to be:

1. focused on the employment of women in tourism or entertainment (given the Saudi preference for this term over 'events');
2. published in an academic peer-reviewed journal;
3. a full-text article;
4. published in either English or Arabic languages;
5. concerned with any of the following variables: attitude towards gender diversity; empowerment of women; gender equality; harassment; environmental variables of society, culture and education; and
6. focused on participants that were members of the tourism or entertainment industries.

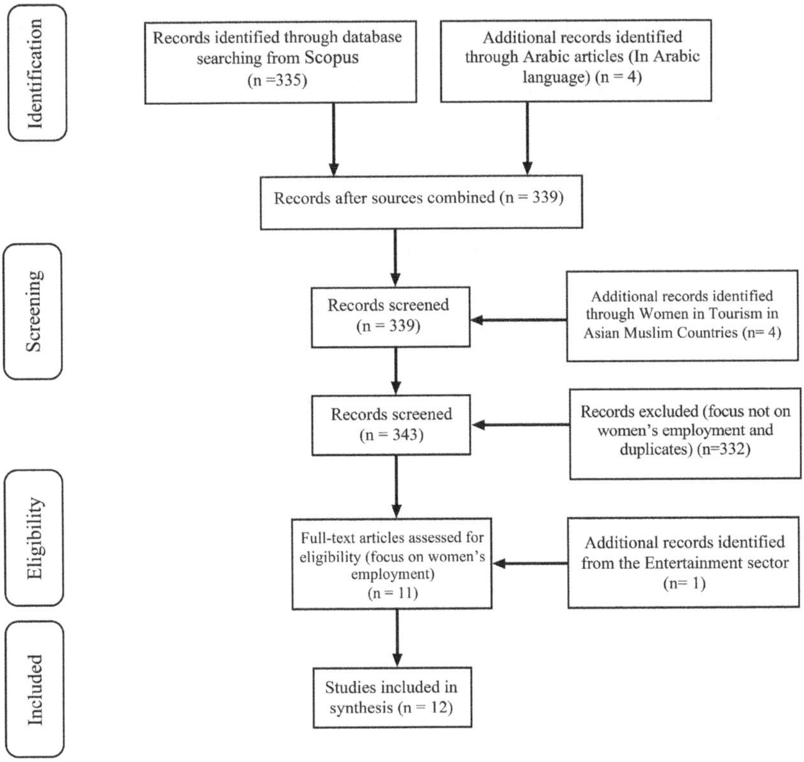

Source: Adapted from Moher et al. (2009).

Figure 5.1 PRISMA flowchart: systematic literature review (SLR)

The three exclusion criteria were: (1) studies which had a general focus on tourism and entertainment without reference to gender; (2) studies which included a gender element but were focussed on women as travellers, rather than as employees; and (3) studies specific to particular hospitality settings (e.g., female chefs).

The initial protocol involved searching the Scopus database for journal articles using the keywords, 'Tourism' and 'Entertainment' and 'women' OR 'female' OR 'gender' OR 'tourism & women' OR 'tourism & gender' OR 'tourism & diversity' AND '1980–2020' (Figure 5.1). Seven databases were used in this research: EBSCO Host, Elsevier, Emerald, ProQuest, Sage, Scopus and Web of Science. The inclusion criteria were English and Arabic language peer-reviewed journals. The researcher screened all the obtained studies' titles, keywords and abstracts to ensure that relevant articles were not omitted. Studies were not selected unless the title or abstract focused on gender in tourism or entertainment; where this was not clear, the full text of each paper was screened according to the eligibility criteria described above.

These search words identified 335 journal articles about gender and tourism and/or entertainment worldwide, which met all the selection criteria. Four additional, Arabic language publications were also added. Therefore, after these sources were combined, there was a total of 339 records. Moreover, in 2021 a book was published about women working in tourism in Asian Muslim countries (Valek & Almuhrzi, 2021). Given the direct relevance of the content, the new publication was added to this study, thus adding four more publications and bringing the total to 343. However, further screening resulted in the removal of 332 articles that were not specific to women's employment in these sectors (e.g., they were about women as tourists, rather than women employed in the tourism industry) or were duplicates; thereafter, 11 publications remained. Further searches focussed on the entertainment sector added one, thus bringing the final total to 12.

5. Findings

The aim of this study was to provide an objective assessment of the research in the field to understand the socio-cultural barriers impacting Saudi women's participation in the tourism and entertainment industry. The systematic literature review unearthed only 12 journal articles over the 40-year period that focused specifically on employment of women in the tourism industry. As noted, papers that focused on women as travellers, or women working in specific hospitality settings were not included in this review. The findings from this review suggest that the most common focus for study has been the barriers that women face in the tourism workplace. These include working conditions, socio-cultural barriers, and work–family conflict.

However, the findings also show that most of the research that has been carried out on women working in tourism has focused on the USA and Australia; thus, democratic and neoliberalist cultures seem to dominate discourses in this field. This correlates with the worldwide lack of research in the subfields of women's employment in both tourism and entertainment, which is confounding given the high proportion of women working in these sectors (Oakley, 2016). This argument is supported by several sources, who state that research in the tourism and entertainment industry is highly masculinized (Tribe, 2010), or dominated by males (Pritchard & Morgan, 2007). It is not clear how relevant the findings of these Western-based studies are to an investigation of the situation for working women in Saudi Arabia.

Literature on women in the tourism workforce in Islamic countries is scant, with even fewer studies being specific to the conditions affecting working women in the tourism and entertainment sectors in Saudi Arabia. Only four studies specific to women in the workplace in Islamic countries were found in this review. Three of the former studies were in the contexts of Oman, Jordan and Iraq and found barriers that affected women in the tourism sector, such as cultural, diversity, social, education, work environment, and demographic factors (Alkharusi & Segumpan, 2021; Alrwajfah et al., 2020; Jassim, 2011). In one study specifically in the Saudi context, Almathami et al. (2020) found several similar challenges facing Saudi women in the event and festival sectors, such as cultural values, workplace environment, gender diversity, education and regulation.

6. Discussion

Given the scarcity of literature in the specific field of interest of this research (women working in the tourism and entertainment industries in KSA), it is necessary to revert to research undertaken in other employment sectors in KSA in order to gain an understanding of the situation for women employed in the tourism and entertainment sectors. Overall, there is a dearth of knowledge about the conditions affecting working women in Saudi Arabia. In response to calls for more research (Henderson & Gibson, 2013; Olesen, 2011; Valentine, 2007) there has been an increase in interest over the last five years on the issues facing women in gaining employment in general in Saudi Arabia (Alasgah & Rizk, 2021; Almathami et al., 2020; World Tourism Organization, 2021).

One of the few studies conducted has been that of Al-Asfour et al. (2017). Using a phenomenological qualitative approach, Al-Asfour et al. (2017) conducted in-depth interviews with 12 women employed in the government, private and not-for-profit sectors, such as teachers, nutritionists, nurses, office managers, assistant school principals, accountants and retailers. These findings identified significant challenges regarding career opportunities and advancement for women, including: lack of work–family balance; restricted mobility and freedom; and workplace discrimination and inequality (Al-Asfour et al., 2017). These issues were found to be much greater for Saudi women than for their counterparts in the Western world. The findings of the SLR reported on in this chapter suggest that these issues are pertinent for women in the tourism and entertainment industries.

Another study by Hakem (2017) into the challenges faced by Saudi women, highlighted gender segregation, the male-orientated society of Saudi Arabia, and the perception of men as leaders and women as followers, as negatively affecting women's careers. One example of this is the Shariah law requiring that women be accompanied by a male at all times, as this restricts the freedom of association of women (Hakem, 2017). Hakem also argued that changes were occurring because exposure to Western cultures has increased the confidence and assertiveness of Saudi women, and royal family support for greater freedoms being given to Saudi women, such as the recent removal of restrictions on women driving. Hakem points out, however, that the process for greater freedoms of women in the KSA workplace is slow and strongly resisted by the conservative religious authorities.

Existing literature also shows that in those sectors which have been examined, traditional cultural values limit Saudi women's ability and desire to participate in the workforce. Women cannot socialize with men that they are not related to in Saudi society. Additionally, they cannot make a major decision without male permission; this includes studying abroad or running a business. This means that women are even required to obtain permission from a male guardian to work (Alhabidi, 2013). Although Saudi women have the ambition and ability, barriers are so great that they are often prevented from attempting to overcome these issues, both within the workplace and amongst society at large (Hakem, 2017).

Nevertheless, Saudi women are now seizing opportunities, presented by national initiatives, to challenge these barriers. One of these changes has seen families travel overseas for tourism and educational purposes (Al-Khateeb, 2007). This international exposure to the possibilities of tourism, along with their improved education and heightened economic status encourages Saudis to be more open-minded (Alghamdi, 2014). Alselaimi and Allui (2018, p. 88) argue that:

> An understanding of the full range of factors that underlie women's progression in the workforce may provide valuable insights into the dynamics of women in the workforce. This issue is not just of academic interest: ensuring that a greater number of women enter and progress in the workforce is a key current issue in terms of the government initiatives, as expounded by the women's empowerment programs advocated by the Vision2030. If we can gain a greater understanding of the positive socio-cultural and legal support, then this will inform the development of better – or different – legislative strategies to help support women's career progression.

Like most Arab nations, Saudi Arabia is a gender-segregated society, where men and women are not allowed to work together. Clearly, this is one of the major obstacles hindering women's participation in the workplace and making it extremely difficult for women to gain work experience (Hakem, 2017). In addition, gender segregation excludes Saudi women from networking opportunities as they are unable to socialize with all-male policymakers in, for example, the event and festival sector (Al-Shehry et al., 2006). This places women at a disadvantage with regards to both finding employment and progressing in their careers. Karolak (2013) concurs, arguing that Saudi Arabia's law of guardianship (women must be accompanied by a male at all times) should be amended soon. Relevant to the SLR which is the focus of this chapter, the work of Almathami et al (2020) found that the gender segregation and issues around a lack of diversity in the workplace are also significant barriers for women in the tourism and events industry.

Some efforts have been made in the Middle East to eliminate restrictions and give women the opportunity to represent themselves. For instance, social movements have attempted to address the issue of women working in public fields by providing gender-segregated facilities (Hakem, 2017). Furthermore, the initiatives allowing Saudi women to travel, study abroad and hold leadership positions should impact on the cultural attitudes towards more integrated environments (Karolak, 2013). Hakem (2017) also points out that Arab women, themselves, have the ability to make changes in society through their communication skills and growing confidence. However, no specific studies examining the implications of easing these restrictions were found in the SLR.

The literature on Saudi working women in general highlights that nepotism is another socio-cultural factor that limits employment opportunities for women in the KSA. Nepotism is defined as the preferential employment of relatives (Ford & McLaughlin, 1986) and, although prevalent worldwide, is more so in developing countries (Abdalla et al., 1998; Arasli et al., 2006). Wirth (2001) confirms that both nepotism and male-oriented norms limit advancement opportunities for women, and according to Vanhanen (1999), nepotism is even more common in cultures that have religious, tribal or nationalist influences. Al-Shehry et al. (2006) explains that:

> the tribal system plays an important role in the workplace as some government officials are fond of giving preference to their relatives while discharging their official responsibilities, even though this act is against their workplace ethics.

The issue of nepotism impacts Saudi women in that gender segregation excludes them from contact with influential male relatives, while their male counterparts are actively advantaged by this cultural norm.

Another significant point that has arisen in the literature on Saudi working women in general is the limited consideration of the issues involved in work–family conflict. There is evidence indicating that the social expectation that women raise and care for children disrupts the career pathways of women (Wirth, 2001) although Small et al. (2011) and Michailidis et al. (2012) note the shortfall in research that has been conducted in this area. In a male-oriented society with highly gendered roles, such as Saudi Arabia, these barriers are likely to be more significant (Allam, 2019). This is confirmed by Almathami et al. (2020), part of the SLR reported on in this chapter, who found that Saudi women working in the event and festival sectors reported significant challenges with conflicting home, family, childcare and work responsibilities.

If the KSA government initiatives to improve the representation of women in the workforce are to be achieved, there needs to be a greater understanding of gender discrimination and other socio-cultural barriers for women in Saudi Arabia, so strategies can be developed to address them.

7. Conclusion

This chapter collates and reflects upon previous studies on the barriers confronting women working in the tourism and entertainment industries with a particular focus on the KSA. The findings of this research identify a clear gap in our knowledge of the circumstances facing working women generally in the KSA, and those impacting women in the tourism and entertainment industries in particular, with only two peer-reviewed academic papers found to have focused on the latter to date. This indicates significant limitations in our understanding of the social, economic and cultural factors that enhance or hinder the situation for women in the tourism and entertainment workplaces in KSA. More broadly, the review found that equally scant research attention has been paid to women in employment in tourism in other Islamic countries and so there are few opportunities to be informed by knowledge from other, somewhat similar, countries.

Taking a lead from research that has been carried out in other employment sectors, it can be surmised that the key issues faced by women in the tourism and entertainment sectors relate to both global challenges and cultural factors specific to the KSA. The generic global challenges include the gender pay gap, harassment and discrimination, gender stereotyping, the glass ceiling, work–life balance, and the effects of the Covid pandemic which are being borne inequitably by women. However, research suggests that these global issues are felt more keenly by Saudi women (Al-Asfour et al., 2017), perhaps because of the additional cultural pressures. Significant cultural factors include the traditional role of women as homemakers in the KSA, the status of Saudi Arabia as a gender-segregated society, the lingering effects of male guardianship (which, although no longer a legal requirement, continues as a cultural norm), the pervasive culture of nepotism (a cultural norm which actively disadvantages women), and ongoing work–family conflict, particularly family and societal views of working women.

Our findings show that there is a need for more research to provide a fuller understanding which can inform the changes needed to address gender inequity within the Saudi tourism and entertainment workforces. Naturally, this SLR has gathered data at one point in time only; ongoing and future research will undoubtedly provide new insights into the phenomena under study. In order to corroborate our findings and reveal additional patterns, we encourage future research to extend and deepen this exploratory analysis.

References

Abdalla, H.F., Maghrabi, A.S., & Raggad, B.G. (1998). Assessing the perceptions of human resource managers toward nepotism: A cross-cultural study. *International Journal of Manpower*, *19*(8), 554–70. https://doi.org/10.1108/01437729810242235

Al Alhareth, Y., Al Dighrir, I., & Al Alhareth, Y. (2015). Review of women's higher education in Saudi Arabia. *American Journal of Educational Research*, *3*(1), 10–15. https://doi.org/10.12691/education-3-1-3

Al-Asfour, A., Tlaiss, H.A., Khan, S.A., & Rajasekar, J. (2017). Saudi women's work challenges and barriers to career advancement. *Career Development International*, *22*(2), 184–99. https://doi.org/10.1108/CDI-11-2016-0200

Al-Khateeb, S. (2007). The oil boom and its impact on women and families in Saudi Arabia. In A. Alsharekh (ed.), *The Gulf family: Kinship policies and modernity* (pp. 83–108). London: Middle East Institute.

Al-Shehry, A., Rogerson, S., Fairweather, N., & Prior, M. (2006). *The motivations for change towards e-government adoption: Saudi Arabia as a case study*. eGovernment Workshop, Brunel University.

Alasgah, A.A., & Rizk, E.S. (2021). Empowering Saudi women in the tourism and management sectors according to the Kingdom's 2030 vision. *Journal of Sustainable Finance & Investment*. https://doi.org/10.1080/20430795.2021.1874217

Aldosari, H. (2016). *The personal is political: Gender identity in the personal status laws of the Gulf Arab States*. Arab Gulf States Institute in Washington.

Alfarran, A. (2016). *Increasing women's labour market participation in Saudi Arabia: The role of government employment policy and multinational corporations* (Unpublished Doctoral Thesis). Victoria University.

Alghamdi, F. (2014). *Saudisation and women's empowerment through employment in the health care sector* (Unpublished Doctoral Thesis). Victoria University of Wellington.

Alhabidi, M. (2013). *Saudi women entrepreneur over coming barriers in ALKhober* (Unpublished Doctoral Thesis).Arizona State University.

Alkharusi, M., & Segumpan, R.G. (2021). Lived experiences of Omani women working in the tourism industry: A phenomenological study. In M. Alkharusic & R.G. Segumpan (eds). *Women in tourism in Asian Muslim countries* (pp. 97–112). Singapore: Springer.

Allahmorad, S., & Zreik, S. (2020). *Education in Saudi Arabia.* World Education News and Reviews (WENR). https:// wenr .wes .org/ 2020/ 04/ education -in -saudi -arabia. (Accessed February 15, 2022).

Allam, Z. (2019). An inquisitive enquiry of work-life balance of employees: Evidences from Kingdom of Saudi Arabia. *Management Science Letters, 9*(2), 339–46. https://doi.org/10.5267/j.msl.2018.11.07

Allen, M. (2017). *The SAGE encyclopedia of communication research methods.* London: Sage.

Almathami, R., Khoo-Lattimore, C., & Yang, E.C.L. (2020). Exploring the challenges for women working in the event and festival sector in the Kingdom of Saudi Arabia. *Tourism Recreation Research.* https://doi.org/10.1080/02508281.2020.1821329

Almohsen, M.A. (2001). *An exploratory study of the views of modernization of educated Saudi women* (Unublished Doctoral Thesis). University of Pittsburgh.

https://www.proquest.com/docview/304631170?pq-origsite=gscholar&fromopenview=true. (Accessed January 10, 2022).

Alrwajfah, M.M., Almeida-García, F., & Cortés-Macías, R. (2020). Females' perspectives on tourism's impact and their employment in the sector: The case of Petra, Jordan. *Tourism Management, 78*, 104069. https://doi.org/10.1016/j.tourman.2019.104069

Alselaimi, R., & Allui, A. (2018, March). Female Employment in Saudi Arabia: Legislative Encouragements and Socio-cultural Support. In *Int'l Conference Proceedings* (p. 88).

Alturki, F., & Alsharif, N. (2018). Tourism and entertainment. *Jadwa Investment.* http:// www .jadwa .com/ en/ researchsection/ research/ thematic ?search = ourism+and+entertainment&year=&Search.x=0&Search.y=0. (Accessed February 10, 2022).

Alzaeem, A. (2016). Eight majors suffer a shortage of graduates. Makkah AlMukarramah. https:// makkahnewspaper .com/ article/ 587441/ أعمال/ 8-تخصصات-تعاني-نقص-الخريجين. (Accessed February 5, 2022).

An-Na'im, A.A. (2002). *Islamic family law in a changing world: A global resource book* (Vol. 2). London: Zed Books.

Arasli, H., Bavik, A., & Ekiz, E.H. (2006). The effects of nepotism on human resource management: The case of three, four and five star hotels in Northern Cyprus. *International Journal of Sociology and Social policy, 26*(7/8), 295–308.

Atkins, B. (2018). Where did all the female CEOs go. *Forbes. com Aug 7th. Retrieved from.* https:// www .forbes .com/ sites/ betsyatkins/ 2018/ 08/ 07/ where -did -all -the -female-ceos-go/ (Accessed January 17, 2022).

Bear, J.B., Cushenbery, L., London, M., & Sherman, G.D. (2017). Performance feedback, power retention, and the gender gap in leadership. *The Leadership Quarterly, 28*(6), 721–40. https://doi.org/10.1016/j.leaqua.2017.02.003

Bierema, L.L. (2016). Women's leadership: Troubling notions of the 'ideal' (male) leader. *Advances in Developing Human Resources, 18*(2), 119–36. https://doi.org/10.1177/1523422316641398

Burkett, E. (2015). What makes a woman? Opinion. *New York Times*. https://www.nytimes.com/2015/06/07/opinion/sunday/what-makes-a-woman.html. (Accessed February 21, 2022).

Business Line. (2017). Women are taking the centre stage in Saudi Arabia. *Business Line*. https://www.thehindubusinessline.com/business-wire/women-are-taking-the-centre-stage-in-saudi-arabia/article9569336.ece. (Accessed February 21, 2022).

Chamberlain, P. (2017). *The feminist fourth wave: Affective temporality*. New York and London: Palgrave Macmillan.

Chan, K.-Y., & Drasgow, F. (2001). Toward a theory of individual differences and leadership: Understanding the motivation to lead. *Journal of Applied Psychology, 86*(3), 481–98. https://doi.org/10.1037/0021-9010.86.3.481

Cole, S. (2018). *Gender equality and tourism: Beyond empowerment*. Wallingford, Oxfordshire: CABI.

Creswell, J.W., & Creswell, J.D. (2017). *Research design: Qualitative, quantitative, and mixed methods approaches*. Thousand Oaks, CA: Sage.

Dainty, A.R., Neale, R.H., & Bagilhole, B.M. (2000). Comparison of men's and women's careers in UK construction industry. *Journal of Professional Issues in Engineering Education and Practice, 126*(3), 110–15.

Darasha, B. (2021). *Higher women's participation in labour force will benefit Saudi Arabia – Moody's*. ZAWYA. https://www.zawya.com/mena/en/economy/story/Higher_womens_participation_in_labour_force_will_benefit_Saudi_Arabia__Moodys-ZAWYA20210307052502/. (Accessed January 21, 2022).

Distelhorst, D. (2007). *A transcultural leader's resource materials for building personal, team, and organizational intercultural competence*. Spokane, WA: Gonzaga University.

El-Sanabary, N. (1994). Female education in Saudi Arabia and the reproduction of gender division. *Gender and Education, 6*(2), 141–50. https://doi.org/10.1080/0954025940060204

Elmulthum, N., & Elsayed, I. (2017). Prospects of Saudi women's contribution to job market under Saudi Vision 2030: An empirical analysis 1999–2015. *International Journal of Applied Sociology, 7*(1), 20–7. https://doi.org/10.5923/j.ijas.20170701.03

Eloubeidi, S. (2020). *Women's rights in Saudi Arabia: A counter-narrative*. The University of Alabama at Birmingham. https://sites.uab.edu/humanrights/2020/03/23/womens-rights-in-saudi-arabia-a-counter-narrative/. (Accessed January 13, 2022).

Figueroa-Domecq, C., de Jong, A., & Williams, A.M. (2020). Gender, tourism & entrepreneurship: A critical review. *Annals of Tourism Research, 84*, 102980. https://doi.org/10.1016/j.annals.2020.102980

First Voluntary National Review. (2018). *Transformation towards sustainable and resilient societies*. https://sustainabledevelopment.un.org/vnrs/ (Accessed February 10, 2022).

Ford, R., & McLaughlin, F. (1986). Nepotism: Boon or bane. *Personnel Administrator, 31*(11), 78–89.

Gazette, S. (2015). Women constitute 13% of Saudi workforce. *AL ARABIYA Middle East*. https://english.alarabiya.net/en/News/middle-east/2015/02/10/Women-constitute-13-of-Saudi-workforce-stats-agency.html. (Accessed February 10, 2022).

Gazette, S. (2020). Qiddiya launches first national scholarship program for Saudi youth. https://saudigazette.com.sa/article/598945. (Accessed January 20, 2022).

General Authority for Statistics Kingdom of Saudi Arabia. (2018). *Tourism Establishments Survey*. https:// www.stats.gov.sa/ en/ 491 -0. (Accessed January 21, 2022).

General Entertainment Authority. (2020). *Diversify and enrich entertainment experiences around the Kingdom of Saudi Arabia*. General Authority for Entertainment Saudi Arabia. https://gea.gov.sa/en/our-role/. (Accessed February 13, 2022).

Gentry, K.M. (2007). Belizean women and tourism work: Opportunity or Impediment? *Annals of Tourism Research*, *34*(2), 477–96. https://doi.org/https://doi.org/10.1016/j.annals.2006.11.003. (Accessed February 10, 2022).

Green, K.A., López, M., Wysocki, A., & Kepner, K. (2002). *Diversity in the workplace: Benefits, challenges, and the required managerial tools*. University of Florida.

Hakem, L. (2017). The challenges Saudi women face at work. *International Journal of Human Resource Studies*, *7*(1), 155–69. https://doi.org/10.5296/ijhrs.v7i1.10697

Hamdan, A. (2005). Women and education in Saudi Arabia: Challenges and achievements. *International Education Journal*, *6*(1), 42–64.

Hameed, N. (2018). How can I help you? More women join Saudi tourism and hospitality industry. *Arab News*. http://www.arabnews.com/node/1219916/saudi-arabia. (Accessed February 9, 2022).

Hammond, J.D. (2003). Women as producers and consumers of tourism in developing regions. *American Anthropologist*, *105*(1), 175–7.

Henderson, K.A., & Gibson, H.J. (2013). An integrative review of women, gender, and leisure: Increasing complexities. *Journal of Leisure Research*, *45*(2), 115–35. https://doi.org/10.18666/jlr-2013-v45-i2-3008

Hymowitz, K.S. (2011). Why the gender gap won't go away. Ever. *City Life Journal*. https:// www.city-journal.org/ html/ why-gender-gap-won%E2%80%99t-go-away-ever-13395.html

Jassim, I. (2011). دور المرأة في النشاط السياحي في العراق. *Journal of Administration and Economics* (89), 259–72.

Jenny, V. (2012). *Week 14: Davis and Lorde*. BCC Feminist Philosophy. https:// bccfeministphilosophy.wordpress.com/ 2012/ 04/ 29/ week-14-davis-and-lorde/ . (Accessed February 16, 2022).

Karolak, M. (2013). Saudi Arabian women's rights and the Arab Spring uprisings: Contextualizing grassroots activism and state reforms. In M.S. Olimat (ed.), *Handbook of Arab women and Arab Spring* (pp. 134–45). Abingdon, UK: Routledge.

Khan, Raheem, A., Ilyas, S., & Mehmood, B. (2017). Does the entertainment industry entertain the economy? Empirical evidence. http://Raheem/cda1940e9bcd6654dd653ed6b877a1944816f6ba. (Accessed February 2, 2022).

Kim, S.Y., & Alghamdi, A.K.H. (2019). Female secondary students' and their teachers' perceptions of science learning environments within the context of science education reform in Saudi Arabia. *International Journal of Science and Mathematics Education*, *17*(8), 1475–96. https://doi.org/10.1007/s10763-018-09946-z

Kotiranta, A., Kovalainen, A., & Rouvinen, P. (2010). Female leadership and company profitability. https://www.semanticscholar.org/paper/Female-Leadership-and-Firm-Profitability-Kotiranta-Kovalainen/73ca770a81de75124a303c66f7a9e48cc1e28081. (Accessed January 25, 2022).

Loeffen, O. (2016). Women in senior leadership: What it took to get to the top. *New Zealand Journal of Human Resources Management*, *16*(1), 5–18.

London, M., Bear, J.B., Cushenbery, L., & Sherman, G.D. (2019). Leader support for gender equity: Understanding prosocial goal orientation, leadership motivation, and power sharing. *Human Resource Management Review*, *29*(3), 418–27. https://doi.org/10.1016/j.hrmr.2018.08.002

Mays, N., Pope, C., & Popay, J. (2005). Systematically reviewing qualitative and quantitative evidence to inform management and policy-making in the health field. *Journal of Health Services Research & Policy*, *10*(1_suppl), 6–20. https://doi.org/10.1258/1355819054308576

Michailidis, M., Morphitou, R., & Theophylatou, I. (2012). Women at workequality versus inequality: Barriers for advancing in the workplace. *The International Journal of Human Resource Management*, *23*(20), 4231–45. https://doi.org/10.1080/09585192.2012.665071

Ministry of Education. (2018). برنامج خادم الحرمين الشريفين للابتعاث الخارجي المرحلة الثالثة *1440 - 1436*هـ. https://departments.moe.gov.sa/Scholarship/RelatedDepartments/KingSalmanScholarship/Pages/default.aspx. (Accessed January 25, 2022).

Moher, D., Liberati, A., Tetzlaff, J., Altman, D.G., & Group, P. (2009). Preferred reporting items for systematic reviews and meta-analyses: The PRISMA statement. *PLoS Medicine*, *6*(7), e1000097. https://doi.org/10.1136/bmj.b2535

Morello, A., Issa, R.R., & Franz, B. (2018). Exploratory study of recruitment and retention of women in the construction industry. *Journal of Professional Issues in Engineering Education and Practice*, *144*(2). https://doi.org/10.1061/(ASCE)EI.1943-5541.0000359

Naseem, S., & Dhruva, K. (2017). Issues and challenges of Saudi female labor force and the role of Vision 2030. *International Journal of Economics and Financial Issues*, *7*(4), 23–7.

National Transformation Program. (2018). *National Transformation Program Delivery Plan 2018–2020*. https://www.vision2030.gov.sa/v2030/vrps/ntp/. (Accessed February 10, 2022).

Oakley, A. (2016). Interviewing women again: Power, time and the gift. *Sociology*, *50*(1), 195–213. https://doi.org/10.1177/0038038515580253

Olesen, V. (2011). Feminist qualitative research in the millennium's first decade. In N. Denzin & Y. Lincoln (eds), *The Sage handbook of qualitative research* (pp. 129–46). Thousand Oaks, CA: Sage.

Pae, C.-U. (2015). Why systematic review rather than narrative review? *Psychiatry Investigation*, *12*(3), 417. https://doi.org/10.4306/pi.2015.12.3.417

Paglis, L.L., & Green, S.G. (2002). Leadership self-efficacy and managers' motivation for leading change. *Journal of Organizational Behavior: The International Journal of Industrial, Occupational and Organizational Psychology and Behavior*, *23*(2), 215–35. https://www.jstor.org/stable/4093732

Pattnaik, L., & Tripathy, S.K. (2014). Diversity management: A tool for competitive advantage. *Training and Development Journal*, *5*(1), 17–24. https://doi.org/10.5958/2231-069X.2014.00776.8

Petrevska, B. (2013). Investigating tourism seasonality in Macedonia. *UTMS Journal of Economics*, *4*(1), 37–44.

Pickering, C., Grignon, J., Steven, R., Guitart, D., & Byrne, J. (2015). Publishing not perishing: How research students transition from novice to knowledgeable using systematic quantitative literature reviews. *Studies in Higher Education*, *40*(10), 1756–69. https://doi.org/10.1080/03075079.2014.914907

Pritchard, A., & Morgan, N. (2007). De-centring tourism's intellectual universe, or traversing the dialogue between change and tradition. In I. Ateljevic, A. Pritchard, & N. Morgan (eds), *The critical turn in tourism studies* (pp. 33–50). London: Elsevier.

Purvis, J. (2004). Grrrls and women together in the third wave: Embracing the challenges of intergenerational feminism(s). *NWSA Journal*, 93–123.

Reich, Sabine. (2021). A systematic gender perspective on entertainment theory. In P. Vorderer, & C. Klimmt (eds), *The Oxford handbook of entertainment theory* (pp. 81–101). Oxford: Oxford University Press.

Richardson, R.B. (2010). *The contribution of tourism to economic growth and food security*. Food Security Collaborative Working Papers 97140, Michigan State University, Department of Agricultural, Food, and Resource Economics.

Ritter-Hayashi, D., Vermeulen, P., & Knoben, J. (2016). *Gender diversity and innovation: The role of women's economic opportunity in developing countries*. Working Paper.Institute for Management Research. https:// research .tilburguniversity .edu/ en/ publications/ gender -diversity -and -innovation -the -role -of -womens -economic -oppor. (Accessed January 20, 2022).

Sabbagh, S. (1996). *Arab women between defiance and restraint*. Northampton, MA: Olive Branch Press.

Saudi Arabia Vision 2030. (2016a). vision2030.gov.sa. http:// vision2030 .gov .sa/ sites/ default/files/report/Saudi_Vision2030_EN_2017.pdf. (Accessed January 12, 2022).

Saudi Arabia Vision 2030. (2016b). *Saudi Arabia Vision 2030*. http:// vision2030 .gov .sa/sites/default/files/report/Saudi_Vision2030_EN_2017.pdf. (Accessed January 12, 2022).

Saudi Arabian Business Council. (2017). *Working in Saudi Arabia: A labor market update*. www.us-sabc.org. (Accessed January 12, 2022).

Saudi Census. (2018). *The total population*. https://www.stats.gov.sa/en/indicators/10.

SCTA. (n.d.). *Tourism investment in Saudi Arabia*. Saudi Commission for Tourism and Antiquities. https:// scth .gov .sa/ en/ TourismInvestment/ Suppo rtTourismI nvestment/Documents/Touristic_investment_eng.pdf. (Accessed January 12, 2022).

Sherbini, A., Aziz, Y.A., Sidin, S.M., & Yusof, R.N.R. (2016). Income diversification for future stable economy in Saudi Arabia: An overview of tourism industry. *International Journal of Economics, Commerce and Management*, *6*(11), 173–89.

Small, J., Harris, C., Wilson, E., & Ateljevic, I. (2011). Voices of women: A memory-work reflection on work-life dis/harmony in tourism academia. *Journal of Hospitality, Leisure, Sport & Tourism Education*, *10*(1), 23–36.

Taylor, C., & Albasri, W. (2014). The impact of Saudi Arabia King Abdullah's scholarship program in the US. *Open Journal of Social Sciences*, *2*(10), 109.

Thompson, M.C. (2015). Saudi women leaders: Challenges and opportunities. *Journal of Arabian Studies*, *5*(1), 15–36.

Toossi, M. (2002). A century of change: The US labor force, 1950–2050. *Monthly Labour Review*, *125*, 15.

Tribe, J. (2010). Tribes, territories and networks in the tourism academy. *Annals of Tourism Research*, *37*(1), 7–33.

UNSDG. (2018). *Goal 5: Achieve gender equality and empower all women and girls*. https://www.un.org/sustainabledevelopment/gender-equality/. (Accessed February 5, 2022).

Valek, N.S., & Almuhrzi, H. (2021). *Women in tourism in Asian Muslim countries*. Springer Nature.

Valentine, G. (2007). Theorizing and researching intersectionality: A challenge for feminist geography. *The Professional Geographer*, *59*(1), 10–21.

Vanhanen, T. (1999). Domestic ethnic conflict and ethnic nepotism: A comparative analysis. *Journal of Peace Research, 36*(1), 55–73.
Wellman, J. (1991). The Seneca Falls women's rights convention: A study of social networks. *Journal of Women's History, 3*(1), 9–37.
Wilcke, C. (2010). *Looser rein, uncertain gain: A human rights assessment of five years of King Abdullah's reforms in Saudi Arabia*. Human Rights Watch.
Williams, B.C., & Plouffe, C.R. (2007). Assessing the evolution of sales knowledge: A 20-year content analysis. *Industrial Marketing Management, 36*(4), 408–19.
Wilson, E. (2014). Diversity, culture and the glass ceiling. *Journal of Cultural Diversity, 21*(3), 83.
Wirth, L. (2001). *Breaking through the glass ceiling: Women in management*. Geneva: ILO: International Labour Organization.
Women UN. (2020). Policy brief: The impact of COVID-19 on women. New York: United Nations.
Workplace Gender Equality Agency. (2020). *Gendered impact of COVID-19*. https:// www.wgea.gov.au/publications/gendered-impact-of-covid-19. (Accessed January17, 2022).
World Bank. (2020). *Labour force participation rate, female (% of female population ages 15)*. https:// data .worldbank .org/ indicator/ SL .TLF .CACT .FE .ZS ?locations = SA. (Accessed January 17, 2022).
World Tourism Organization. (2021). *Women in tourism: Middle East (2nd ed.)*. WTO.
Yang, E.C.L., Khoo-Lattimore, C., & Arcodia, C. (2017). A narrative review of Asian female travellers: Looking into the future through the past. *Current Issues in Tourism, 20*(10), 1008–27.
Zhang, J., & Zhang, Y. (2020). Tourism and gender equality: An Asian perspective. *Annals of Tourism Research, 85*(4), 103067.

PART II

Gender, tourism and work

6 Gender, empowerment and tourism in Iran: a Muslim perspective

Seyedasaad Hosseini, Abolfazl Siyamiyan Gorji, Rafael Cortés Macías and Fernando Almeida García

1. Introduction

Tourism is often viewed as a significant source of employment and income (Nikraftar & Hosseini, 2016). As a consequence, it is argued that involvement in the tourism industry has the potential to empower women (Vujko et al., 2019), and provide opportunities for women entrepreneurs (Haugen & Vik, 2008). For example, the United Nations World Tourism Organization (UNWTO) (2020) argues that the tourism industry could empower women through income-generating opportunities in small and giant tourism enterprizes. Similarly, 10 per cent of the world's GDP is generated by global tourism (WTTC, 2019).

However, employment opportunities for women in the tourism industry are generally of lower quality than in other industries (Santero-Sanchez et al., 2015). Moreover, the low quality of employment in the tourism and hospitality industry is associated with gender differences. While women's participation in the tourism industry has improved in both quality and quantity, women continue to face a variety of barriers due to discrimination in the labour market (Alrwajfah et al., 2020). Much attention has been paid to the role of tourism in increasing women's income and employment in promoting gender equality. Cole (2018) argues that women's empowerment is undergoing a positive shift through the tourism industry and that women can and should use tourism wisely to improve their position. Rinaldi and Salerno (2020) have also claimed that tourism offers opportunities for gender equality and that the tourism industry has been instrumental in creating new jobs for women. Duffy et al. (2015) have shown that women have gained social and economic autonomy through employment in the tourism sector. Once women start working and earning a living through tourism, the dominant patriarchal culture slowly begins to be challenged (Farmaki, 2019). Furthermore, to reduce financial poverty, tourism provides an opportunity for women to escape poverty (Xu et al., 2018).

Gender inequality is a major obstacle to development in many developing countries (Alrwajfah et al., 2020). One of the most critical aspects of achieving the Millennium Development Goals (MDGs) is to bridge the gap between men and women in terms of capacity, access to services and opportunities, and vulnerability to violence and conflict (WTTC, 2019). Gender issues can play a significant role in the development of the tourism industry, given that numerous tourist studies highlight the critical relationship between tourism, peripheral development, and women's empowerment (Seyfi et al., 2020).

However, religious and cultural expectations have led to lower participation of many Muslim women in particular in the tourism industry. Cultural norms in Muslim societies may hinder women's participation in the tourism industry and play a crucial role in creating gender inequality (Seyfi & Hall, 2018). In addition, Muslim-majority countries face challenges related to social justice and gender inequalities in the workplace (Masadeh et al., 2018). While tourism may not be the only solution, it can provide opportunities for all countries with an oil-based rental economy. This is particularly the case when it comes to women, who make up half of society and continue to overcome the difficulties resulting from gender inequality.

The strict impact of Islamic rule in some Muslim countries and cultures, like Iran, has resulted in constraints for women (Gorji et al., 2022). In the specific case of Iran, Islamists took control of the country following the 1979 revolution and enforced a number of ideological rules, which had a particular impact on women (Ehteshami, 1995). Despite the fact that many Iranian women have received higher education (Hosseini et al., 2022), their job prospects have not improved significantly since the revolution, with women's unemployment remaining significantly low: Iranian women between the ages of 15 and 29 are predominantly unemployed (Seyfi et al, 2022). The number of women participating in Iran's labour market is very low (only 17 per cent), owing to a number of legal and social barriers that work to limit their livelihood and economic contribution (Shahidian, 2002).

In more recent years, Iran has witnessed a number of changes in women's rights, due mainly to the ubiquity of the internet and the emergence of a new middle class of educated young women who are increasingly seeking new lifestyles, including travel (Fadaee, 2018; Tavakoli and Mura, 2017). Further, Iranian feminist movements have undergone a significant shift towards gender equity and women's empowerment (Khalajabadi-Farahani et al., 2019). At the same time, there has also been a noticeable increase in international tourists to Iran. Tourist arrivals have increased from 5.2 million in 2015 to 9.1 million in 2019. Iranian tourist departures have also increased in recent years, rising from 6.6 million in 2015 to 10.5 million (2017) and 7.2 million in 2018 (this decrease may be due to the start of the economic crisis caused by international sanctions) (UNWTO, 2020). The demand for female-led holidays has also grown in Iran and created more opportunities for women to work in non-traditional positions, such as travel guides. Well-managed, equitable tourism can empower all individuals in the community and for marginalized and disadvantaged groups, such as women. By providing better opportunities for women's participation in the workforce, by strengthening female entrepreneurship and female leadership, tourism can contribute to gender equality.

Despite the poor condition of women's rights in Iran, little research has been conducted on the barriers to gendered impacts on Iranian women's empowerment in the tourism context. Furthermore, the negative economic context and outcomes in Iran have had a significant negative impact on Iranian women's labour force participation and has hampered their involvement capabilities. Drawing upon the theoretical framework of empowerment developed by Scheyvens (1999, 2000), this study sought to examine the barriers to empowerment and enhancement of women of tourism in a patriarchal society and a masculinized political Iranian culture.

2. Women, Tourism and Empowerment

Tourism development has an important impact on the economy of the destination, especially in developing countries (Sheng & Tsui, 2009). According to Sharpley (2002), tourism creates new jobs, investment opportunities, restaurants and lodging establishments, and improves the quality of life for residents. Gender has always been a critical issue in the sociological study of tourism (Cohen & Cohen, 2019). However, despite the importance of tourism in understanding residents' perceptions and support for tourism development, little attention has been paid to the role of gender (Janta & Christou, 2019; Trupp & Sunanta, 2017). Látkova and Vogt (2012) state that understanding these perceptions is crucial for successful tourism development and to improve positive and reduce negative impacts. In promoting gender equality, much emphasis has been placed on the impact of tourism on increasing women's employment and income. For example, Nyaruwata and Nyaruwata (2013) argued that tourism is an important source of employment for women.

Boonabaana (2014) found that women in Uganda prefer to seek employment in tourism. According to Duffy et al. (2015), women have gained economic and social independence through employment opportunities in the tourism industry. Nonetheless, the scope of literature in Muslim countries is limited. In particular, in Muslim countries, gender can be a salient issue when it comes to hiring. (Huh & Vogt, 2008; Mason & Cheyne, 2000). For example, in Islamic societies in particular, women continue to be discriminated against in tourism employment, largely due to social and cultural factors that discourage women from participating in tourism (Alrwajfah et al., 2020; Masadeh et al., 2018; Uduji et al., 2020).

Empowerment is a multidimensional social mechanism that enables people to control life-influencing factors (Scheyvens, 1999; Trommlerová et al., 2015). Concepts such as empowerment, and in particular the empowerment of women, have increasingly become central to the understanding of sustainability and the Sustainability Development Goals (SDGs). The prevailing patriarchal culture is quickly challenged when women begin to work and earn money in tourism. Indeed, tourism can help all people in a community, especially marginalized groups such as women, by promoting women and supporting large affiliated businesses (Kimbu et al., 2019; Yim et al., 2018). Consequently, many global institutions, such as the UNWTO *Global Report on Women in Tourism*, have addressed women's empowerment (UNWTO, 2019). Nonetheless, tourism has been talked about almost exclusively as a promising strategy for women's empowerment, often overlooking the highly gendered nature of tourism. According to the Global Gender Gap Report 2018 (WEF, 2020), there is still a significant gender gap in Asia and the Middle East. In Japan, Korea and India, for example, women spend much more time on average in unpaid work. In addition, women in Muslim countries, including Syria, Lebanon, Saudi Arabia, Yemen, Jordan, and Pakistan, do not have the same access to employment opportunities and leadership positions as men.

Cole (2018) argues that the discussion of empowerment in the development literature needs to move beyond financial and masculinist conceptual frameworks. Further, Cole (2018) points out that 'empowerment, as it is so often conceptualized, refers only to products and not reproductive labor, and does not respond to the structural inequalities that underlie enterprises built on patriarchal symbolic and normative codes'. According to the United Nations Commission on the Status of Females (United Nations Women, 2014), 'almost 15 years after the adoption of Millennium Development Goals, hardly any country has achieved equal rights for women' (p. 12). This is especially true in the area of education, which makes a significant contribution to 'achieving gender equality and women's empowerment' (United Nations, 2014, p. 20).

In light of this situation, various tourism industries are attempting to close the gender gap in their respective countries. To this end, Romo et al. (2019) argue that equal opportunities for men and women should be a central focus of corporate social responsibility. The tourism industry can help to lessen if not eliminate gender bias in hiring and promoting staff.

Empowerment through tourism refers to enabling the community to reap the economic benefits of tourism, whereby the income generated is shared and distributed among households in a community, resulting in an improved quality of life for residents (Scheyvens, 1999). Tourism fills the gender gap through higher levels of increased female income, promotion of employment, leadership development, and better education for women (Ferguson & Alarcon, 2015). Tourism has the potential to contribute to economic empowerment by creating jobs, revenue, and business opportunities; however income equality and distribution are critical aspects of the empowerment process. Social empowerment, according to Scheyvens's (1999) framework, consists of improvements in integration, collaboration, and community cohesion (Boley et al, 2017; Moswete & Lacey, 2015). Gender research in the tourism industry also helps us to understand the current situation of the role of women in the sector (Costa et al., 2017). Some studies have outlined the difficulties women face when working in tourism, and in different parts of the world, for example, in Mexico (Chant, 1994), Dominican Republic (Grasmuck & Espinal, 2000), Middle East (Sönmez, 2001), Turkey (Cave & Kilic, 2010; Tucker, 2007), Thailand (Trupp & Sunanta, 2017) and Jordan (Alrwajfah et al, 2020). These authors have attributed the barriers to traditional and religious constraints, political restrictions on women's participation in decision-making, women's role in the family, and gender characteristics.

Through this lens, therefore, this study aims to explore how these dimensions of women's tourism-related empowerment may be influenced by traditional and religious patriarchal society and a masculinized political culture.

3. Women and the Tourism Sector in Iran

Iran is a large, Middle Eastern country where trade routes (such as the Silk Road) and varied weather and landscape have created a rich resource for tourism development (Gorji et al., 2021). Iran has long been a popular destination for religious and cultural travellers, and after the 1979 Islamic Revolution and the subsequent establishment of a theocracy, the country has attracted large numbers of religious tourists and pilgrims from neighbouring countries (Seyfi & Hall, 2018). Islamists have ruled Iran since the 1979 Revolution.

The interpretation of women's rights among current Iranian politicians is based on Islamic texts that state that women's main responsibilities are in the home and that they must be protected by their husbands (Abedinifard, 2019). Therefore, men are given priority in education, work, and many other areas of society that generate wealth and power (Rafatjah, 2012). Because of this Islamic interpretation of women's participation, Iran was placed among the lowest-ranking performers in the World Economic Forum's *Gender Gap Report* (2020). Abedinifard (2019) noted that in addition to political pressures on women, society is also strongly patriarchal in nature, as men have traditionally been the financial providers for the family and are therefore generally seen as the head of the family and have privileged access to decisions for themselves, their wives and children. Therefore, due to the lack of a reliable statistical system, little reliable information is available on the employment rate of women in the tourism and hospitality sector in Iran.

Outbound and domestic tourism in Iran have recently increased, exposing Iranians to a wider range of cultures as a result (Tavakoli & Mura, 2017). Despite the legal, religious, and cultural judgements against women, Iranian society has shifted somewhat in favour of women's status in society (Davoodi et al., 2019). According to Seyfi and Hall, (2018), such changes in women's rights are primarily the result of the widespread emergence of a new middle class of educated young women who are increasingly seeking new lifestyles, work and leisure activities. Fadaee (2018) mentions that the number of Iranian women who reject men's control over their lives and strive for greater agency and emancipation is increasing. In particular, Iranian women are attempting to redefine the position of women in Iranian society by challenging what they see as outdated stereotypes imposed by tradition, religion and law. In addition to that, thanks to globalization and increased access to social media platforms (Instagram, Facebook, Twitter), women have become more aware of gender, empowerment and related issues, such as in the way they spend their leisure time or their rights. If Iranian women gain education and economic independence, they are more likely to challenge societal gender norms because these factors increase their bargaining power.

4. Methodology

4.1 Research Design

This study employed an exploratory, qualitative paradigm based on an interpretive approach Given the exploratory and multi-faceted nature of the empowerment study, qualitative methods were chosen to explore the personal and subjective interpretations (Creswell & Poth, 2016; Riley & Love, 2000). Furthermore, feminist scholarship has suggested that qualitative epistemology is best suited for obtaining data on a sensitive study (Caprioli, 2004; Figueroa-Domecq et al., 2015). The analytical framework used in this study aided us to explore the subjective nature of women's experiences in Iran.

4.2 Data Collection and Analysis

Despite two of the authors being Iranian, the researchers did not have access to extensive networks of women working in tourism in Iran, so a purposive and snowball sampling technique was used to develop an interviewee base (Flick, 2018). Initial contact was made via email and social media, with an explanation of the purpose of the research. All those who responded definitively were contacted to explain the format of the interview and to enquire about their availability for a telephone, Whatsapp or Skype converzation. It was recognized that the use of new digital technology as a research medium in qualitative research methods is more convenient for some hard-to-reach and geographically dispersed groups (Hanna, 2012).

The researchers recruited five participants for semi-structured pilot interviews in January 2021.

A final interview guide was then developed based on the basic pilot interviews. All interviews were conducted via WhatsApp between January 2021 and February 2021 and lasted between 25 and 40 minutes. Qualitative research usually aims at a relatively small and concentrated sample in order to understand the individuality of the phenomenon under study and the uniqueness of its circumstances (Maxwell, 2008). This research followed the principle of 'saturation of data' (Creswell & Poth, 2016), and theoretical saturation appeared to be reached after 15 interviews. These 15 participants included women working in a tourism-related role representing different sectors of the tourism and hospitality industry. The selected age group was between 20 and 45 years old. Table 6.1 summarizes the characteristics of the participants.

Table 6.1 Participants' socio-demographic characteristics

Name	Age	Sector	Position	Interview	Duration (mins)
Fataneh	24	Hotel	Marketing department	WhatsApp	30′
Fatemeh	28	Travel agency	incoming	WhatsApp	34′
Maryam	32	Travel agency	Domestic tour	Skype	39′
Zainab	34	Tour guide	International tour guide	WhatsApp	32′
Sahar	37	Travel agency	Domestic tour guide	WhatsApp	27′
Farzana	28	Tour guide	Domestic tour guide	WhatsApp	25′
Shima	41	Travel agency	Social media	WhatsApp	31′
Mohadaseh	39	Hotel	Food and beverage manager	Skype	36′
Farzaneh	26	Travel agency	Technical manager	WhatsApp	26′
Ima	38	Tour guide	International tour guide	WhatsApp	27′
Sajedeh	37	Tourism school	Teacher	WhatsApp	25′
Roya	29	Hotel	Marketing department	WhatsApp	25
Ziba	34	Hotel	Marketing department	Skype	38′
Afsaneh	32	Tour guide	International tour guide	WhatsApp	33′
Farideh	31	Travel agency	Marketing department	WhatsApp	29′

Semi-structured, in-depth interviews were utilized to capture the experiences of the respondents (Bradford & Cullen, 2013). Questions were formulated in accordance with the study's focus and were drawn from a variety of related studies (Aghazamani et al., 2020, 2000; Seyfi et al., 2020) and adapted to the Iranian context. For instance, questions included: 'What are the obstacles and challenges encountered by women working in the tourism sector? What are the negative impacts on the role and empowerment of women in the tourism sector in Iran?'. We were willing to hear more spontaneous opinions to avoid the potential bias of limiting responses to the researcher's established categories (Creswell & Poth, 2016). The semi-structured interviews were conducted in Persian. All interviews were transcribed verbatim and translated back into English by the lead author to ensure consistency of meaning.

Qualitative thematic analysis was adopted for data analysis. Thematic analysis is the most widely used qualitative approach to interview analysis (Alhojailan, 2012; Braun & Clarke, 2006), and it is useful when working within realist or constructivist social science paradigms and attempting to gain a more comprehensive and nuanced understanding of the empirical material (Braun & Clarke, 2006; Nowell et al., 2017). Thematic analysis is a systematic method which involves defining key themes, classifying theme-based data, and evaluating the categorized themes by identifying commonalities, relationships, and critical issues. The focus of this step is on a broad theme and involves categorising various codes into possible themes in the five steps. In the focused coding phase, the most relevant and frequent initial codes were identified and the main category was determined. Based on the theoretical framework of the study, the interview transcripts were thematically examined into employer attitudes, social and cultural barriers, personal and family barriers, and political barriers. The researchers began the coding process together by coding line by line and identified 87 initial codes. After conducting the interviews, the transcripts were reread by the researchers and initial findings were noted.

5. Findings

This study examines how women are perceived in Iranian tourism hospitality organizations and the issues and challenges they face in the workplace due to the intersectionality of gender, ethnicity and religion. The opportunities, structures and barriers surrounding the Iranian tourism industry provide context for women's roles, constraints, and barriers. This chapter engages with the concepts of inequality regimes and intersectionality to explain inequality in the workplace and the complex challenges faced by Iranian women workers in the tourism sector. The findings indicate that for the women we spoke to, they continue to face a variety of challenges in the workplace, and it is important to consider the intersection of gender and culture.

5.1 Employers' Attitudes

Apart from the difficulties of working in tourism and dealing with the initial adjustment to the work situation, many women continue to face some negative attitudes in the workplace. The first topic deals with the negative attitude they experienced from their employers. Employers are concerned about women leaving the company after they get married. The main reasons given were additional responsibilities, or lack of spousal support (Belwal & Belwal, 2017). Employers believe that many women quit their jobs after marriage. In a Muslim conservative society, the decision to become a mother often poses an additional challenge (Tariq, & Syed, 2018). Most of these women reported that employers have a negative attitude toward female employees because they are more likely to marry, and have and raise children. They believe that employers' views have harmed their ability to work. A female tour guide stated:

> It is a problem when there are married women in a department. Because if she gets married, she needs to leave, and if she gets pregnant, she needs maternity leave... employers avoid having her. (Farzana)

This was echoed by her colleague:

> The employers continued to believe that I would quit at any time. I'm not sure if employers think hiring women is a threat or if they look at her and think she will plan to get married and have children, 'the problem of being pregnant every year' (Maryam).

Our interviewees also claimed that employers' perceptions of women lead to higher unemployment and subsequently an insecure business environment for women in Iran. One of the interviewees stated:

> Employers prefer men, who are considered more reliable and productive workers. As a woman, this can sometimes be a problem in Iran. They always pay women less and would rather have certain jobs done by a man than a woman (Roya).

5.2 Social and Cultural Barriers

Due to negative social stereotypes and discrimination, Muslim women's labour force participation is significantly impacted (Hopkins, 2009). Gilliat-Ray (2010) argued that negative religious and ethnic connotations contribute to the underestimation of women's abilities in the workplace. In addition, some Islamic countries do not allow their daughters to pursue higher education or work for fear that it will distract them from their domestic duties or expose them to non-traditional culture and values (Esposito & DeLongBas, 2001; Mossière, 2012). Almost all of the participants stated that as women, they are primarily responsible for domestic and caregiving tasks at home, such as raising children and caring for other family members, as well as working. In addition, many talked about societal attitudes and how they filtered their situation. For example, they discussed negative attitudes towards women working in environments with male staff and international visitors:

> In some communities in Iran, like my hometown, women are not allowed to be active outside the home. The negative male attitude regarding women working outside the home is the reason for the poor representation of women in the workforce (Fataneh).

Religious attitudes and family members also have a significant influence on women's career decisions in many Muslim societies. Family members, for example, may be concerned about the type and conditions of work women do. Shift work, working late at night, rigid schedules, and certain work environments are often considered inappropriate:

> I grew up in a religious family. In these families, parents play a significant role in influencing their daughters by giving them advice. My parents are very religious and strictly conservative. Working at night was fine for me, but since I live with my parents, my father had a problem with me working the night shift. As a result, I had to move my previous workplace to another hotel (Ziba).

This sentiment was also expressed by another respondent, Farideh:

> ...it is not acceptable to work with men in a workplace. Generally, our culture doesn't accept this workplace atmosphere. We are under pressure by our masculine community.

All respondents felt that these perceptions have a negative impact on their social empowerment. They believe that the development of tourism will change the passive role of women into an active role that will empower them to manage their social life. They also mention that tourism provides good access to opportunities and greater participation in decision-making through social interactions. For example, Shima, who works in a travel agency stated that:

> My job as a tour manager has helped me make new foreign friends, understand other cultures, share experiences, and expand my social networks. So, in general, I can say that my experience in the tourism industry has changed my perception of the role of women in society. It gives me a sense of empowerment as a woman (Shima).

Indeed, intersectionality and discrimination are not limited to one aspect of Iranian women in the tourism sector; these women argued that they face socio-cultural challenges as a whole. Role conflict was also an important issue for the women. Participants talked about the difficulties of balancing work and family responsibilities. Even when many women start working outside the home, they are still wholly responsible for the household.These obstacles arise from society's current beliefs and cultural and traditional approaches to the role of women in the family and the nature of work in the tourism industry. Further, general government policies, norms and values, and political culture and structures contribute to the reinforcement and reproduction of these kinds of barriers against women, for example, social attitudes towards the way girls are portrayed in society and society's expectations of the presence of boys in the public sphere, as well as the lack of individual independence of girls before and after marriage, who are under the control of their parents and their husbands.

5.3 Personal and Family Barriers

The family can, in some cases, be an obstacle to the development of women's activities in the tourism industry. Women working in the tourism industry often face resistance from their families due to the Iranian family form and structure and women's lack of independence before marriage (Farahani & Dabbaghi, 2018). Families are concerned about the safety of girls in the tourism industry due to a lack of familiarity with the nature of the industry and a high degree of separation from family (Seyfi et al., 2018). Married women working in the tourism industry are constantly told that marriage is an obstacle to their career and professional advancement. Additionally, religious, cultural and family beliefs about the nature of women's work in tourism affect women's personal lives.

The often unstable nature of work in the tourism industry, such as regular absence from home at certain times of the day, has exacerbated traditional family resistance to women working in tourism and has challenged their capabilities (Farahani & Dabbaghi, 2018). Moreover, family and work are the main issues in the lives of both men and women. Nevertheless, in many communities, family responsibilities are considered to be primarily the responsibility of women, while men are considered to be the main breadwinners (Brush, 1992). This shows that men and women have different priorities and challenges when it comes to work and family. For example, Ima commented:

> The most difficult challenges I faced were outside the organization, such as my family's expectation that I get married and start a family. After I married, I took a job to support my family financially, but I soon found that my household responsibilities – teaching my children, cooking, cleaning, and other chores – had not diminished.

A local tour guide also commented:

> It is very difficult for us to strike a balance between work and life because it is believed that women are responsible for the children and we have less time for empowerment activities (Farzaneh).

Some of the women's husbands also displayed negative attitudes. Again, this was related to the nature and conditions of work, such as being on the front lines, working long hours, shift work, and other job responsibilities, as Sahar found:

> Some men think that if a woman goes to work, they are incompetent. As a result, they think that if their wife goes to work, others will think the same of her and have a special prejudice against her, asking, are we starving that you want to go to work?

This was echoed by another respondent:

> ... we are sometimes under pressure to make our husband satisfied. In fact, the need for us as wives to please our husbands is an obstacle to feeling more comfortable in our workplace (Mohadaseh).

Despite the difficulties posed by family barriers, most respondents expressed optimism about societal reform efforts and an understanding of the long time required for women's empowerment in the workplace. In addition, the most frequently mentioned family empowerment issues by respondents in this study were women's financial independence and income generation. The participants indicated that the tourism industry has contributed to the social and economic empowerment of their families.

5.4 Political Obstacles

In some conservative Muslim countries, women have a minimal role in participating in political decision-making compared to men; thus women are vastly underrepresented in political arenas and policy-making (Seyfi et al., 2020). The existence of specific cultural stereotypes poses challenges for women in this respect. Female participants reported facing stereotypes of 'poor ability' and often being asked about their level of competence simply because they are women. As a result, these women earn lower salaries and are not given equal opportunities to display their full potential. This form of stereotypical behaviour acts as an identity threat for these women. Consequently, women face a double handicap, as they not only have to prove themselves as women in the workplace in the fight against general forms of discrimination, but also have to prove their skills and competences as women. One of the interviewees commented:

> We can see the great absence of women's decision-making in tourism activities when local and national organizations want to decide on women's activities. In my opinion, women in Iran are less likely than men to have access to the training, contacts, and resources necessary to become effective leaders in the tourism sector (Sajedeh).

This was echoed by another interviewee:

> I feel a lack of practice and engagement through a transparent and effective political system, where women can participate and engage freely in the tourism market without any social and political restrictions (Maryam).

Nonetheless, increasing women's employment is critical to reducing poverty, sustaining economic development and promoting women's equality and autonomy. Mohadaseh, who works in a hotel, commented on this by saying that tourism development has given women more opportunity in decision making, empowerment and tourism development:

> I believe that the tourism industry provides a significant opportunity for Iranian women to demonstrate their skills, as well as a significant opportunity to change stereotypes about women's work force. Consider how difficult it is for us to change old traditional opinions about our society, and how we are trying to change men's thinking by actively participating in tourism activities (Mohadaseh).

The respondents believed that providing necessary and specialized training can increase women's awareness and skills in the area of women's skills in the tourism industry. More obviously, tourism organizations have too few plans or policies to increase the use of women in their organizational mission. Indeed, it can be argued that the participation of women makes an important contribution to the development of the skills and knowledge of local residents and has a positive economic impact on the growth of the local and national economy.

6. Discussion

One of the most important aims of the Sustainable Development Goals is the economic empowerment of women (UN Women, 2020). According to Kimbu et al. (2019), tourism is recognized as a sector that promotes gender equality, women's empowerment, and higher levels of economic autonomy for women. The role of women in preserving, managing, and raising families for the next generation is important. Consequently, a better understanding of individual and social rights will boost economic activity, support exit from the cycle of poverty, raise educational levels in society, support control and access to resources, promote health, and support social and economic development in the community (Farahani & Dabbaghi, 2018).

Nonetheless, as the results of this study have shown, social and cultural constraints have led to direct effects on the employment and entrepreneurship of women in the tourism industry. These restrictions curtail avenues of empowerment for women and thus serve to reinforce conservative gender roles. Such an exacerbation of women's powerlessness is rarely discussed in the existing literature, and this study has highlighted the significance of this phenomenon, which has been little studied in the field of tourism in Muslim countries.

The responses of the Iranian women interviewed in this study reveal a number of barriers and challenges that hinder their career advancement in the tourism industry. These findings demonstrate that a complex web of stressors affects Iranian women in the workplace, including employers' attitudes, social and cultural barriers, personal and family barriers, and political obstacles and a lack of equity, and gender discrimination in the workplace. Moreover, women in Iran encounter a number of cultural, religious, and political obstacles, and they live in a predominantly traditional and patriarchal society (Taheri & Guven-Lisaniler, 2018). These obstacles are the consequence of beliefs, traditional and cultural challenges to society, and the nature of work in the tourism sector. Furthermore, the organization of the tourism authority identifies and enforces the national, cultural, and religious systems of the community, which is a major challenge for the growing participation of women in tourism in Iran. Nonetheless, the number of women interested in tourism sector employment opportunities is growing as the development of the tourism industry is being prioritized in Iran these days.

Women are trying to fill positions that are different from those that women have held in the tourism industry in the past, contrary to public opinion. Of course, these public perceptions have changed over time. It shows that the speed of transformations is relatively high. Perhaps the term 'generation gap' is appropriate to describe the pace of the shifts. In traditional cultures, fathers, brothers, husbands, and male colleagues are the men who set and define permissions and boundaries. However, women in Iranian society, as in other countries in the Middle East and North Africa, are beginning to challenge these typically accepted roles.

7. Conclusion

This study represents an attempt to explore the gender implications of problems and challenges faced by women in the workplace. The structural effects of social barriers in Iran should not be overlooked. As a result of these challenges, Iran's security approach to civil society has become tougher, creating barriers for women. According to Tavakoli and Mura, (2017), 'women's rights activists are often accused by hardliners of wanting to adopt Western values that undermine the country's Islamic values'. Many of the challenges the women in this study faced while working in tourism were accepted or overcome, allowing them to continue working in the industry. This could enable a more positive and supportive tourism working environment. These advantages were not apparent at the beginning of the career path, but seem to play a major role later in terms of the effectiveness of tourism work. The gain in strength, confidence, independence and status seemed to lead to a sense of empowerment and the opening of new doors. The women also reported greater job satisfaction than at the beginning of their careers, and some described their work in tourism as a life-changing experience.

Finally, the contributions of this chapter to the literature on women in Iran empowerment lie in its focus on religious and cultural constraints on women in Iran as an Islamic country in the tourism sector. Moreover, this research reveals insights into the dynamics between gender and tourism activity in Iran, which is highly susceptible to domestic (religious–patriarchal) factors and highlights the main challenges faced by Iranian women. Considering the nature of the tourism industry, despite the technological advancement in the world, this industry is still based on the significant role of human resources. Therefore, the tourism industry can be seen as the solution to the unemployment crisis, inequality and poverty.

For tourism development to be successful and sustainable, women must benefit equally from the visitor economy and participate in decision-making and planning. According to the concept of equality in sustainable development, the inclusion of all strata of society, especially those with less effective power, in the development process is important, and women are one of these strata.

References

Abedinifard, M. (2019). Asghar Farhadi's nuanced feminism: Gender and marriage in Farhadi's films from *Dancing in the Dust* to *A Separation*. *Asian Cinema*, *30*(1), 109–27.

Aghazamani, Y., Kerstetter, D., & Allison, P. (2020). Women's perceptions of empowerment in Ramsar, a tourism destination in northern Iran. *Women's Studies International Forum*, *79* (March), 102340.

Alhojailan, M.I. (2012). Thematic analysis: A critical review of its process and evaluation. *West East Journal of Social Sciences*, *1*(1), 39–47.

Alrwajfah, M.M., Almeida-García, F., & Cortés-Macías, R. (2020). Females' perspectives on tourism's impact and their employment in the sector: The case of Petra, Jordan. *Tourism Management, 78*, 104069.

Belwal, R., & Belwal, S. (2017). Employers' perception of women workers in Oman and the challenges they face. *Employee Relations, 39*(7), 1048–65.

Boley, B.B., Ayscue, E., Maruyama, N., & Woosnam, K.M. (2017). Gender and empowerment: Assessing discrepancies using the resident empowerment through tourism scale. *Journal of Sustainable Tourism, 25*(1), 113–29.

Boonabaana, B. (2014). Negotiating gender and tourism work: Women's lived experiences in Uganda. *Tourism and Hospitality Research, 14*(1–2), 27–36.

Bradford, S., & Cullen, F. (eds). (2013). *Research and research methods for youth practitioners*. New York: Routledge.

Braun, V., & Clarke, V. (2006). Using thematic analysis in psychology. *Qualitative Research in Psychology, 3*(2), 77–101.

Brush, C.G. (1992). Research on women business owners: Past trends, a new perspective and future directions. *Entrepreneurship Theory and Practice, 16*(4), 5–30.

Caprioli, M. (2004). Feminist IR theory and quantitative methodology: A critical analysis. *International Studies Review, 6*(2), 253–69.

Cave, P., & Kilic, S. (2010). The role of women in tourism employment with special reference to Antalya, Turkey. *Journal of Hospitality Marketing & Management, 19*(3), 280–92.

Chant, S. (1994). Women, work and household survival strategies in Mexico, 1982–1992: Past trends, current tendencies and future research. *Bulletin of Latin American Research, 13*(2), 203–33.

Cohen, S.A., & Cohen, E. (2019). New directions in the sociology of tourism. *Current Issues in Tourism, 22*(2), 153–72.

Cole, S. (ed.). (2018). *Gender equality and tourism: Beyond empowerment*. CABI.

Costa, C., Bakas, F.E., Breda, Z., Durao, M., Carvalho, I., & Caçador, S. (2017). Gender, flexibility and the 'ideal tourism worker'. *Annals of Tourism Research, 64*, 64–75.

Creswell, J.W., & Poth, C.N. (2016). *Qualitative inquiry and research design: Choosing among five approaches*. Thousand Oaks, CA: Sage.

Davoodi, Z., Fatehizade, M., Ahmadi, A., & Jazayeri, R. (2019). Culture and power: How do culture and power influence Iranian couples. *Journal of Couple & Relationship Therapy, 18*(4), 353–65.

Duffy, L.N., Kline, C.S., Mowatt, R.A., & Chancellor, H.C. (2015). Women in tourism: Shifting gender ideology in the DR. *Annals of Tourism Research, 52*, 72–86.

Ehteshami, A. (1995). *The politics of economic restructuring in post-Khomeini Iran*. Working Paper. University of Durham, Centre for Middle Eastern and Islamic Studies, Durham.

Esposito, J.L. (2001). *Women in Muslim family law*. Syracuse, NY: Syracuse University Press.

Esposito, J. & DeLong-Bas, N. J. (2001). *Women in Muslim family law*. New York: Syracuse University Press.

Fadaee, S. (2018). Ecotours and politics of fun in Iran: From contested state–society relations to emancipatory nature–society relations. *The Sociological Review, 66*(6), 1276–91.

Farahani, B.M., & Dabbaghi, H. (2018). Tourism and the empowerment of women in Iran. *Tourism in Iran: Challenges, Development and Issues*, 36.

Farmaki, A. (2019). Women in Airbnb: A neglected perspective. *Current Issues in Tourism*, 1–5.

Ferguson, L., & Alarcon, D.M. (2015). Gender and sustainable tourism: Reflections on theory and practice. *Journal of Sustainable Tourism, 23*(3), 401–16.
Figueroa-Domecq, C., Pritchard, A., Segovia-Pérez, M., Morgan, N., & Villacé-Molinero, T. (2015). Tourism gender research: A critical accounting. *Annals of Tourism Research, 52*, 87–103.
Flick, U. (2018). *An introduction to qualitative research*. London and Thousand Oaks, CA: Sage.
Gilliat-Ray, S. (2010). Body-works and fieldwork: Research with British Muslim chaplains. *Culture and Religion, 11*(4), 413–32.
Gorji, A.S., Almeida-García, F., & Mercadé Melé, P. (2021). Analysis of the projected image of tourism destinations on photographs: The case of Iran on Instagram. *Anatolia*, 1–19.
Gorji, A.S., Hosseini, S., Garcia, F.A., & Macias, R.C. (2022). Complexities of women solo travelling in a conservative post-Soviet Muslim society: The case of Uzbek women. In S. Seyfi, M. Hall, & S. M Rasoolimanesh (eds), *Contemporary Muslim travel cultures* (pp. 155–69). London: Routledge.
Grasmuck, S., & Espinal, R. (2000). Market success or female autonomy? Income, ideology, and empowerment among microentrepreneurs in the Dominican Republic. *Gender & Society, 14*(2), 231–55.
Hanna, P. (2012). Using internet technologies (such as Skype) as a research medium: A research note. *Qualitative Research, 12*(2), 239–42.
Haugen, M.S., & Vik, J. (2008). Farmers as entrepreneurs: The case of farm-based tourism. *International Journal of Entrepreneurship and Small Business, 6*(3), 321–36.
Hosseini, S., Macías, R.C., & García, F.A. (2022) The exploration of Iranian solo female travellers' experiences. *International Journal of Tourism Research, 24*(2), 256–69.
Hopkins, P. (ed.). (2009). *Muslims in Britain: Race, place and identities*. Edinburgh: Edinburgh University Press.
Huh, C., & Vogt, C.A. (2008). Changes in residents' attitudes toward tourism over time: A cohort analytical approach. *Journal of Travel Research, 46*(4), 446–55.
Janta, H., & Christou, A. (2019). Hosting as social practice: Gendered insights into contemporary tourism mobilities. *Annals of Tourism Research, 74*, 167–76.
Khalajabadi-Farahani, F., Månsson, S.A., & Cleland, J. (2019). Engage in or refrain from? A qualitative exploration of premarital sexual relations among female college students in Tehran. *The Journal of Sex Research, 56*(8), 1009–22.
Kimbu, A.N., Ngoasong, M.Z., Adeola, O., & Afenyo-Agbe, E. (2019). Collaborative networks for sustainable human capital management in women's tourism entrepreneurship: The role of tourism policy. *Tourism Planning and Development, 16*(2), 161–78.
Látková, P., & Vogt, C. A. (2012). Residents' attitudes toward existing and future tourism development in rural communities. *Journal of Travel Research, 51*(1), 50–67.
Masadeh, M., Al-Ababneh, M., Al-Sabi, S., & Allah, M.H. (2018). Female tourist guides in Jordan: Why so few? *European Journal of Social Sciences, 56*(2), 89–102.
Mason, P., & Cheyne, J. (2000). Residents' attitudes to proposed tourism development. *Annals of Tourism Research, 27*(2), 391–411.
Maxwell, J.A. (2008). Designing a qualitative study. In L. Bickman & D.J. Rog (eds), *The Sage handbook of applied social research methods* (pp. 214–53). Thousand Oaks, CA: Sage.
Mossière, G. (2012). Modesty and style in Islamic attire: Refashioning Muslim garments in a Western context. *Contemporary Islam, 6*(2), 115–34.

Moswete, N., & Lacey, G. (2015). 'Women cannot lead': Empowering women through cultural tourism in Botswana. *Journal of Sustainable Tourism*, *23*(4), 600–17.

Nikraftar, T., & Hosseini, E. (2016). Factors affecting entrepreneurial opportunities recognition in tourism small and medium sized enterprises. *Tourism Review*, *71*(1), 6–17.

Nowell, L.S., Norris, J.M., White, D.E., & Moules, N.J. (2017). Thematic analysis: Striving to meet the trustworthiness criteria. *International Journal of Qualitative Methods*, *16*(1), 1–13.

Nyaruwata, S., & Nyaruwata, L.T. (2013). Gender equity and executive management in tourism: Challenges in the Southern African Development Community (SADC) region. *African Journal of Business Management*, *7*(21), 2059–70.

Rafatjah, M. (2012). Changing gender stereotypes in Iran. *International Journal of Women's Research*, *1*(1), 61–75.

Rinaldi, A., & Salerno, I. (2020). The tourism gender gap and its potential impact on the development of the emerging countries. *Quality & Quantity*, *54*(5), 1465–77.

Riley, R.W., & Love, L.L. (2000). The state of qualitative tourism research. *Annals of Tourism Research*, *27*(1), 164–87.

Romo, R.S., Gabriel, L.P.M., & Soares, J.R.R. (2019). Gender equality in access to management in the tourism industry. In D Tuzunkan & V. Altintas (eds), *Contemporary human resources management in the tourism industry* (pp. 85–103). Hershey, PA: IGI Global.

Santero-Sanchez, R., Segovia-Pérez, M., Castro-Nuñez, B., Figueroa-Domecq, C., & Talón-Ballestero, P. (2015). Gender differences in the hospitality industry: A job quality index. *Tourism Management*, *51*, 234–46.

Scheyvens, R. (1999). Ecotourism and the empowerment of local communities. *Tourism Management*, *20*(2), 245–9.

Scheyvens, R. (2000). Promoting women's empowerment through involvement in ecotourism: Experiences from the Third World. *Journal of Sustainable Tourism*, *8*(3), 232–49.

Seyfi, S., & Hall, C.M. (eds). (2018). *Tourism in Iran: Challenges, development and issues*. London: Routledge.

Seyfi, S., Hall, C.M., & Vo-Thanh, T. (2020). The gendered effects of statecraft on women in tourism: Economic sanctions, women's disempowerment and sustainability? *Journal of Sustainable Tourism*, 1–18.

Seyfi, S., Hall, C. M., & Vo-Thanh, T. (2022). The gendered effects of statecraft on women in tourism: Economic sanctions, women's disempowerment, and sustainability? *Journal of Sustainable Tourism*, *30*(7), 1736–1753.

Shahidian, H. (2002). *Women in Iran: Gender politics in the Islamic Republic* (No. 197). Greenwood Publishing Group.

Sharpley, R. (2002). Tourism: A vehicle for development? In R. Sharpley & D.J. Telfer (eds), *Tourism and development: Concepts and issues* (pp. 3–30). Bristol: Channel View.

Sheng, L., & Tsui, Y. (2009). A general equilibrium approach to tourism and welfare: The case of Macao. *Habitat International*, *33*(4), 419–24.

Sönmez, S. (2001). Tourism behind the veil of Islam: Women and development in the Middle East. In Y. Apostolopoulos, S.F. Sönmez, & D.J. Timothy (eds), *Women as producers and consumers of tourism in developing regions* (pp. 113–42). Westport, CT: Praeger.

Taheri, E., & Guven-Lisaniler, F. (2018). *Gender Aspect of Economic Sanctions: Case Study of Women's Economic Rights in Iran*. 19 December.

Tariq, M., & Syed, J. (2018). An intersectional perspective on Muslim women's issues and experiences in employment. *Gender, Work & Organization*, *25*(5), 495–513.

Tavakoli, R., & Mura, P. (2017). Iranian women traveling: Exploring an unknown universe. In C. Khoo-Lattimore & E. Wilson (eds), *Women and travel: Historical and contemporary perspectives* (pp. 109–24). New York: Apple Academic Press.

Trommlerová, S.K., Klasen, S., & Leßmann, O. (2015). Determinants of empowerment in a capability-based poverty approach: Evidence from The Gambia. *World Development*, *66*, 1–15.

Trupp, A., & Sunanta, S. (2017). Gendered practices in urban ethnic tourism in Thailand. *Annals of Tourism Research*, *64*, 76–86.

Tucker, H. (2007). Undoing shame: Tourism and women's work in Turkey. *Journal of Tourism and Cultural Change*, *5*(2), 87–105.

Uduji, J.I., Okolo-Obasi, E.N., & Asongu, S.A. (2020). Sustaining cultural tourism through higher female participation in Nigeria: The role of corporate social responsibility in oil host communities. *International Journal of Tourism Research*, *22*(1), 120–43.

United Nations Women. (2014). *Commission on the status of women*. Fiftieth Session, 27.

United Nations Women. (2020). *Progress of the world's women, 2019–2020*.

United Nations World Tourism Organization (UNWTO). (2020). *UNWTO World Tourism Barometer* (Vol. 18, Issue 2, May 2020).

Vujko, A., Tretiakova, T.N., Petrović, M.D., Radovanović, M., Gajić, T., & Vuković, D. (2019). Women's empowerment through self-employment in tourism. *Annals of Tourism Research*, *76*, 328–30.

World Economic Forum (WEF). (2020). *Global gender gap report 2020*. http://www3.weforum.org/docs/WEF_GGGR_ 2020.pdf

World Travel and Tourism Corporation (WTCC). (2019). *Travel & tourism: Driving women's success*. WTTC.

Xu, H., Wang, C., Wu, J., Liang, Y., Jiao, Y., & Nazneen, S. (2018). Human poverty alleviation through rural women's tourism entrepreneurship. *Journal of China Tourism Research*, *14*(4), 445–60.

Yim, F., Cheung, C., & Baum, T. (2018). Gender and emotion in tourism: Do men and women tour leaders differ in their performance of emotional labor? *Journal of China Tourism Research*, *14*(4), 405–27.

7 Shift working in the hotel industry: experiences of female migrant workers in Macao

Sandeep Basnyat and Carmen Pau Ka Mun

1. Introduction

Globalization of the economy and the increased demands for services have extended working time to non-standard business hours in many countries (Kang et al., 2017; Tai et al., 2014). Consequently, working round-the-clock shifts has been a practice in several industries including healthcare, transportation, communication and hotels, among others (Tai et al., 2014). Hotels across the world rely heavily on migrant workers, and a significant number of these migrant workers are female. Many consider hotel jobs as precarious and challenging, particularly for female migrant workers. However, the contextual conditions and situations of female migrant workers who work shifts, and the challenges they face while maintaining their family and work life have been largely underresearched. This chapter presents issues faced by female migrant workers who do shift work in luxury hotels focusing on Macao, a Special Administrative Region of China.

Macao's economy is highly dependent upon the gaming sector, and casinos in particular. Most casinos in Macao reside within luxury hotels, which are open 24 hours a day, seven days a week. Findings of a few previous studies have revealed that hotel and casino employees in Macao routinely experience burnout, job dissatisfaction, work-related stress and work–family conflicts due to the nature of their work (Chan et al., 2015; Chau, 2019; Vong & Tang, 2017); however, the effects of shift work on hotel employees, especially female migrant workers, have been largely ignored and underresearched. One recent study by Liu (2020) has examined the impact of social support on job stress of shift-working mothers in Macao casinos. Liu's (2020) study found that emotional and instrumental supports from families and friends are the most important social support for shift-working mothers to cope with their job stress in casinos. Although Liu's study was based on the issues faced by female employees in the hotel sector in Macao, it did not delve into the subject of shift work and its effects on migrant workers in particular. This chapter aims to fill this gap.

The first section of this chapter conceptualizes shift work, discussing its benefits and challenges. The second section sets the study context by discussing the current situation of, and employment conditions in, the luxury hotels (and casinos) in Macao. It also discusses the existing practices of shift work in the luxury hotels in Macao. The third section analyses the issues faced by female migrant workers, who do shift work, in the luxury hotels in Macao, and finally the chapter concludes by highlighting important implications of shift work for female migrant workers and hotels. Measures that can be taken to address the issues faced by the female migrant workers who work shifts are also suggested.

2. Understanding Shift Work

While there is little in the documented history of the evolution of shift work, scholars believe that shift work has existed since ancient times, especially among shepherds, camp guards, soldiers and sailors who had to be awake and vigilant during normal sleeping hours (Vaughn & Kataria, 2020). Particularly, after the nineteenth century Industrial Revolution, followed by urbanization, the demand for shift work increased. The modern-day concept of shift work arose in the early 1980s as part of increasingly industrialized economies, including the USA and UK, when new machinery and equipment were being developed and used for the production of goods and services (Vaughn & Kataria, 2020). Increasing demands required factories to operate continuously for 24 hours a day, thus necessitating the idea of a shift system (or a continuous shift system), under which different groups of workers were assigned to work various shifts. Until the early twentieth century, because of union pressure, many companies across the world usually structured shift works in eight-hour windows, for example, from morning to afternoon (8.00 am to 4.00 pm), afternoon to night (4.00 pm to 12.00 pm), and night to morning (12.00 pm to 8.00 am). Today, however,, companies allocate their workers various shifts that range anywhere from 8 to 12 hours (Vaughn & Kataria, 2020). To suit their requirements, some companies have also introduced the idea of a rotating shift system, under which workers are assigned to work shifts that vary regularly between morning and night (ILO, 2004).

The International Labour Office (ILO), headquartered in Geneva, Switzerland, provides guidelines to conceptualize shift work, protect workers and regulate shift work. In 1990, the ILO defined shift working, holistically, as a method of organization of working time in which workers succeed one another at the workplace so that the establishment can operate longer than the hours of work of individual workers at different daily and night hours (ILO, 2004). Therefore, regardless of the arrangement of time-slots, shift work can be understood as an arrangement of working hours other than the regular day work, or a work schedule beyond that of the conventional office hours (e.g., 9.00 am to 5.00 pm).

Shift work is now widespread across industries throughout the world. For example, while 27 per cent of all U.S. workers worked alternative shifts (i.e., not a regular day shift) and 7 per cent regularly worked a night shift in 2015 (Centers for Disease Control and Prevention, 2020), 21 per cent of the workers in the European Union worked in some type of a shift system in the same year (Alali et al., 2018). In the UK, 18.6 per cent of the total workers employed in all industries worked in shifts in 2017 (Office for National Statistics, 2018). The Korean Ministry of Employment and Labor found that around 15.2 per cent of all industries and 22 per cent of all manufacturing companies had a shift system in place in 2011 (Kang et al., 2017). The Statistics and Census Service bureau reported that shift workers accounted for 94.6 per cent of the total number of full-time employees in the fourth quarter of 2019 in the highly dominant gaming sector of Macao, China (DSEC, 2020b).

Although the practice of shift working began in the manufacturing industry, it is also widely used in various sectors of the service industry. One of the most common service sectors which uses shift work is the transportation sector where the networks of airlines, railways, and buses often share variable tasks, start times, locations and end times that result in variable transportation work timetables (Office for National Statistics, 2018). Hospitals that provide 24 hours of continuous healthcare services to their patients also use shift systems of working. Public services providers such as police and fire departments also regularly schedule their employees' work in shifts. Traditionally, it has been a common practice in hotels to schedule their employees' work shifts since many of them, across the world, operate their businesses 24 hours (Office for National Statistics, 2018). More recently, hotels have also been increasing the number of in-house services, such as in-room dining, bars, pools, spas and gyms, that are available 24 hours to satisfy the demands of their customers. This, in turn, has increased the necessity of more employees who work in shifts (Moon et al., 2015).

While it has been generally regarded that female workers are less likely than their male counterparts to work in shift work because of a variety of social and cultural reasons and domestic responsibilities including the existence of legal prohibitions against night work for women in some countries (ILO, 2004), the perceptions of the general population as well as the social reality are changing. Recent trends show that not only male, but also a significant percentage of female employees are involved in shift working, and in some sectors, the percentages of female employees are larger than their male counterparts. The data reported by the Office for National Statistics (2018) show that in the UK, the percentages of male and female shift workers, across all industrial sectors, were consistent around 16 per cent and 19 per cent between 2007 and 2017. In the US, while 28.23 per cent of all male workers and 24.78 per cent of all female workers worked alternative shifts (i.e., not a regular day shift), 9.11 per cent of all male workers and 5.57 per cent of all female workers regularly worked a night shift in 2015 (Centers for Disease Control and Prevention, 2020).

Kang et al. (2017) reported that out of 14,241 employees surveyed in an electronic manufacturer in South Korea, between 9 April and 21 May, 2015, 60 per cent (8,469) of employees reported that they worked in shifts. Among these 8,469 employees who worked in shifts, 66 per cent were female. In Macao, female employees account for 57.5 per cent and 44.03 per cent of the total number of full-time employees in the gaming and hotel sectors, respectively (DSEC, 2020b). Since shift workers comprise 94.6% per cent among them (as mentioned above), it is safe to assume that the percentage of female shift workers is significant in these sectors. In fact, in some sectors of the service industry, such as healthcare and hospitality, where the number of female employees often outnumbers male employees, the number of female shift workers is also usually greater than that of male shift workers.

2.1 Benefits and Costs

The economic benefits of shift work are predominantly associated with two perceived aspects: higher earnings for workers, and enhanced organizational productivity and capacity management (ILO, 2004). The rationale for higher earnings for workers through shift work can be understood with the help of the economic theory of compensating differentials. The theory of compensating differentials argues that since workers can easily find jobs with desirable characteristics, compensating wages are necessary to induce workers to take up jobs that are not usually desirable, including those that frequently require workers to work in shifts (alternating between day and night), among others (Trent & Mayer, 2014). Consequently, industrial sectors in many countries provide additional economic benefits (allowances) to those who work in shifts, especially during nights. Although such additional economic benefits provide incentives to many employees to work in shifts, some studies have found that the idea of additional and higher–earning does not hold, generally. For example, in countries where the economic condition of the larger population is generally poor and the jobs are relatively scarce, the compensating wage differentials may be less of a motivating factor (Trent & Mayer, 2014). Additionally, many workers may be satisfied with working for less than the desired compensation.

Higher earnings enabled by working in shifts is not always an indicator of the economic wellbeing of workers. A US study involving General Social Survey (GSS) data by Golden (2015) reported that the variability of work hours contributed by irregular shifts not only caused income instability but also affected household consumption of US consumers. Often, these last-minute schedule changes, which are considered normal in many hospitality enterprises, cost employees money on their paycheck. This usually happens as they have to pay additional expenses if, for example, they want to obtain or purchase certain services such as childcare, medical, vacation and so on (TSheets, 2018). Sometimes, legal and institutional policy arrangements in a country also dictate the way additional compensations are paid or not. For example, in Macao, shift workers are entitled to receive the normal remuneration for the work performed plus an increase of 10 per cent, and 20 per cent in the case of a night shift, provided that the worker has not been specifically hired to provide shift work (DSAJ, 2020).

Another reason why many organizations schedule work in shifts is based on the idea of enhancing organizational productivity and managing capacity. Productivity is considered essential for the success of all enterprises, particularly in hospitality organizations such as hotels (Pullman & Rodgers, 2010). The working environment in hotels is often fast-paced, and employees are required to be ever ready to attend to the demands of their customers. Hotels usually require outstanding customer services from their dynamic pool of employees, and this, in turn, necessitates the evaluations and maintenance of their organizational productivity. Enhancing organizational productivity is related to the extent to which an organization, such as a hotel, utilizes and manages its production capacity (Pullman & Rodgers, 2010).

Enhancing productivity and managing capacity is also important for many hospitality organizations because they require a significant amount of capital investment and expenditure for establishment and operation. Efficient management of capacity ensures that the hotel is able to sufficiently meet the demands of its customers. The extent to which capacity satisfies demand has an impact on visitor experience, employee satisfaction, profitability, and long-term sustainability of both the resources and the hotel itself (Pullman & Rodgers, 2010). One of the key strategies that hotel managers implement to maximize the utilization of existing capacity is by operating the hotel as long as possible using various means including organising work in shifts. The concept of capacity management by engaging employees over shifts has been so pervasive in the hospitality industry, especially hotels, that most hotels across the world consider it as a regular practice, irrespective of the demands of their customers. However, it is also important to recognize that organizational capacity utilization is a holistic concept and cannot be achieved only by extending work in shifts. For example, the nature and characteristics of employees who work at shifts differ, and thus may affect their productive output. During the night shifts, it has been observed that supervision is normally reduced and there may be no maintenance or technical personnel available to ensure that the problems that arise are efficiently solved (Folkard & Tucker, 2003).

Existing studies have identified that employees who work irregular shift times, in contrast with those with more standard, regular shift times, have higher chances of experiencing physical and mental health conditions including some serious health conditions such as cardiovascular disease, diabetes and obesity (Griffin, 2010). Alvionita et al. (2017) examined the significance of different working shifts in affecting job fatigue levels among 120 employees who worked at the front office, housekeeping, and food and beverage (service, kitchen, and pastry) department in the morning, afternoon, and night shift in hotels in Surabaya. Their findings revealed that the participants who worked at the shift, especially at night shift, usually experienced a very high level of job fatigue. As a result, the night shift employees usually reported being tired. The job fatigue not only affected them physically and mentally but also deteriorated their skills to a large extent. A survey of 506 hotel workersat two first-class hotels in Seoul showed that shift work was significantly related to their depression (Moon et al., 2015). TSheets, a company that develops web-based time tracking and employee scheduling application named TSheets, reported that a large number of respondents who worked in restaurants and hotels expressed that they were not only experiencing sleeping disorders and stress because of their irregular shift work patterns, but also finding it harder to exercize, pursue hobbies or stick to a healthy diet plan (TSheets, 2018).

Employees who often work in an irregular schedule also experience greater work-family conflicts. Golden (2015) reported in their study that the work-family conflicts were particularly strong for salaried workers even though they were able to control their relatively longer working hours. Golden's research found that generally having to be constantly available for work, not just long hours per se, had created a daily struggle for those workers to reconcile competing caregiving and workplace demands. Many employees who worked irregular shifts have also reported that they were not able to participate in important family and social events because of their irregular work schedules, and consequently, negatively affected their family and social relationships (TSheets, 2018).

3. Setting the Study Context: Macao

Macao is a Special Administrative Region (SAR) of China and lies in the Western Pearl River Delta and by the South China Sea, 60 kilometres south-west of Hong Kong. It is a small Chinese city with a land area of 32.9 square kilometres. In 2019, the population of Macao was 679 600, of which 196 538 were migrant (non-resident) workers (DSEC, 2020a). While around 62 per cent of these migrant workers were from Mainland China (122 357), the remainder came from various other Asian regions including the Philippines (33 781 – 17 per cent), Vietnam (14 804 – 7.5 per cent), Indonesia (6 043 – 3 per cent) and Hong Kong (4 598 – 2.3 per cent), among others (DSEC, 2020a). Females generally constitutes about 45 per cent of the total number of migrant workers in Macao (DSEC, 2020a), however, the percentages are very high for some countries. Although the percentage of female migrant workers from Mainland China seemed relatively lower (35 per cent) compared to other countries, the absolute number was high (43 156) (as 62 per cent of the total migrant workers came from Mainland China).

The economy of Macao is highly dependent upon tourism, especially casino gambling (generally referred to as gaming and junket activities), most of which are operated within luxury hotels. The World Travel and Tourism Council (2019) estimates that the total travel and tourism contribution to employment in Macao is around 65.5 per cent. Macao has the largest gaming industry in the world, generating about US$37 billion in revenue, and about seven times larger than that of Las Vegas (DSEC, 2020a). Currently, there are six casino license holding companies in Macao that operate 41 casions at various hotels. In 2019, a total of 39.4 million tourists visited Macao, among which, visitors from Mainland China, Hong Kong and Taiwan constituted more than 91 per cent (Mainland China, 27.92 million, Hong Kong, 7.35 million, Taiwan, 1.06 million) (DSEC, 2020a).

Macao has around 69 luxury hotels (3 stars and above), whose occupancy rate in 2019 was above 91 per cent, and where most gaming activities were/

Table 7.1 Average earnings of full-time resident and non-resident (migrant) employees in Macanese patacas

		Gaming industry				Hotel			
		Resident		Non-resident		Resident		Non-resident	
Year	Types of workers	Male	Female	Male	Female	Male	Female	Male	Female
2017	Total	24 430	22 220	18 440	19 430	23 020	18 600	15 400	12 400
	Unskilled	13 210	11 850	6 760	7 350	11 340	10 120	9 900	9 660
2018	Total	26 800	23 500	24 860	24 150	24 180	19 760	15 980	13 190
	Unskilled	14 280	13 010	7 850	8 140	11 890	10 750	10 700	10 240
2019	Total	26 240	23 750	22 140	21 560	25 190	20 770	16 220	13 560
	Unskilled	15 150	13 860	8 300	8 660	12 560	11 300	10 960	10 650

Source: Government of Macao Special Administrative Region, Statistics and Census Service, Survey on Manpower Needs and Wages - Gaming Industry, Manufacturing, Hotels, Restaurants, Financial Activities except Banking, Child-care, Elderly Care, various years. https://www.dsec.gov.mo/en-US/Statistic?id=302

are organized (DSEC, 2020a). Females account for 51 per cent of the total employed population in Macao, and this proportion is also reflected in other sectors (DSEC, 2020b). For example, in 2019, females accounted for 57.5 per cent and 44.03 per cent of the total number of full-time employees, including migrant workers, in the gaming and hotel sectors, respectively. As of 2021, the average salary in Macao is Macanese patacas (MOP) 21 000 or approximately US$2 630 (Stotz, 2021). Those who work in certain sectors, including gaming and recreational services, are able to earn higher than the minimum salary. Table 7.1 shows the average earnings of full-time resident and non-resident (migrant) employees in Macao from 2017 to 2019 in the gaming and hotel sectors. As seen in Table 7.1, not only do migrant workers earn considerably less than the residents, but there is a significant difference between the incomes earned by male and female employees (including migrant workers). Except for a few cases when female migrant workers were able to earn a slightly higher income than male migrant workers in the gaming sector, female employees, generally, earn less than their male counterparts.

Not all workers earn the average salary mentioned above. Security workers and cleaners in Macao receive a minimum wage which is MOP6 656 per month (equivalent to approximately US$833) (Stotz, 2021). The domestic helpers are excluded and fall outside of the scope of the minimum wage. Statistics and Census Service data of the government of Macao shows that, as of 2020, there were about 30 100 domestic workers in Macao. While half of these domestic workers were from the Philippines, the remainder were from various other Asian countries including Indonesia and Vietnam among others. A majority of domestic workers, who are mostly female, earn between MOP 3 500 and 5 000, and several of them earn less than MOP 3 500 (equivalent to approximately US$437) (Asia Times, 2017).

Hotels and casinos are open 24 hours a day, seven days a week in Macao. Therefore, it is obvious that hotel, as well as casino management, schedule their employees' work in various shifts. Macao Labour Relations Law identifies shift work as the one that must be performed without a fixed schedule and at a different time (DSAJ, 2020). Shift work can be scheduled by the organization whose business hours are longer than the maximum limits of the normal working hours and should respect the hourly limits of no more than eight hours per day and 48 hours per week (DSAJ, 2020). In practice, hotel and casino managements typically allocate staff to daily operations based on customer demand; however, the customer demands can vary depending on factors including the individual venue, the time of day, the day of the week and the season. Consequently, even if the gaming tables are empty, for example, the dealers are still allocated there to sit through a full eight-hour shift. In 2015, about 88 per cent of the total full-time employees in the gaming sector were engaged in shift work; however, this figure has increased and reached 94.6 per cent by the fourth quarter of 2019 (as mentioned above) in Macao (DSEC, 2020b). The proportion of employees working shifts in the non-gaming sector is around 24 per cent. The next section discusses the experiences of female migrant workers while working in shifts in the luxury hotels in Macao.

4. Method

The empirical data for this study were collected through semi-structured interviews with 23 female migrant workers who worked in shifts in the luxury hotels in Macao. Since casions were situated within the hotels in Macao, where the participating female migrant workers were working, they were also considered a part of hotels for the purpose of this study. Several migrant workers, who are from Mainland China, live in Zhuhai, a neighbouring Chinese city of Macao and commute to Macao daily for work. Therefore, the data for this study were collected from two types of female migrant workers: those who were living and working in Macao, and those who were working in Macao but were living in Zhuhai. The age of the participants ranged between 25 and 49. All participating female migrant workers in this study except four were married, and were working in the luxury hotels for between one and eight years. Married female migrant workers, particularly, shared their unique experiences and distinct perspectives on shift-working in Macao. Out of 23 participating female migrant workers, ten were from Mainland China (commuting between Zhuhai and Macao), five were from the Philippines, two were from Indonesia, three were from Vietnam, two were from Taiwan and one was from Myanmar; 15 out of 23 female migrant workers' spouses/families were in their hometown/country. The participating female migrant workers were working in various positions including as a security guard, clerk, housekeeping staff, receptionist, waitress, and assistant manager in the luxury hotels (including gaming sector) in Macao.

During her undergraduate study in 2019, the second author had an opportunity to complete an internship in a luxury hotel in Macao, where she obtained first-hand knowledge of how the manager scheduled shifts for employees. Her female colleagues (especially migrants) sometimes shared the difficulties that they faced during shift works. In the initial phase of data collection for this study, the second author contacted three of those female migrant workers for interviews. Later, other participants were recruited through their referral (using a snowball sampling method) (Saunders, 2012).

Scholars have argued that qualitative approaches that use semi-structured interviews are appropriate for conducting workplace-related research, not only because they can provide rich, insightful accounts but also to explore issues in depth (such as speaking about difficulties that are caused by organizational practices including shift works) (Alvesson & Ashcraft, 2012; Saunders & Townsend, 2016). The interviews were conducted between October 2018 and January 2019. The questions that were asked to the participants revolved around three issues: what they thought and felt about working in shifts in the hotel; what challenges they faced while working in shift, particularly being a female migrant worker; and the effects of shift work on their life as female migrant workers. The interviews were conducted in English and Mandarin. Since the second author was fluent in both languages, she translated the interviews that were conducted in Mandarin into English by herself. All interviews were transcribed verbatim and an inductive thematic approach was used to analyse the data (Braun & Clarke, 2012).

5. Findings

5.1 A Compromise for Economic Benefits

Most female migrant workers reported that changes in shifts often created an imbalance in their daily routine. Although female migrant workers did not appreciate shift working in general, they believed that it was a compromise for the economic benefits they were receiving. A Filipino migrant worker reported:

> Ideally, I am willing to work in standardized and fixed work hours, irrespective of whether day or night. However, I am also aware of the fact that, since hotels and casinos are operated 24 hours a day, such an operation would require the staff to work in shifts. In addition, the monthly income [including salary and other allowances] are mostly higher in Macao than in my own country.

Recovering recruitment fees that migrant workers had paid to employment agencies and accumulating enough money to pay back debts were also the factors that forced migrant workers to follow the work arrangements scheduled by employing hotels. Therefore, regardless of the imbalances that shift work had created in their daily routine and life, the participating female migrant workers had no objection to working in shifts. In fact, most female migrant workers felt it natural (and sometimes felt compelled) to compromize. An Indonesian migrant worker clarified:

> I paid recruitment fees to an employment agency in Indonesia and also in Macao before landing a job in Macao. The total recruitment fee was equal to three months' salary for me. Besides, I have debts to pay back in my country, and I have no other source of income in their hometown. I have come to Macao to increase my income and therefore, I would work for all types of shift arrangements.

All of the female migrant workers reported that they were able to earn extra income by working in shifts. In addition, the chances of earning extra income increased substantially for workers who worked during mandatory public holidays as the hotels compensated with salary for that day, plus triple the amount of paid compensation. Several participating female migrant workers affirmed that they were also earning additional income by working night shifts or overtime hours. However, one concern that the majority of the female migrant workers expressed was related to differences in remuneration between male and female employees, and more particularly between resident and migrant workers, in many companies, in Macao. A Vietnamese migrant worker expressed her dissatisfaction this way:

> Hotel and gaming works are equally challenging for both males and females as well as for residents and migrant workers like us. So why we [female migrant workers] are paid less than other female workers [residents] and often even less than male workers from our own countries? Companies should eliminate such a differential remuneration practice.

Some female migrant workers argued that the differential remuneration practice was the result of the persistence of traditional Chinese culture, among some employers, who view that women have a lower status than men in terms of power, wealth and prestige. Nevertheless, as the female migrant workers believed, elimination of such a differential practice may help female migrant workers earn more, and live a slightly more comfortable life, as well as solve their financial problems. The female migrant workers reported that the living cost in Macao was generally higher compared to their country of origin, especially, the rental price of housing was reported to be the most expensive in Macao. Therefore, to reduce the housing expenditure, while most of the participating migrant workers from Mainland China rented an apartment in Zhuhai, migrant workers from other countries shared an apartment with their friends/colleagues or lived in a boarding house (hostel).

5.2 Constrained Social and Family Relationships

The participating female migrant workers reported that they were mentally prepared for all types of situations that they might face, including shift work, before accepting employment at the hotel and gaming sectors in Macao. However, only a few of them had considered the costs associated with shift-working. Almost all of the female migrant workers were concerned about the fact that not only were they unable to mingle with the people in the society where they work (Macao), but also they had trouble managing their family relationships, because of shift work. As a Filipino migrant worker mentioned:

> For the majority of the migrant workers like us, the only social circle that we have, apart from the people from our own country, includes the colleagues we work together with in the same company.

A female migrant worker from Mainland China reported how the shortage of time constrained social relationships for most of them who commuted between Zhuhai and Macao for work:

> I am always in a rush while commuting between Zhuhai and Macao, which usually takes about four hours, altogether. Consequently, I have very little time to go around Macao with other colleagues. I do have some friends outside of my company here [in Macao]; however, because of the irregular schedules due to shift work, it is often difficult for me to find a common time when I can hang out with them. Instead, I prefer to hang out with my friends in Mainland China.

Most female migrant workers from other countries (other than Mainland China) found it difficult to mix in society, especially because of the language barrier, and the lack of time and motivation to learn the language. Although many young locals can communicate in English, Cantonese is the preferred and widely used language in Macao. A Filipino migrant workers explained:

> Learning Cantonese is difficult. I tried a couple of times, but it is not an easy language to learn. It needs a considerable amount of time and persistence to learn this language. Because of the irregular work time and shift work, I find it hard to commit myself to learn this language.

A few non-Chinese female migrant workers, however, reported that, although not fluent, they could communicate in Cantonese. However, because of the absence of local friends, their social circle was also mostly limited to the people from their own countries. As the female migrant worker from Myanmar reported, and also experienced by a number of female migrant workers, 'Generally, residents in Macao preferred to have local friends, than to have someone from other countries.' In addition, to make local friends, the female migrant workers should be available at times when locals are comfortable and can socialize. Because of shift work, it was often difficult for these migrant workers to find a common time and develop social relationships. An Indonesian migrant worker clarified that:

> We want to make friends, develop a social relationship with locals, and mix in this society. But for that, we should be available, generally, in the evening, because that's the time when locals go around and hang out. However, we can be available in the evening, for a couple of hours, only when we work in the morning shift, and this is not something that is under our control or usually happens.

All of the female migrant workers reported having some type of difficulty in their family life because of shift work. Not only were they unable to spend a sufficient amount of time with their family members, but also, at times, they could not extend the necessary support, which is expected from a family member. Spouses of the several migrant workers, who were from Mainland China, were living and working in other Chinese cities. Because of their irregular schedules due to shift work, many of these female migrant workers faced the difficulty of communicating with their partners. Irregular communication with their partners often caused misunderstanding in their relationships. A female migrant worker from Mainland China explained:

> My husband works in Shenzhen. I visit my husband, once or sometimes twice a month; however, these visits are usually short. They are very unfulfilling in all aspects including physically, mentally, and emotionally. Sometimes we argue with each other and I feel so bad. For example, my husband wants a child. But he thinks that I am not giving enough time for this. I think the whole misunderstanding comes because we are not able to spend time with each other because of my work schedule.

Another female migrant worker from Mainland China, who was single, reported that she liked to sleep most of the time in her apartment, whenever she had her week off. Because of her behaviour, her mother was always upset with her, as she was not able to help her mother in performing daily chores at home. Family conflicts, caused by mistrust and misunderstanding, were also common among the non-Chinese female migrant workers. One Filipino migrant worker, while feeling sad, reported:

> I often have bitter arguments with my boyfriend. He lives in the Philippines and never understands the nature of my [shift] work. He is suspicious all the time whenever I go out of my apartment, for work, especially during a night shift. The problem is I can neither leave him, because I love him, nor convince him that what he thinks is not true.

Another female migrant worker reported that her children complained that she was not spending enough time with them, whenever they were talking over the phone or chatting through Skype. Consequently, her children often got angry with her, which, eventually made her feel guilty. While some female migrant workers could not be present (on online social media) on their children's birthday, others reported that they were not able to discuss important problems with their husband on family matters. Furthermore, their own cultural values also constrained some non-Chinese migrant workers' family relationship. A few non-Chinese female migrant workers remarked that their parents and family members often got angry with them because they were doing night shifts. In their culture, their parents argued, women should not go out and work at night, because, people may think negatively about their character.

5.3 Physical Tiredness and Mental Stress

All of the female migrant workers reported that they experienced physical tiredness and mental stress because of the shift work. As a female migrant worker from Taiwan stressed, 'Because of changes in shift work schedules, for example, when altered between morning, afternoon and night, it is hard for me to get enough, peaceful and quality sleep.' Lack of enough and quality sleep made them feel lazy, dizzy and low in energy. Furthermore, hotel jobs required them to work for long hours, and often without taking breaks. As a result, female migrant workers often felt tired and exhausted. A female migrant worker, who lived in Zhuhai and travelled to Macao for work every day, informed, 'I feel extreme tiredness as I generally have to spend four hours, every day, just to commute between Macao and Zhuhai, and this is really exhausting.'

Most female migrant workers reported that they experienced mental stress, either because they were not able to fulfil their family responsibilities, had conflicts with friends and families or were unable to cope with work–life balance as a consequence of shift work. The Filipino migrant worker who earlier mentioned about conflicts with her boyfriend, reported that she always 'felt extremely stressed', and 'could not focus' on her work, and 'constantly felt angry' with herself thinking why she migrated to Macao to work. Another Filipino migrant worker expressed:

> I often feel lonely and sad after I return from my work because I miss my family. I miss the time I spent with them and the events we used to celebrate together. I especially feel bad when it's my children's birthday. Then, I cry sitting alone in my boarding house. Once my husband was sick and hospitalized in my hometown. But I was not even able to talk to him properly because of my work. You can imagine how I felt at that time.

A number of married female migrant workers also reported that they were stressed because their relationship with their spouse was falling apart, but because of shift work, they were unable to spend enough time to communicate with them and resolve their problems. A Vietnamese migrant worker felt stressed because her parents and family members could not understand the nature of her (shift) work. She reported:

> They [parents and other family members] are putting pressure on me either to find a job where I can work stably at regular (day) shift or quit the job and return home. I can not follow any of those suggestions because I know that it is not easy to find a stable day-shift-only job in the hotel sector in Macao. Also, I can not return to my home country. I would have to live a life of struggle and scarcity there.

The feeling of being unable to cope with work–life balance because of shift work also caused mental stress among female migrant workers. A Chinese female migrant worker said:

> Although I was aware of the nature of work in hotels and casinos when I started the work, I did not expect that the shift working would change my lifestyle entirely. I was freer and had a bigger social circle with many friends, which, because of this work, has narrowed down to a few people. Whenever I remember my life before the shift working, I feel stressed as I know that I would not be able to go back again to the same life.

Another Chinese female migrant worker informed that shift working had 'shortened her life' as she was 'always in a rush commuting between Zhuhai and Macao'. She had been able to neither 'properly take care of food and healthy eating habits' nor continue physical exercize. In fact, she had isolated herself from the rest of society and often stayed alone in her apartment during her weeks off. She felt stressed thinking that she was 'locked' into her lonely life.

6. Discussion

Shift work is a longstanding part of the hospitality industry, especially in hotel and casino sectors where the businesses are run 24 hours a day, seven days a week. While from an economic standpoint, shift work can be beneficial for both the employers and the employees, the desire to increase wealth and income often comes with costs that are not socially desirable, and which are gendered in nature. Further, employees' wellbeing, which should be an essential prerequisite for running successful service enterprises, may be compromized. The effects can be detrimental to female migrant workers who leave their hometown and commute to, or stay in, another city in the hope of earning more money and enhance their standard of living.

As revealed by the empirical data of this study conducted in Macao, many female migrant workers experienced physical and mental conditions as their relationships with family and friends were falling apart, and many of them were unable to strike a balance between work and personal life, and/or were physically weaker. Indeed, shift-working male migrant workers may also experience similar physical and/or mental challenges in their life. However, as the Macao case demonstrated, certain social stereotypes associated with gender roles of women, prevalent in many societies, such as 'women should not go out during nights', 'women should be available for family events and when their family needs them' and 'women should also help and support in household chores irrespective of how hard they work outside of their house', seem to play a critical role in exacerbating these challenges experienced by female migrant workers (Basnyat et al., 2021). Earlier studies (e.g., Oakes et al., 1994; Poria, 2008) have found that such gendered occupational segregation has been prevalent in various cultures, especially in many Asian countries.

While examining the impacts of shift work on work–family conflicts Mills and Rosiello (2015) found that, historically, shift work has been highly gendered, although it became less so during World War II when women were called into manufacturing roles. Existing social and economic systems that are commonly practised, such as remunerations paid to employees in hotels and gaming sectors in Macao, sometimes subconsciously create differences between men and women, as well as between resident and non-resident workers (Abubakar et al., 2019; Forseth, 2005). Therefore, the impact of such practices may not be limited to female migrant workers who do shift work.

7. Conclusion

Considering the negative effects that shift-work, holistically, has brought into the lives of female migrant workers in Macao – both the Chinese and the non-Chinese – it is essential that companies that hire them develop a practice that aims to minimize such differences. The development of such a practice would not only act as a gesture of goodwill towards women in general, who constitute more than half of the employed population in many countries, including Macao, but it would also financially help many female migrant workers who struggle to make ends meet while trying to support their families, back in their home countries. Although increasing remuneration may not entirely compensate for their losses (physical, mental and social) caused by shift work, it would surely make them feel better, and help them positively connect with the host country, as well as with the companies where they work.

Developing an equitable system is also necessary for the hospitality industry, especially in the hotel sector, because of their dependence upon a large number of female and migrant workers (Adib & Guerrier, 2003). A significant majority of unskilled workers, including female and migrant workers, is employed by the sector and also do most of the shift work. However, unfortunately, they are the ones who earn the least among the employees. Because of the existence of these practices, across the countries, the turnover rate in the hotel sectors is considered one of the highest in the world. Though shift working by their employees is considered essential for the smooth running of hotels, the long-term sustainability of these hotels highly depends upon how they respond to the needs and conditions of their shift-working female migrant workers.

References

Abubakar, A.M., Anasori, E., & Lasisi, T.T. (2019). Physical attractiveness and managerial favoritism in the hotel industry: The light and dark side of erotic capital. *Journal of Hospitality and Tourism Management*, *38*(2019), 16–26.

Adib, A., & Guerrier, Y. (2003). The interlocking of gender with nationality, race, ethnicity and class: The narratives of women in hotel work. *Gender, Work & Organization*, *10*(4), 413–32.

Alali, H., Braeckman, L., Van Hecke, T., & Abdel Wahab, M. (2018). Shift work and occupational accident absence in Belgium: Findings from the 6th European Working Condition Survey. *International Journal of Environmental Research and Public Health*, *15*(9), 1811.

Alvionita, C.P., Angelina, T.F., & Wijaya, S. (2017). Working shift differences and their effects on employees' job fatigue levels: An empirical evidence from hotel industry in Surabaya. *KINERJA*, *19*(1), 42–53.

Alvesson, M., & Ashcraft, K. (2012). Interviews. In G. Symon & C. Cassell (eds), *Qualitative organizational research: Core methods and current challenges* (pp. 239–57). Los Angeles: Sage.

Asia Times. (2017). Macau should include maids in minimum wage plan: Scholar. https:// asiatimes .com/ 2017/ 12/ macau -include -maids -minimum -wage -plan -scholar/ date accessed 28 January 2021.

Basnyat, S., Che, I.T., & Ip, K.H. (2021). Gender roles and the commodification of beauty and physical attractiveness in restaurants: Perspectives of female servers. *Tourism and Hospitality Research*, 1–14. https://doi.org/10.1177/14673584211000086

Braun, V., & Clarke, V. (2012). Thematic analysis. In H. Cooper, P.M. Camic, D.L. Long, A.T. Panter, D. Rindskopf, & K.J. Sher (eds), *APA handbooks in psychology®. APA handbook of research methods in psychology, Vol. 2. Research designs: Quantitative, qualitative, neuropsychological, and biological* (pp. 57–71). American Psychological Association.

Centers for Disease Control and Prevention. (2020). *Work organization characteristics (NHIS-OHS) charts*. https://wwwn.cdc.gov/NIOSH-WHC/chart/ohs-workorg/work?OU=*&T=OU&V=R

Chan, S.H., Wan, Y.K.P., & Kuok, O.M. (2015). Relationships among burnout, job satisfaction, and turnover of casino employees in Macau. *Journal of Hospitality Marketing & Management*, *24*(4), 345–74.

Chau, S.-l. (2019). The impact of work-family conflict on work stress and job satisfaction among Macau table game dealers. *International Journal of Tourism Sciences*, *19*(1), 1–17.

DSAJ. (2020). *Labour relations law*. Legal Affairs Bureau, Macao SAR Government.

DSEC. (2020a). *Macao in figures: 2020*. Statistics and Census Service, Government of Macao Special Administrative Region.

DSEC. (2020b). *Survey on manpower needs and wages: Gaming sector*. Statistics and Census Service of the Government of Macao Special Administrative Region.

Folkard, S., & Tucker, P. (2003). Shift work, safety and productivity. *Occupational Medicine, 53*(2), 95–101.

Forseth, U. (2005). Gender matters? Exploring how gender is negotiated in service encounters. *Gender, Work & Organization, 12*(5), 440–59.

Golden, L. (2015). Irregular work scheduling and its consequences. *EPI Briefing Paper No. 394*. https://www.epi.org/publication/irregular-work-scheduling-and-its-consequences/

Griffin, R.M. (2010). *The health risks of shift work*. https://www.webmd.com/sleep-disorders/features/shift-work date accessed 27 January 2021.

ILO. (2004). *What is shift work?*https://www.ilo.org/wcmsp5/groups/public/---ed_protect/---protrav/---travail/documents/publication/wcms_170713.pdf date accessed 1 June 2021.

Kang, M.-Y., Kwon, H.-J., Choi, K.-H., Kang, C.-W., & Kim, H. (2017). The relationship between shift work and mental health among electronics workers in South Korea: A cross-sectional study. *PloS One, 12*(11), 1–10.

Liu, S. (2020). The impact of social support on job stress of shift working mothers: A study of casino employees in Macao. *Asian Education and Development Studies, 11*(3), 559–70. https://doi.org/10.1108/AEDS-02-2020-0037

Mills, M.J., & Rosiello, R.M. (2015). Shiftwork as gendered and its impact on work–family balance. In M.J. Mills (ed.), *Gender and the work-family experience* (pp. 251–70). New York: Springer.

Moon, H.J., Lee, S.H., Lee, H.S., Lee, K.-J., & Kim, J.J. (2015). The association between shift work and depression in hotel workers. *Annals of Occupational and Environmental Medicine, 27*(1), 1–11.

Oakes, P.J., Haslam, S.A., & Turner, J.C. (1994). *Stereotyping and social reality*. Hoboken, NJ: Blackwell.

Office for National Statistics. (2018). *Tables looking at numbers and percentages undertaking shiftwork, and numbers by type of shift, by sex for 2007 to 2017 for selected industry groups*. https://www.ons.gov.uk/employmentandlabourmarket/peopleinwork/employmentandemployeetypes/adhocs/008452tableslookingatnumbersandpercentagesundertakingshiftworkandnumbersbytypeofshiftbysexfor2007to2017forselectedindustrygroups date accessed 30 May 2021.

Poria, Y. (2008). Gender—a crucial neglected element in the service encounter: An exploratory study of the choice of hotel masseur or masseuse. *Journal of Hospitality & Tourism Research, 32*(2), 151–168.

Pullman, M., & Rodgers, S. (2010). Capacity management for hospitality and tourism: A review of current approaches. *International Journal of Hospitality Management, 29*(1), 177–87.

Saunders, M.N. (2012). Choosing research participants. In G. Symon & C. Cassell (eds), *Qualitative organizational research: Core methods and current challenges* (pp. 35–52). Los Angeles, CA: Sage.

Saunders, M., & Townsend, K. (2016). Reporting and justifying the number of interview participants in organisation and workplace research. *British Journal of Management, 27*, 836–852.

Stotz, J. (2021). *Average and minimum salary in Macau, China*. https://checkinprice.com/average-and-minimum-salary-in-macau-china/

Tai, S.-Y., Lin, P.-C., Chen, Y.-M., Hung, H.-C., Pan, C.-H., Pan, S.-M., Lee, C.-Y., Huang, C.-T., & Wu, M.-T. (2014). Effects of marital status and shift work on family function among registered nurses. *Industrial Health, 52*(4), 296–303.

Trent, C., & Mayer, W.J. (2014). Working the night shift: The impact of compensating wages and local economic conditions on shift choice. *Economics Research International, 2014*, 1–15. https://doi.org/10.1155/2014/632506

TSheets. (2018). How shift work affects restaurant and hotel workers. https://www.hospitalitynet.org/news/4086289.html date accessed 30 May 2021.

Vaughn, B.V., & Kataria, L. (2020). Shift work disorder. https://www.medlink.com/articles/shift-work-disorder

Vong, L.T.-N., & Tang, W.S.-L. (2017). The mediating effect of work–family conflict in the relationship between job stress and intent to stay: The case of tourism and hospitality workers in Macau. *Journal of Human Resources in Hospitality & Tourism, 16*(1), 39–55.

World Travel and Tourism Council (2019). Key highlights – economic impact of cities 2019. www.wttc.org. accessed March 1, 2021.

8 Negotiating gender and power during COVID-19: women and tourism in San Gil, Colombia

Claudia Becerra-Gualdrón, Karolina Doughty and Margreet van der Burg

1. Introduction

The comparatively high participation of women is one of the reasons that tourism has been presented as a sector with high potential to benefit them (UNWTO-UN Women, 2011). However, scholars working in the field stress that tourism is providing neither a necessary nor a sufficient condition for gender equality (Zhang & Zhang, 2021). Existing gender power hierarchies and dynamics are instead often reproduced in tourism spaces (Vizcaíno-Suárez & Díaz-Carrión, 2018), and sometimes intensified in ways that limit women's opportunities (Morgan & Winkler, 2019).

International evidence underlines that women in the tourism sector are more likely than men to face poorer working conditions (Guimarães & Silva, 2016), exploitation, sexual harassment and violence (World Tourism Organization, 2019). Further, women carry expectations in the home to shoulder the majority of the domestic labour, resulting in 'double working' days (Gentry, 2007). The advent of the COVID-19 crisis has exacerbated existing gendered dimensions of inequality, through its impact on women's ability to retain and continue their paid work, the increased loads of unpaid domestic and caring work resulting from lockdown measures that most often fall to women, and the heightened risk of domestic violence against women that often accompany economic downturns and societal crises (Guterres, 2020).

San Gil – the empirical focus of this chapter – is a small city located in the centre east of Colombia in the department of Santander. The city has a warm climate and due to its geographical location, has waterfalls, wells, caves and rivers, making it particularly attractive for adventure tourism (Pérez-Pinzón & Serrano-Ruíz, 2018). San Gil is considered one of the most dynamic tourism cities in Colombia (Forero, 2017), holding 9 per cent of the hotel capacity while only 0.2 per cent of the region's population. In 2018, San Gil received approximately 45 000 tourists (La Cometa, 2019), yet the local tourism sector is still not well documented nor researched, and there is little understanding of the situation and experiences of women tourism workers. This chapter addresses this gap, with a view to better understanding women's experience of tourism work, coupled with the impact of the coronavirus pandemic.

In March 2020, Colombia endorsed a strict lockdown to contain the COVID-19 outbreak. This first national measure lasted until September 2020, when a more flexible and regional approach was taken. Since then, local governments interspersed measures according to the spikes of infections, until gradually after July 2021 all restrictions were lifted. However, Colombia has had almost 5 million people infected and 126 000 deaths. The quarantines and curfews, capacity limits, social distancing and restrictions on mobility had a severe negative impact on the country's economy, especially in sectors like tourism (Alon et al., 2020), which disproportionally affected women. It has been broadly recognized that the COVID-19 crisis has also served to intensify existing gendered divides more generally (Manzo & Minello, 2020).

In this chapter, we examine how women working in tourism experienced and coped with the challenging circumstances of the coronavirus pandemic while navigating gender power relations at home and at work. This focus responds to calls for nuanced site-specific research that examines gender issues at the microscale (Boley et al., 2016), taking into account that these play out in place-specific ways (Tucker & Boonabaana, 2012). In addition, the chapter takes a comparative approach in its focus on women across different labour positions, to address the lack of studies in the field of gender and tourism that engage comparatively with women's lived realities across the spectrum of employment, entrepreneurship and leadership. As we shall demonstrate, women's labour positions affected how they experienced the COVID-19 crisis and its direct impacts on their work and home life, the coping mechanisms upon which they relied, and how they navigated intimate gender power relations, such as those affecting the distribution of freedoms, responsibilities and tasks in the home.

In the following section, we outline the conceptualization of gendered power that we employ in our analysis. We specifically present the articulation of the different modalities of power in 'power over', 'power to', 'power with' and 'power within', which draw analytical attention to women's agency within different sets of gender relationships (Yount et al., 2016) at work and at home, and how these experiences and practices relate to each other. We then detail the qualitative methodology employed, and introduce the 19 women we interviewed for this research. Empirical findings are then presented and discussed, illustrating the diverse ways that women working in tourism have experienced and coped with the challenging circumstances of the pandemic. The findings highlight a heterogeneous process of empowerment in the face of these circumstances. Based on the San Gil adventure tourism case, conclusions are then drawn in light of the conceptualization of gendered power and gender dynamics.

2. Conceptualising Gender Power Relations in Tourism

The subfield of tourism gender research is broadly concerned with women's contributions as producers and consumers of tourism (Swain & Momsen, 2002), the gender dimension of tourism development (Ferguson & Moreno, 2015), and women's participation and integration into the tourism labour market (Guimarães & Silva, 2016). In the Latin American context, tourism gender studies emerged at the beginning of the twenty-first century, with a strong focus on the gendered impacts of tourism development in host communities (Vizcaíno-Suárez & Díaz-Carrión, 2018), and efforts to make gender and power relations visible in a region characterized by social, political and economic inequalities (Díaz-Carrión, 2012). This literature has recently been enriched with counter-hegemonic contributions, especially postcolonial approaches (Barboza, 2017).

2.1 Modalities of Power Relations and Notions of Empowerment

Theorizations of power relations within gender tourism literatures have gone beyond the traditional dominance model of *power over* (such as the structural subjugation of women within patriarchal societies) in favour of a more nuanced understanding of the modalities of power and agency, where women are able to exercize within a broader landscape marked by gender inequality (Kabeer, 1999; Rowlands, 1997). The notion of *power to* acknowledges the capacity of a person to act in spite of or in response to the power wielded over them by others, and is closely related to the concept of empowerment(e.g., Allen, 1999). We follow Fuente (2013) in making a distinction between *power to* as a capacity, and empowerment as a process of change that includes psychic, cultural, political and relational aspects. Empowerment involves a process of different degrees of personal development through different times and phases, from growing awareness to actions aimed at removing inequities (Van Eerdewijk et al., 2017). Further, *power with* refers to collective capacities for action (Allen, 1999), while *power within* signals the internal intangible assets of self-esteem and self-confidence (Nikkhah et al., 2012). *Power within* is associated with individual capacities for self-awareness, assertiveness and reflexive analysis of experiences allowing individuals to recognize how power operates in their lives, and to gain confidence to improve their situation in the context of gender power relations (Williams et al., 1994).

Perhaps not surprisingly, the notion of empowerment is often central in efforts to examine the transformative potential of tourism as a driver for gender equality. However, the concept has been criticized because it tends to celebrate microscale expressions of agency without sufficient attention to wider structures of domination (Fuente, 2013). This is evident in the tourism literature which has shifted its focus from social justice, equity and power relations to an emphasis on the neoliberal values of individualism and competitiveness (Small et al., 2017). Instead, considering empowerment is entangled with, and tempered by, the dominant modality of *power over*, research on gender and tourism can address both aspects of domination and individual agency.

2.2 Work-Home Interactions and Labour Positions

The analysis of gender power relations in Latin America has focused on the empowerment of women through increased job opportunities offered in tourism (UNWTO, 2019). Some studies stress the empowering capacity of tourism (Chablé et al., 2007; Sánchez et al., 2019). Others have found that structures of domination prevent women from benefiting from tourism (Barkin, 2003; Belsky, 1999), particularly due to family and housekeeping expectations and demands (Morgan & Winkler, 2019). However, these studies seldom address how women navigate and negotiate interconnected power relations at work and at home. Relations between home and work have typically been addressed in terms of 'work–family conflict' (Edwards & Rothbard, 2000) and the strategies that women develop to make their work in tourism compatible with their family responsibilities, especially in Latin America (Vizcaíno-Suárez et al., 2016). This notion has been criticized for focusing exclusively on women (Emslie et al., 2004), for considering the work–family conflict as an external objective and homogenous reality, detached from women's lived experiences (Grünberg & Matei, 2019) and for perpetuating the discourse that women are individually responsible for achieving a 'happy work–family balance', ignoring the broader landscapes of inequality in which they are immersed (Rottenberg,

2018). It also focuses exclusively on the heteronormative notion of family, that is, heterosexual couples with children.

To address these critiques, we draw on the analytical typology of Grünberg and Matei (2019) in considering the multifaceted and contingent relations between home and work. They identify that these are typified as separate, contrasting or complementary realms. As separate realms, rigid boundaries between home and work are drawn; each one exhibits distinct cultures and forms of social organization. As contrasting realms, home is understood in relation to workplace, and vice versa. This view looks at how the differences between the two spheres appear to be meaningful. And last, as complementary realms, they are considered to exhibit a relation of mutual enhancement and completion.

In our comparative focus across labour positions, we seek to understand the complexity of relations between work and home for women working in tourism. We argue that different labour positions can greatly affect the way in which women experience their participation in tourism and the gender power relations they must navigate. Existing research on labour positions in relation to gender power relations in tourism has mainly focused on the gendered nature of employment (Madera et al., 2009) and entrepreneurship (Byrne et al., 2019).

However, in this chapter we focus on the role of various labour positions in how women navigate gender power across spaces of work and home. Further, we wish to understand how these intersect with other axes of potential disadvantage such as the rural–urban divide, the role of religion in perpetuating traditional gender roles, and the impact of marital status and motherhood.

3. Methodology

3.1 In-Depth Interviews

This research put women themselves in the centre of research, employing a qualitative design using in-depth interviews to obtain first-hand subjective interpretations from women working in tourism. The interviews were semi-structured with open-ended questions aiming to fully capture the experiences, perceptions, feelings, decisions, concerns and desired changes in the women's lives. Participating women were encouraged to use all their senses, feelings and emotions (Hunjan & Pettit, 2011) to talk about their everyday life experiences and practices.

Participants were asked about their careers in tourism, their relations and the decision-making processes at work. To link their realities at work and home, they were asked about experiences of conflict or support between work and home. Questions on women's daily routines were useful to link practices and experiences at home and at the workplace, as well as the changes in both spheres due to the COVID-19 restrictions. Follow-up questions were asked to identify situations of constraints, control, discrimination, harassment, violence, etc. Women were asked to elaborate on their experiences, actions, reactions, decisions and whether they had felt limited in their options in relation to their physical integrity, self-esteem, dignity, self-confidence, etc. Women were also invited to talk about ways to overcome difficulties or injustices and the changes in self-determination, self-confidence and their ability to make choices. In order to capture the implications of different labour positions, participant answers were differentiated according to certain social and demographic dimensions, such as family status, age, class and religion, to acknowledge intersectionality.

Due to the COVID-19 restrictions, all the interviews were conducted over telephone by the first author in her and the participants' mother tongue, Spanish. Most of the interviews were conducted in the strictest phase of quarantine, which provided more time and availability for answering the questions. The interviews lasted between 45 and 120 minutes; the quotes included in the chapter have been translated into English by the first author. All interviews were recorded and transcribed. Pseudonyms are used to assure anonymity.

The data was analysed following the substantive phases set out by Braun and Clarke (2006). The transcripts were carefully read and organized, and a list of initial codes was generated. This process was constructed both inductively and deductively. After sorting the different codes into potential themes, relations between codes, themes and different levels of themes were considered, reviewed and refined. Considering the research question and the literature on gender power relations in tourism three main themes and seven sub-themes were identified which captured differentiated impacts of the pandemic, navigation between work and home relations and coping strategies.

3.2 Research Participants

The sample consisted of women working in the tourism industry in San Gil, Colombia. These women were recruited through snowball sampling (Goodman, 1961). A balanced sample of women of different labour positions, ages, social classes, and family constellation was sought. Regarding labour positions, there were three groups – employees, entrepreneurs and self-employed –

the first group with some type of contract or labour subordination, the second owning their companies and the third as sole workers in their own informal businesses. The number of entrepreneurs was unfortunately lower than the number of employees or self-employed women. A total of 19 interviews were conducted between March and August 2020.The characteristics of the participants are summarized in Table 8.1.

4. Findings

4.1 Impact of the Pandemic on Women in Different Labour Positions

The restrictions introduced by the Colombian government in response to the pandemic had a devastating effect on the tourism sector in San Gil, much as elsewhere across the globe. Government aid packages were declared for tourism workers but have been accompanied by criticism and corruption scandals. For example, income aid was made available for three months to those who worked in tourism, provided they had an up-to-date registration in the National Tourism Registry (at 15 April, 2020), were in possession of a professional card, and not already receiving other government benefits. Due to these requirements, many tourism workers were not able to claim any support; only four of the 19 participants got financial support of approximately 150 euros since many worked informally. Another six women among the participants accessed the more general 'solidarity income' of approximately 40 euros per month, which was directed to the poorest families according to the databases of the National Planning Department. However, there were complaints about the reliability of the databases used to assign it. Despite the broad participation of women in tourism, there has been no governmental or media exposure about gender-related impacts of the pandemic at the local or national level, or differentiation by gender in terms of aid packages. Women have been invisible to the political agenda during the crisis and therefore also to targeted actions.

The study revealed that all interviewed women endured a loss of income due to the pandemic but experienced the COVID-19 pandemic differently relative to labour position, socioeconomic status, age, family setup and location. The women also managed their household finances and loss of income in different ways.

Table 8.1 Characteristics of San Gil research participants

ID	Pseudonym	Labour position	Age	Family setup	Location	Education level
1	Celmi	Employee	48	Single, 1 child	Urban	University
2	Daisy	Employee	25	She lives with her parents, single, 1 child	Rural	Primary school
3	Diana	Employee	25	Married, 1 child	Rural	High school
4	Ema	Employee	39	Married, 2 children	Urban	Technical college
5	Femy	Employee	40	Married, 2 children	Urban	High school
6	Gloria	Employee	44	Married, 1 child	Urban	University
7	Hilda	Employee	43	Single, 1 child	Rural	Primary school
8	Julia	Employee	25	She lives with her parents, no children	Urban	Technical college
9	Lily	Employee	53	Single, 1 child	Urban	High school
10	Maria	Employee	60	Widow, 2 children	Urban	Primary school
11	Naty	Employee	30	She lives with her father, no children	Urban	Technical college
12	Sara	Employee	38	Divorced, 2 children	Urban	High school
13	Nely	Entrepreneur	38	Married, 2 children	Urban	University
14	Nora	Entrepreneur	40	Divorced, 2 children	Urban	University
15	Alba	Entrepreneur	36	Married, 3 children	Urban	University
16	Ana	Self-employed	62	Single, 2 children	Urban	Technical college
17	Lucy	Self-employed	35	Single, 1 child	Urban	University
18	Lyda	Self-employed	55	Divorced, 2 children	Urban	Technical college
19	Rosa	Self-employed	65	Widow, 5 children	Urban	Primary school

4.1.1 *Women Entrepreneurs*

The interviewed women entrepreneurs had higher incomes, higher levels of existing savings, and easier access to credit than employees and the self-employed, and sometimes had income from other businesses. All entrepreneurs interviewed were managing their own companies, were included in the payroll, and enjoyed benefits such as family allowances, healthcare, retirement plan, etc. The entrepreneurs, having financial back-up resources, used the time of the pandemic to plan new projects, prepare for the reopening or dedicate themselves to leisure activities. For example, Alba, a middle-aged married formal entrepreneur and her husband, thanks to the profits of the companies they own, bought a place to let: 'We have leased a commercial space here in San Gil and with that we are practically making a living.' She also sells dollhouses and is expanding her business.

4.1.2 *Employees and Self-employed*

In contrast to the entrepreneurs, the vast majority of the interviewed women employees and self-employed had no other sources of income and little savings which made it difficult for them to find money for rent, food and basic necessities. Exceptions were women living on farms in rural areas, most of them employees. These women were able to subsist on farming activities, livestock and crops, as they either owned the land or could live there in exchange for their work on it. For example, Hilda, a 43-year-old employed woman, bought a farm with her husband and kept it after the divorce. Women employees who were living in rural areas expressed that their daily routines and general lifestyle hardly changed due to the pandemic. For example, Diana, a 25-year-old married employee living in a rural area considered her location a benefit:

> Here in the countryside it is different, it is better than in the city; because on the farm at least one has a bit more freedom. The pandemic has been more difficult in the city ... I missed my job, but here in the countryside one does other activities.

Contrary to entrepreneurs and women living in rural areas, the main concern of other interviewed employees and self-employed women was finding resources to support themselves and their families. This was especially necessary for those on a so-called service contract. This type of contract provides only payment for activities carried out without employment benefits such as healthcare or retirement plan, and is commonly used in the tourism sector to enable companies to hire seasonally, but leaves workers in a vulnerable situation. However, most employees interviewed were resigned to this reality. Gloria, a middle-aged married employee, for instance, said that 'When the pandemic began, they made a definitive closure for tourism activities, then I automatically accepted that I could not have more work there.'

Women who were not living in nuclear families experienced more pressure, especially when they had dependants to support. Sara, a 38-year-old divorced employee and mother of two young children, expressed how her economic situation changed:

> [The pandemic] has been a very hard blow. My work in the hotel generated the necessary income to live with my children and give them what they need. Now our only source of income is what I can do as cleaning some houses and what my children's father sends them, but almost always we have to argue with him.

Many of the employees and self-employed women mentioned they became increasingly dependent on financial support from relatives such as parents or children, depending on their age. For example, Julia, a 25-year-old single employee who lives with her parents, said 'my father is a rancher and he takes care of most of the household expenses.' She is an example of young women who live with their parents and consider their income as an extra contribution to the household and for their personal expenses. In the case of Daisy (25, single mother living with her parents and brothers), only her father and brother kept their jobs: 'I am not earning the same, so right now I am not contributing to the groceries or services; then my brother and dad have to do that.' At the other end of the spectrum, older participants generally received financial support from their children, as in the case of Maria, a 60-year-old widow with two adult children: 'My children help me monthly for my expenses.'

In most families where men were present, it was the man who continued to receive some form of income, also in families where the husband and wife both worked full-time in tourism. For instance, Gloria (44, a married employee with one child), said that although she and her husband both worked in activities related to tourism, only her husband had kept his job. Femy (40, employee married with two children) had the same experience: 'Thank God my husband has had something to do.'

As these findings show, women working in tourism in San Gil were affected differently according to their labour position, age, economic status, location and family setup. Overall, employed or self-employed, middle-aged women, especially single mothers (which account for almost half of the participants in this study) in urban areas, have borne the brunt of the financial impacts of the pandemic.

4.2 Navigating Work–Home Relations

Looking to work–home relations, we found other aspects of impact and vulnerability across the labour positions. The changes due to the pandemic generated renegotiations of work–home relations and responsibilities for most of the participants, mainly evidenced in the use of time, domestic tasks and sources of household income. Although the majority of the interviewed women stated they were satisfied with the new distribution of tasks and income, the renegotiation occurred in two main ways. In some cases, the participants spoke explicitly of negotiation processes within their homes, either with their parents, children or partners and used terms such as equity, equality and teamwork. In other cases, most commonly for employed and self-employed married women, the (re)distribution reinforced traditional gender roles.

4.2.1 Being Confined to the Home

Lockdown measures in response to COVID-19 meant that the vast majority of the women interviewed could not continue their work, or had to reduce time spent on work. There were clear differences in how women used the increased time spent at home. Mainly entrepreneurs and women with external economic support were able to use available extra time for self-development, such as thinking about future projects, or learning new skills. For example, Alba, a 36-year-old entrepreneur, shared that together with her husband she had been planning an ambitious new project:

> In this time … we are working with the Vice Ministry of Tourism and the Vice Ministry of Sport so that in 2023 we can create the rafting world championship here in San Gil.

Ana (self-employed tour-guide) used the lockdown to study English to be able to get a certificate as a professional guide: 'We are on standby due to the pandemic, we will see when that can be solved but in the meantime we have to study.' The entrepreneurs and self-employed women were already accustomed to using the off-season time to prepare for the next season, and could fall back on this pattern of activity. Alba explained:

> Normally … we have strong times of the year such as December and January, Easter, July holidays, October recess and holidays … In low season, one dedicates the time to improving equipment, maintaining equipment, making location improvements; all this matters.

However, employees with financial constraints were more focused on trying to survive while hoping things would return to normal. For them the pandemic was much less an opportunity for self-development, but some valued the extra time to spend with their families.

Family structure and age of the participants often affected what activities could be carried out during confinement. For instance, middle-aged women with small or school-age children had to meet the new challenge of virtual education and spent more time with their children. This was also the case for entrepreneur Nely, a 38-year-old married bakery owner, who shared how her routine changed:

> My son no longer goes to school, so since then everything has changed, because my son is at home, so I have to help him with his homework and everything related to school.

4.2.2 Household Chores

More time spent together at home during the pandemic often led to a change in the distribution of household chores. Particularly the employees who could not continue work outside the home, ended up being responsible for the tasks in the home instead, as the family fell back on traditional gender norms. For example, Femy (40-year-old married employee) explained:

> With the pandemic I have taken away my sons' chores because before my children were practically the ones who did everything at home. Since I am at home I have reduced their household chores.

These changes were less pronounced for women like Hilda, a single mother of 43, in a rural location, who shared that she got extra help from her daughter who had to stay at home: 'Now I don't get up so early because my daughter is here with me so she gets up and helps me clean and cook.'

Several women (mainly employees and self-employed) used the word 'collaboration' or 'help' to refer to the household chores that men perform. This may indicate that they see household chores as their responsibility to which their partners or the men of the house collaborate when the women lack time due to their work outside the home. When the women returned home due to the pandemic, they returned to 'normal', which is for them to carry out housework. Likewise, the women's income as economic contribution to the home is also termed 'collaboration'. For instance, Ema, a married employee said: 'Thank God I have my job; at the moment I am using that to help with the cost of groceries.'

In a second group of especially, but not exclusively, entrepreneurs, the distribution of tasks at home was allocated in a more equitable way. Alba and her husband used to employ a maid, and when she no longer could come due to the COVID-19 restrictions, they distributed the tasks among all family members: 'Now that we no longer have a person to help us around the house, we distribute the housework; we begin to teach the children that it is important to help with the housework.'

Similarly, Gloria, a 44-year-old married employee with one child, shared:

> Here is teamwork ... We are training our children to be like that so that they get used to it. While I do one thing they must do another and my husband has cooked all the time ... and I take care of the part of the organization of the house.

4.3 Networks

The networks that the interviewed women have woven in their work and their extended families have been fundamental to cope not only with the changes of the pandemic but also to balance their family and work demands. All the participants spoke positively about their work relationships, although the employees put more emphasis on collegiality than self-employed and entrepreneurs. For example, Daisy, a 25-year-old employee, mentioned that 'I started to work and two months later I got pregnant. I didn't expect it, but my colleagues encouraged and supported me, so I felt better.' Ema, whose daughter has health problems, said that her co-workers and her work in general 'have been essential in many situations, especially in my daughter's illness, to attend medical appointments to other cities and pay expenses'. Some women shared that they often turned to female colleagues for support with personal or work-related challenges.

The relationship with female relatives was mentioned as important, especially in interviews with employed or self-employed women. Mothers, daughters, sisters, sisters-in-law, cousins and aunts support each other; especially in caring arrangements such as childcare. Daisy said: 'My mother is the one who takes care of my daughter so that I can go to work, if I hadn't someone I trust, I couldn't work.' She expressed that the support of her mother has been essential for her during the pandemic. Lucy (35, a single mother, self-employed) mainly relied on her mother: 'We always support each other when, for example, I have to go on a trip, my daughter can stay with my mother.'In addition to this type of help, Nely found that 'Emotional support and advice are important to maintain balance in my life.'

4.4 Coping with the Pandemic

Although individual circumstances and experiences varied, the coping strategies of the interviewed women followed similar patterns. Resourcefulness, flexibility, optimism and learning were common to almost all. However, how these women from San Gil talked about their faith and themselves highlighted differences between entrepreneurs on the one hand, and employees and self-employed women, on the other.

4.4.1 Resourcefulness and Flexibility

Many of the participants, across labour positions, appeared to be used to working in an unstable sector. The following quote from Alba illustrates this: 'We still have many times that we do not have tourists, so that is (constantly) happening during all these years ... there are times where there is no income.'

Although the pandemic did catch women off-guard, some had savings because they were used to relying on peak season earnings. They were aware that the sector is unstable and that a person who works in tourism in San Gil has to learn to distribute the money throughout the year. As a result, women are flexible and grab the opportunity to do a wide range of jobs. For instance, 30-year-old single employee Naty said: 'I am a very active person. If you say to me: can you help me by distributing chocolate, I say ok … if I don't know, I find the way, I find out and I do it.' Thus, it seems that the instability of the sector requires women to have, or develop, both flexibility and ingenuity.

4.4.2 Optimism and Learning

Despite the difficulties that the participants have faced during the pandemic, almost all emphasized positive aspects and lessons learned. Whenever they mentioned something negative, it was followed by a positive sentiment: 'but the good thing is…' or 'despite that…', etc. The possibility to spend more time with their family was most mentioned as positive. Employee Celmi said 'I am a single mother … and until now we have spent more time together thanks to the pandemic.'

Most interviewed women pointed out that the pandemic generated useful life lessons. For instance, that it is possible to live well with less income. As Julia (employee) stated: 'Although my income has decreased ... and my father's as well with what we have, that is enough.' Alba (entrepreneur) also mentioned the positive side of being distracted and not wanting to consume so much:

> In this pandemic, we learned to be a little more thrifty, because since we have no income then we start to see things from a different way ... The pandemic has been very positive on understanding that ... even if one does not want to be in the circle of our economy, one is there; because you want to buy and buy things.

However, while for some women (mainly entrepreneurs) optimism was related to a sense of keeping control of the situation, for others (mainly employees and self-employed), it was rather about acceptance. They tried to stay calm and positive in the face of an external event over which they felt little control.

4.4.3 Faith

Religious beliefs played a significant role in dealing with the challenges of the pandemic. The vast majority of those interviewed were Catholic and most of them framed the challenges of the pandemic in relation to their beliefs, which provided emotional strength, as Alba expressed:

> I have God in my heart and my joy and happiness lies in that. If I have him, I have everything. He gives me everything, he provides everything to me (...) My husband and I live 100 percent off tourism and I can say that every day God has given us what we have needed.

The entrepreneurs used more expressions of gratitude while self-employed and employees were more likely to use words like 'I beg or ask God'. For example, Nora, a middle-aged divorced entrepreneur, repeats throughout the interview her gratitude to God:

> I have to thank God for all the blessings he has given me. I go back and repeat it: Thank God. Thanks to him I have two wonderful daughters, I have a roof to sleep under, a plate of food every day at my table, many privileges that unfortunately many people do not have at the moment.

Differently, Rosa, an older self-employed widow, begged for the crisis to end quickly: 'I beg with the power of God, the Holy Virgin and the Holy Spirit eliminate this pandemic soon.'

4.4.4 Self-perception

The participants expressed different ideas about what the pandemic crisis has meant for them. Especially the employees, who lost their main source of income, have experienced it as an economic and personal crisis in their lives.

They hope it ends soon so that their life can go back to the way it was before. For example, Lyda (55-year-old divorced, self-employed tour guide): 'This was not expected by absolutely anyone and it changed our lives... we must be patient and hope that it will end soon so that we return to our life as it was before.'

Others, especially, but not exclusively, entrepreneurs, considered the crisis as one more obstacle to overcome in their lives. For instance, Nora, a middle-aged divorced entrepreneur expressed:

> We have been able to reinvent ourselves, get ahead. It has not been easy indeed but as good Santanderians we carry in our blood a race of vigorous, enterprising, hardworking people and for us it is easy to be exigent and get ahead regardless of the situations we are going through, not only in our department but in our country in the entire world.

The way women talked about the pandemic was closely linked to their self-perception. The group of mainly entrepreneurs who referred to the pandemic as one more obstacle to overcome also described themselves as leaders, strong and who throughout their lives have been able to overcome difficulties and solve problems.

In general terms, entrepreneurs expressed more confidence in their capabilities than employees. They were more likely to individualize their situation and hold themselves solely responsible for their results. For instance, Nora characterized herself as 'vigorous, enterprising, and hardworking' and related it directly to her response to the pandemic: 'For us it is easy to be strict and get ahead regardless of the situations.' The entrepreneurs manifested a greater sense of control over the crisis and placed a role of leadership in their hands. Alba talked about herself as a leader: 'I think that I am a very entrepreneurial woman in the sense that I am always looking for leadership of the processes.' She considered herself as an example to follow: 'It seems to me that this is healthy, because it is that one is an example to follow, an example of growth.' Many families depend on her and her company: 'We want to transcend in the tourism, we in our jobs always want to move tourism forward, so it seems to me that I am a woman who can be an example for many.' She responded accordingly in the pandemic, and tried to initiate new projects. Likewise, they considered their companies not only as generating profits but also helping other people as Alba explained to 'create with them [employees] a bond of growth, transformation, emotional support ... I see the company as a way to help many people.'

This is related to self-awareness, self-esteem and identity. Those women with a positive self-perception of their own capabilities talked more about new possibilities. It seems clear that when assigning meaning to the changed pandemic circumstances, the women interviewed made use of elements such as previous experiences of problem solving, which made some see it as another challenge among many others, while for others it was a very difficult crisis.

5. Discussion

This chapter has offered insights into how women working in tourism in San Gil experienced and coped with the challenging circumstances of the COVID-19 pandemic. All participants experienced a loss of income but navigated and negotiated differently in their heterogeneous realities based on their labour position, socioeconomic status, age, family setup and location. In general, employees and the self-employed were worse affected compared to entrepreneurs.

When we look at how their various responses are related to empowerment processes, the emotional strength that many women expressed suggests that they could rely on 'power within', and their control over the situation points at 'power to' when facing difficulties. Nevertheless, we could identify two groups. For the first group of women, mainly consisting of entrepreneurs, we could relate professional achievements, self-confidence and a feeling of control over the crisis to fair processes of renegotiation. Within the home this concerned the distribution of time dedicated to the career and household tasks, as well as the responsibility for family income. In Grünberg and Matei's (2019) terms, work and home were experienced as complementary realms. Moreover, the comparatively higher self-confidence of entrepreneurs may be related to positive characteristics associated with entrepreneurship (Nicholson & Anderson, 2005). Running a business successfully can be an important source of empowerment for women, which can be enhanced by 'succeeding' in an area that many still consider masculine (Ahl, 2007). However, these characteristics are also aligned with discourses that encourage citizens to be autonomous, positioning them as unconstrained by external forces transferring responsibility almost exclusively to the individual (Rottenberg, 2018).

For the second group, consisting mainly of employees and self-employed women, expressions of self-esteem, self-confidence and positive perception of their own career appeared much lower. In this group most women took a more passive position and were hoping for the pandemic to end soon. Their renegotiations tended to be tacit and generally resulted in traditional distributions of tasks within the home. In these cases, male work was privileged, and work and home were played out as contrasting and separate realms, accentuating traditional gender roles.

Our findings also support Grünberg and Matei's (2019) argument about the importance of using multifaceted and contingent notions of these relations and of addressing family types other than heterosexual couples with children. In our study, less than half of the interviewees have such a family setup. Therefore, the theorizations focused on this type of family fall short to understand and analyse the realities of most of our participants.

Our study strongly supports the claims for the need to perform intersectional analyses. We found that the labour position intersected with age, family setup and the rural–urban divide to generate differentiated experiences. Employed or self-employed middle-aged single mothers in urban areas were the most vulnerable in terms of existing resources to cope with loss of income. Younger and older women, even before the pandemic, had been receiving financial support from parents, siblings and children, which made it easier to adjust and to cope with the loss of income. Women living in rural areas had an advantage over women living in the cities in terms of freedom and access to housing and food. Our results also reveal the important, although differentiated roles of religion in experiences of and coping with the crisis.

Network management illustrated how participants turn to other women to cope with challenges of work and family demands, which is closely associated with the concept of 'power with'. Mutual support went both ways from home to work and vice versa. The work-to-home support network was naturally much more evident among employees than among the self-employed and employers. Although 'power with' is generally understood in terms of collectively achieving ends, this study found that camaraderie and mutual support – without collective action – have positively impacted the lives of the participants, thus mutual support could be considered as an end in itself.

6. Conclusion

This chapter's results show that very few of the women we interviewed mentioned structural factors that limit their possibilities. Explicit exemplifications of 'power over' were scarce in the interviews and most participants individualized their own situation. However, our data shows that in most cases there are subtle mechanisms and tacit agreements about how women and men are expected to behave. This resulted in a greater burden of the household falling to women and male work being privileged. Nevertheless, evidencing structural 'power over' relationships through interviews is difficult.

Future studies are necessary to explore more detailed mechanisms of 'power over'. The study also calls for more research on site-specific gender and tourism in San Gil and Colombia. Despite the increase in literature that makes visible the different realities of women in tourism in the world, in Colombia, and in Latin America in general, they remain scarce. Research on the mechanisms of gender power relations and intersectional analysis may support tailoring interventions and help to cope with future crises.

References

Ahl, H. (2007). A Foucauldian framework for discourse analysis. In H. Neergard & J.P. Ulhoj (eds), *Handbook of qualitative research methods in entrepreneurship*. Cheltenham, UK and Northampton, MA, USA: Edward Elgar. 216–250.

Allen, A. (1999). *The power of feminist theory: Domination, resistance, solidarity*. Boulder, CO: Westview Press.

Alon, T., Doepke, M., Olmstead-Rumsey, J., & Tertilt, M. (2020). The impact of COVID-19 on gender equality. *NBER Working Paper Series 26947*.

Barboza Núñez, E. (2017). El enclave turístico y la imagen del 'buen salvaje' americano. Un abordaje iconográfico. *Estudios y Perspectivas en Turismo,26*(4), 760–80 [fecha de Consulta 29 de Agosto de 2021]. https://www.redalyc.org/articulo.oa?id=180752919001

Barkin, D. (2003). Alleviating poverty through ecotourism: Promises and reality in the Monarch Butterfly Reserve of Mexico. *Environment, Development and Sustainability, 5*(3–4), 371–82.

Belsky, J. (1999). Misrepresenting communities: The politics of community-based rural ecotourism in Gales Point Manatee, Belize. *Rural Sociology, 64*(4), 641–66.

Boley, B., Ayscue, E., Maruyama N., & Woosnam, K. (2016). Gender and empowerment: Assessing discrepancies using the resident empowerment through tourism scale. *Journal of Sustainable Tourism,25*(1), 113–29. https:// doi .org/ 10 .1080/ 09669582 .2016.1177065

Braun, V., & Clarke, V. (2006). Using thematic analysis in psychology. *Qualitative Research in Psychology, 3*(2), 77–101.

Byrne, J., Fattoum, S., & Diaz, M. (2019). Role models and women entrepreneurs: Entrepreneurial superwoman has her say. *Journal of Small Business Management, 57*(1), 154–84. https://doi.org/10.1111/jsbm.12426

Chablé, E., Gurri, F., Molina, D., & Schmook, B. (2007). Fuentes de ingreso y empoderamiento de mujeres campesinas en el municipio de Calakmul, Campeche. *Política y Cultura, 28*, 71–95.

Díaz-Carrión, I. (2012). Turismo de aventura y participación de las mujeres en Jalcomulco (México). *Pasos, 10*(5), 531–42. https://doi.org/10.25145/j.pasos.2012.10.068
Edwards, J., & Rothbard, N. (2000). Mechanisms linking work and family: Clarifying the relationship between work and family constructs. *Academy of Management Review, 25*(1), 178–99. https://doi.org/10.2307/259269
Emslie, C., Hunt, K., & Macintyre, S. (2004). Gender, work–home conflict, and morbidity amongst white-collar bank employees in the United Kingdom. *International Journal of Behavioral Medicine, 11*(3), 127–34. https://doi.org/10.1207/s15327558ijbm1103_1
Ferguson, L., & Moreno, D. (2015). Gender and sustainable tourism: Reflections on theory and practice. *Journal of Sustainable Tourism, 23*(3), 401–16. http://dx.doi.org/10.1080/09669582.2014.957208
Forero, L. (2017). Propuesta de generación de marca para San Gil, Santander (Colombia), como base para marca región. *Revista de Investigación de la Ciencia Turística -RICIT* (11), 54–77.
Fuente, M. (2013). Poder y feminismo: Elementos para una teoría política. *Tesis doctoral*. Universitat Autònoma de Barcelona.
Gentry, K. (2007). Belizean women and tourism work: Opportunity or impediment? *Annals of Tourism Research, 34*(2), 477–96. https://doi.org/10.1016/j.annals.2006.11.003
Goodman, L.A. (1961). Snowball sampling. *The Annals of Mathematical Statistics, 32*(1), 148–70.
Grünberg, L., & Matei, Ș. (2019). Why the paradigm of work–family conflict is no longer sustainable: Towards more empowering social imaginaries to understand women's identities. *Gender, Work & Organisation, 27*(3), 289–309. https://doi.org/10.1111/gwao.12343
Guimarães, C.R. & Silva, J. (2016). Pay gap by gender in the tourism industry of Brazil. *Tourism Management,52*, 440–50. https://doi.org/10.1016/j.tourman.2015.07.003
Guterres, A. (2020). A greater impact on women. *The Hindu*. Retrieved 3 March 2021 from https://www.thehindu.com/opinion/op-ed/a-greater-impact-on-women/article31465962.ece
Hunjan, R., & Pettit, J. (2011). *Power: A practical guide for facilitating social change*. London: Carnegie Trust/IDS.
Kabeer, N. (1999). Resources, agency, achievements: Reflections on the measurement of women's empowerment. *Development and Change, 30*(3), 435–64.
La Cometa. (12 de Julio de 2019). *Turismo en San Gil, incremento este año 2019*. La Cometa San Gil. (accessed August 13, 2022) https://lacometaradio.com/turismo-en-san-gil-incremento-este-ano-2019/
Madera, J., Hebl, M., & Martin, R. (2009). Gender and letters of recommendation for academia: Agentic and communal differences. *Journal of Applied Psychology, 94*(6), 1591–9. https://doi.org/10.1037/a0016539
Manzo, L., & Minello, A. (2020). Mothers, childcare duties, and remote working under COVID-19 lockdown in Italy: Cultivating communities of care. *Dialogues in Human Geography, 10*(2), 120–3.
Morgan, M.S, & Winkler, R. (2019). The third shift? Gender and empowerment in a women's ecotourism cooperative. *Rural Sociology,85*(1), 137–64.
Nicholson, L., & Anderson, A. (2005). News and nuances of the entrepreneurial myth and metaphor: Linguistic games in entrepreneurial; sense making and sense giving. *Entrepreneurship Theory and Practice, 29*(1), 153–164.

Nikkhah, H., Redzuan, M., & Abu-Samah, A. (2012). Development of 'power within' among the women: A road to empowerment. *Asian Social Science,8*(1) 39–46. https://doi.org/10.5539/ass.v8n1p39

Pérez-Pinzón, L., & Serrano-Ruíz, C. (2018). El turismo patrimonial como conmemoración del nacimiento de las repúblicas bolivarianas: el caso de Socorro, Colombia. *International Journal of Scientific Management and Tourism, 4*(2), 445–76.

Rottenberg, C. (2018). Women who work: The limits of the neoliberal feminist paradigm. *Gender, Work & Organisation,26*, 1–10.

Rowlands, J. (1997). *Questioning empowerment*. Oxford: Oxfam.

Sánchez, Y., Pérez, E., Pérez, M., Rodríguez, G., & Munguía, M. (2019). Organización y empoderamiento de mujeres en el Turismo Rural Comunitario: Red Ecoturística Calakmul, Campeche, México. *Sociedad y Ambiente,19*, 217–39. https://doi.org/10.31840/sya.v0i19.1943

Small, J., Harris, C., & Wilson, E. (2017). Gender on the agenda? The position of gender in tourism's high ranking journals. *Journal of Hospitality and Tourism Management, 31*, 114–17. http://dx.doi.org/10.1016/j.jhtm.2016.11.002

Swain, M.B. & Momsen, J.H. (eds). (2002), *Gender/tourism/fun(?)*. New York: Cognizant Communication.

Tucker, H., & Boonabaana, B. (2012). A critical analysis of tourism, gender and poverty reduction. *Journal of Sustainable Tourism, 20*(3), 437–55. http://dx.doi.org/10.1080/09669582.2011.622769

UNWTO. (2019). *Global report on women in tourism (2nd edn)*. Madrid: World Tourism Organization.

UNWTO-UN Women. (2011). *Global report on women in tourism 2010*. Madrid: World Tourism Organization, United Nations Entity for Gender Equality and the Empowerment of Women.

Van Eerdewijk, A., Wong, F., Vaast, C., Newton, J., Tyszler, M., & Pennington, A. (2017). *White paper: A conceptual model of women and girls' empowerment*. Amsterdam: Royal Tropical Institute (KIT).

Vizcaíno-Suárez, L., & Díaz-Carrión, I. (2018). Gender in tourism research: Perspectives from Latin America. *Tourism Review,74*(5), 1091–103.

Vizcaíno-Suárez, L.P., Serrano-Barquín, R., Cruz-Jiménez, G., & Pastor-Alfonso, M.J. (2016). Teorías y métodos en la investigación sobre turismo, género y mujeres en Iberoamérica: Un análisis bibliográfico. *Cuadernos de Turismo,38*, 485–501.

Williams, S., Seed, J., & Mwau, A. (1994). *Oxfam gender training manual*. Oxford: Oxfam.

World Tourism Organization. (2019). *Global report on women in tourism (2nd edn)*. Madrid: UNWTO. (accessed March 12, 2020): https:// doi .org/ 10 .18111/9789284420384

Yount, K.M., VanderEnde, K.E., Dodell, S., & Cheong, Y.F. (2016). Measurement of women's agency in Egypt: A national validation study. *Social Indicators Research, 128*(3), 1171–92.

Zhang, Jiekuan, & Zhang, Yan. (2021). A qualitative comparative analysis of tourism and gender equality in emerging economies. *Journal of Hospitality and Tourism Management,46*, 284–92. https://doi.org/10.1016/j.jhtm.2021.01.009

PART III

Gendered experiences in tourism

9 Gender-based violence and risk in tourism field research

Heike Schänzel and Brooke Porter

1. Introduction

Gender-based violence and risk in tourism field research is an uncomfortable and under-discussed phenomenon. Thus, there is a need to open the discussion on occurrences of gender-associated risks in fieldwork and report on the unexpected dangers and risks for the inexperienced fieldworker. For many tourism researchers, fieldwork involves immersing oneself in an unfamiliar social, cultural and political environment. Though under-acknowledged, fieldwork 'involves entering into a new gender and sexual economy in which different understandings of reciprocity and exchange may be at play' (Clark & Grant, 2015, p.1). As a result of these nuanced exchanges, the broader socio-political aspects of fieldwork very much include sexual politics (Huang, 2016), highlighting fieldwork as a gendered experience (Porter & Schänzel, 2018a; Porter et al., 2021). While this has been acknowledged and debated in other subjects, such as anthropology (e.g., Clark & Grant, 2015), ethnography (e.g., Kloß, 2017), geography (Ross, 2015), and conservation (e.g., Rinkus, et al., 2018), there has been little research conducted in the field of tourism, and more specifically, on the female fieldwork experience in tourism studies.

The aim of this chapter is to critically analyse gender-based violence, risks and sexual harassment experienced by women when conducting tourism research. The research is based on semi-structured interviews with 13 female tourism researchers from around the world and from diverse ethnic backgrounds and at various career stages. Tourism, being cross-cultural and cross-disciplinary, often requires individual/single-researcher fieldwork that exposes one's gender, often in more remote locations. While many fieldwork experiences are without issue, the traumatising experiences in the field are deliberately omitted by women not only from their doctoral theses but also, by more experienced researchers, from the academic tourism literature. Recent publications have acknowledged that gender-based violence in tourism is embedded within wider social structures of gender inequalities and discrimination (see Eger,

2021; Vizcaino-Suárez et al., 2020) and gets 'down-played' in travel guidebooks (Thornhill, 2021), thus normalising harassment. In addition to exposing the gendered violence in tourism, we must also consider how these incidents are impacting the female researcher. To do this we first unpack the literature on gendered field research, voluntary risk taking and violence in the field before outlining the qualitative methodology used to further explore the occurrence of gender-based violence and inherent risk encountered by female researchers. The findings are used to produce a series of recommendations for immediate action.

2. Gender and Fieldwork

Caroline Criado Perez (2019) in her book, *Invisible women: Exposing data bias in a world designed for men*, states that there are three themes that crop up again and again for women: the female body; women's unpaid care burden; and male violence against women. These are issues of such significance that they touch on nearly every part of women's lives, including conducting research in the field. But the same is not true for men, because men do not have female bodies or, often, the same care responsibilities. Such gender-specific issues become insignificant to the male experience. While men may have to contend with harassment in the field, this violence typically manifests itself in different ways from violence faced by women. Though all researchers are potentially vulnerable to gender-based violence (Green et al., 1993), ingrained gender inequalities and gender differences (Eger, 2021) along with considering the traditional 'fieldworker' as a lone male figure conducting objective research makes the field space a largely masculine construct (Porter & Schänzel, 2018a), which exposes female researchers to greater risks.

To date, the gendered experiences of tourism researchers have been largely ignored, and academia has proceeded as if the male body and its attendant life experience are the gender-neutral default. This also acknowledges that spaces and places are increasingly regarded as socio-cultural constructions (in this case, leisure sites and tourism landscapes) that are gendered and subject to the 'male' gaze (Pritchard & Morgan, 2000) and its inherent power differential. It is only through more reflective and exploratory exercizes that the gendered nature and risk of field research is beginning to emerge in tourism debate for female and male researchers (Porter & Schänzel, 2018a; Porter, et al., 2021). While this chapter focuses on the female experience, there is much scope to also expand on the male experience, especially when it comes to having to conform to a heteronormative masculinity as a gay or non-binary researcher (Aquino, 2021; Ooi, 2021).

It became obvious from the reflections of the female researchers (see Porter & Schänzel, 2018a) that these often-confronting experiences in the field were enshrouded in silence. From unsolicited marriage proposals, verbal harassments, incidents of sexual harassment and assault, to increased research costs due to safety concerns, gender has a significant influence on the field experience, or what Frohlick (2002) refers to as:

> The embodied entanglements that play out between our selves or subjectivities and our research sites, both before and while we are in the field. (p. 50)

Not just in tourism, but gendered violence in the field has been systematically overlooked in academic literature for multiple reasons (Cai, 2019). In addition to general concerns about blaming and stigmatising the victims, researchers have been inhibited from speaking about sexual problems encountered while conducting field research for fear that it may undermine their academic credibility and professional standing (Huang, 2016; Moreno, 1995). As Sundberg (2003, p. 188) notes, the peculiar silence implies academia 'fails to provide adequate guidance for students preparing for research, leading many to individualize and therefore conceal the challenges they encounter'. This lack of institutional support discourages victims from reporting gendered violence encountered when conducting field research. As Huan (2016, p. 3) points out when reflecting on her experience of being raped during fieldwork, the researcher's body is institutionally recognized as 'merely a liability', with institutional concern for researcher safety largely revolving 'around the university not wanting to be held responsible if something grave were to happen'.

To date, safety guidelines of ethics committees largely focus on the potential physical risks to research participants, paying less attention to the pervasive structural and gendered violence female researchers must negotiate. These oversights may include risks associated with unaccompanied research and increased accommodation costs due to safety considerations. Despite gendered violence during fieldwork being quite common (Gibbons, 2014; Porter, & Schänzel, 2018b), it has yet to lead to the institutionalization of pre-fieldwork training, budget considerations or post-trauma mental support. In 2019, Cai's experiences based in geography (p. 2) led her to call for a more open dialogue on gendered threats and risks faced by field researchers and to better prepare research students 'to anticipate and negotiate sexual politics in hetero-patriarchal settings'. Similar sentiments on the risks for sexual harassment/assaults in the field and the need for measures to ensure personal safety and emotional wellbeing were found amongst the contributions from tourism scholars to Porter and Schänzel's (2018a) book compilation, thus indicating that this is a broad phenomenon affecting social research.

Unfortunately, an open dialogue is not a straightforward solution as managing the professional distance between the researcher and the research subject is often tricky (Cai, 2019). Previous research has reported researchers struggling to navigate (or end) field-relationships with powerful participants perpetrating gendered violence, considering that perpetrators are often key informants or gatekeepers (Clark & Grant, 2015; Műgge, 2013). As the researcher is expected to cultivate a comfortable and encouraging atmosphere to facilitate data collection (Kaspar & Landolt, 2016), making efforts to engage participants may be misinterpreted as sexual bargaining. The common view of 'researchers as cultural penetrators exercising power over their subjects' is framed in the masculine. Instead, female researchers are often left vulnerable due to their 'subordinate position as a woman in sexist-patriarchal settings' (Cai, 2019, p. 3). This subordination may translate to increased responsibilities in the field where women must balance fieldwork progress while maintaining a hyper focus on their personal safety, daily.

Despite the lack of formal institutional preparation of female researchers for fieldwork, women are not necessarily unprepared for encountering gendered violence in the field. Discreet converzations occur amongst women (both researchers and gatekeepers) on who to avoid in the field (Hamilton & Fielding, 2018), how wearing wedding rings and avoiding alcohol consumption or going out at night are wise choices (Usher, 2018), or what one should wear to avoid unwanted advances (Martinez & Peters, 2018; Swanson, 2018; Usher, 2018). Similarly, concerns with attire extend beyond female researchers to female travellers. For example, participants in Yang et al.'s (2018) study on Asian female solo travellers found that women were attempting to dress 'butch', or gender-neutral, to avoid sexual harassment. With most, if not all of these absent from the male researcher's radar, it becomes obvious that these 'preventative strategies' are essentially victim-blaming and body-disciplining through which female researchers 'internalise the male gaze and patriarchal logic' (Cai, 2019, p. 4). Such defensive strategies are not without cost; they are often time, energy and emotion consuming (Cai, 2019) and the defence may further come at a financial cost (Porter & Schänzel, 2018b).

The lack of research into the gendered violence and risk encountered by women when conducting field research in tourism led us to this exploratory study. It is apparent that sexual violence and risk during fieldwork is a reality for women and is deserving more research and discussion, thus forming the aim of this chapter. Through interviews with 13 women we asked questions such as: How does one's gender influence fieldwork? Where are 'violence', 'danger' and 'risk' located? How did you negotiate these risks? And, how can we better prepare female fieldworkers to cope with and negotiate these realities?

3. Methodology

To gain a deeper understanding of women's gendered fieldwork experiences, including gender-based violence, such as harassment or any inherent risks encountered, participants were invited to share their research stories. Utilising the interpretivist paradigm and exploratory research approach, smaller samples can be used to generate theories from the results, with both the researcher and the participants involved within the study (Carson, 2001). Epistemologically, this study was conducted through a constructivist frame where the individual seeks to construct their meanings through experiences of interactions with others and society (Neuman, 2014).

Semi-structured interviews with 13 female tourism researchers were conducted in-person and virtually between 2019 and 2020. These types of interviews encourage participants to express rich, descriptive narratives of the enquiries of the study (Jordan & Gibson, 2004). In other words, they aim to establish a rapport with participants, offering them the opportunity to provide subjective and multiple realities. The participants were recruited through a global snowball sampling with the intent to interview researchers from diverse ethnic backgrounds and at various career stages, with many of the researchers also working and living in a second culture. This involved contacting colleagues known to us as well as being referred to scholars who conducted field research that might have exposed them to gendered risks. We note that the LGBTQ community was represented in our sample and that all participants identified as cisgender. As a result of an academically diverse sample, some participants reflected on their doctoral research while others had years of research experiences themselves and as supervisors to reflect upon. To ensure anonymity of the participants no further demographic details, affiliations or career stages are provided to prevent identification as most of the women were only willing to disclose their experiences with assurance of complete confidentiality. The research deliberately invited reflections on personal safety, sexual harassment, sexual assault and risk mitigations when conducting research in the field.

All interviews were recorded and transcribed verbatim. Transcripts were subjected to thematic analysis by the first author, an approach compatible with interpretivist research, following the conventions of Braun and Clarke (2006). This involved familiarization with the data, coding, identification, organization and development of themes from the data manually until key themes emerged. The resultant themes were then scrutinized by the co-author for consistency. The study had a broader aim of exploring gendered fieldwork experiences, including care and wellbeing in the field, but the focus of this chapter is on gender-based violence and risk in tourism field research.

The authors are both women of European descent who have reflected on their own positionality regarding field research as part of their book compilation (Porter, 2018; Schänzel, 2018). Schänzel, as someone who entered academia in mid-life and with children, has not experienced violence in the field but has had to modify research practices to keep herself safe. Porter entered academia in her early 30s and had children shortly thereafter. She experienced sexual harassment (even while pregnant), though through accompanied research with children, such encounters have been drastically reduced. As described by Schänzel, accompanied research requires significant modifications to fieldwork. Even in her late 30s she has been asked, on multiple occasions, if she was a student by male colleagues and remains the frequent recipient of mansplaining episodes.

This is an exploratory study that sought out participants who might have encountered risks or violence in the field and as such is not representative of female academics as a single group. Most of the participants were Western women conducting research in Western countries as well as developing countries along with three participants of Asian descent. Despite our aim to recruit participants from diverse ethnic backgrounds, the "whiteness" of our sample is likely a reflection of our own white ethnicities and what Thomas (2019) describes as structurally induced homophily. There is scope to expand this study to include a more ethnically diverse pool of participants to get a better understanding of the scale and proportion of risks and violence encountered.

4. Findings and Discussion

The exploration of gendered violence in fieldwork amongst female researchers led to the following broad themes: attire and conduct; sexual harassment; race and gender; physical and emotional field preparations; and strategies for risk minimization and gender equality. Using excerpts from the interviews to support our interpretations of the data, each theme is discussed individually.

4.1 Attire and Conduct

Depending on the field situation, attire and conduct can be challenging. For example, in a remote field situation or in a situation with formidable weather our clothing options may be limited for researchers. While we study destination cultures and begin preparations before embarking on the research trip, the lack of access to our regular infrastructures (and wardrobes) can pose a challenge. For our female participants, appropriateness of attire and proper conduct were repetitive concerns. Many reported putting forth significant efforts to 'blend in' and play by the 'rules'. This effort in going unnoticed often took the form of conservative dress and restrained conduct in fieldwork. For example, one participant conducting research on a Pacific island stated:

> I was also very conscious of the way that I dressed and even though it was a tropical island I always made sure no skimpy sundresses, no short shorts ... I had to swim in my clothing. (Participant 1)

For this same participant, blending in included the consumption of unwanted (or possibly spoiled) food and drink from the local community because she was reliant on them for her research:

> The food sat out in the sun all day and it was fish and seafood and things like that, but I had to eat it ... I was really sick [afterwards] but I had to do it because otherwise I risked being excluded from the community. (Participant 1)

Another participant who conducted her research in North Africa tried to blend in through various means with notably limited success:

> A lot of my research now happens in Muslim contexts, so I'm always very careful about what I wear just to try and be respectful. ... I'm blonde, so I stand out like a sore thumb in most of the places that I research, so people know that I'm not from there, it's obvious that I'm not from there. When I was in [North African country] I actually dyed my hair brown ... It didn't really work. I'm too pasty. I don't look like I'm a local. (Participant 5)

She also remarked about the internal conflict of feeling forced to wear more gender-neutral clothing:

> I do think about the kinds of clothes that I'm wearing. I wouldn't wear a miniskirt; I wouldn't show too much cleavage but again I don't know if I agree with that from a feminist perspective, but I suppose it's something that I do to try to not attract that kind of unwanted attention. (Participant 5)

A participant, who has conducted several research studies in Asia, spoke about the specificity of her field attire:

> I have a wardrobe full of clothes to wear doing fieldwork that I don't wear generally but they're my fieldwork clothes because I know they're totally acceptable under all circumstances. (Participant 7)

Further, this participant remarked about the modifications to her dietary choices while in the field:

> I drink coffee without sugar in it. I didn't know only witches drink with no sugar. ... If you're drinking six or seven cups of coffee a day and all of them are loaded up with four teaspoons of sugar, it's like you're taking a lot of sugar on board, which I don't want. But I realised that actually you get a very different acceptance, like the closeness, the initial making of the relationship is very different when you've refused sugar. It's like – oh – and you can sense it whereas if you accept it with the sugar then you're just normal. (Participant 7)

These stories from participants detail some of the resignations female researchers make to ensure success in the field. Opting to accept getting food poisoning rather than offending the food customs of the local community or accepting sugary drinks to avoid the label of a witch are extreme examples of trying to 'blend in' and playing by the 'rules'. They also signify potential health risks and dangers for the participants that need to be acknowledged much more when preparing women for field research. Similarly, the steps taken by many of the women regarding their attire confirm the body-disciplining taking place when negotiating the male gaze in these foreign countries (Cai, 2019). The current response to the objectification of the female body is conservative dress and restrained conduct in fieldwork (see also Porter & Schänzel, 2018b). The participants' responses exemplify the thought and time that goes into defensive field strategies for female researchers confirming the findings in Cai (2019) which reported the planned avoidance of sexual harassment in the field as all-consuming. The notable efforts of the participants to blend in and follow local customs did not stop the occurrences of unwanted sexual advances. Incidences of sexual harassment are discussed as the next emergent theme.

4.2 Sexual Harassment

Decades ago, Warren (1988) opened the discussion of the "sexual politics" in the field. The lack of attention given to acknowledging related issues in fieldwork is surprising given that sexual harassment in higher education has been referred to as an epidemic (Bondestam & Lundqvist, 2020). Numerous incidents of sexual harassment and sexual assault were recounted by the participants from unwanted attention, catcalling, groping of their genitals, to forced kissing, marriage proposals and attempted kidnapping. Often the perpetrators were known to the women, further complicating the situations. Beyond issues of general sexual harassment, our data also revealed complexities associated with non-heteronormative sexual identities. Despite the inappropriateness of any unwanted sexual advances, a lesbian participant recounted the difficulties with an unwanted advance from a male acquaintance:

> He started trying to guilt me into feeling bad for him and I'm like – hang on – and then it was complicated as I'm actually married to a woman; and at the time, I was dating my girlfriend ... I wasn't out in that culture. So, that added another layer of complexity of not being able to identify my own sexuality in that space because that would've been an easy out for me, but I was more worried about upholding cultural values I thought [lesser-developed region] might have against gays. (Participant 6)

Recent explorations on normative masculinities have revealed similar issues of male researchers hiding non-heteronormative sexual identities (see Aquino, 2021; Ooi, 2021); however, this phenomenon is largely unreported for women.

Unsurprisingly, there were many other examples of sexual harassment that the participants reported compartmentalising as part of their field experience; most had not recounted these experiences prior to our interviews. For example, multiple incidents related to accommodations are surprisingly similar despite happening in completely different parts of the world (one in the South Pacific, two in different Asian countries and one in North Africa):

> I had one guy in the community who took a shine to me and he showed up where I was staying one night really quite drunk and being quite demanding around wanting to marry me ... I actually felt quite threatened by it because I was on my own. He knew where I lived, and I didn't really know him. (Participant 1)

Another participant who had checked herself into a resort instead of backpacker accommodation out of safety precautions was met with harassment by the porter:

> On the way he sorts of hit on me and asked me out and things like that. I felt totally unsafe because my room was so far away ... he knows exactly where my room is, and he knows that I am by myself. (Participant 2)

Similarly, another participant in speaking about her doctoral research at a heritage site referred to budgetary issues and accommodation:

> I was actually living onsite because I couldn't afford accommodation and transport to get there. So, when all the visitors went home, I would go into one of the old cottages and I would live upstairs and it was really, really spooky. (Participant 1)

Other participants reported issues of sexual assault at or in their accommodations:

> One (local) approached me, hit on me and the guy barged into my room, yanked my face over and started kissing me out of nowhere. (Participant 6)
> (Local) men would follow me around or follow me up the stairs to the apartment where I was staying and tried to kiss me.... This guy just came out of nowhere, pinned me against the wall and tried to stick his tongue in my mouth. (Participant 5)

Another participant was out at a bar one night when the security guy advized her to not walk home but take a taxi instead:

> So, I took a taxi, and the taxi driver took me back to his house. I kind of got my phone out and pretended to call people but I didn't know anyone. There wasn't really anyone that I could call and eventually the guy kind of freaked out and drove me home. (Participant 5)

These participant experiences are demonstrative of the issues of sexual harassment women encounter in the field. They also demonstrate the increased financial costs for female researchers, such as choosing to stay at a more expensive and more secure accommodation or the need to call a taxi rather than walk alone. Unfortunately, while such choices may mitigate the risk of being sexually harassed, they do not eliminate it. These examples highlight that there is no respite for a woman in the field and that safety concerns are omnipresent leading to a kind of resignation as expressed by a participant, 'It really shaped my behaviour and I kind of stopped doing a lot of things that I would've done otherwise.' (Participant 5)

The participants' responses confirm that sexual violence and risks are real for women and need to be factored in to their research design and field preparation. More attention is needed for the vulnerable positions female researchers are entering when embarking on field research (Cai, 2019; Porter & Schänzel, 2018b) and what it "costs" to balance fieldwork progress and reduce the risk of sexual harassment. In the next section, we explore the intersection of race and gender as it relates to gendered violence in the field.

4.3 Race and Gender

The results of the objectification of women in the media have been gaining attention in general media for some time now (e.g., #Metoo movement). Similarly, the discussion on gender continues to grow and evolve in many academic disciplines. While this attention is needed and overdue, some of our participants note that this momentum glosses over the intersection of race and gender as it relates to fieldwork. For example, one participant reflects on skin colour:

> It is my race, my skin colour does make a difference. I feel like especially coming from South East Asia, we do not have a lot of Western white women backpacking in our country ... they might look at them but it's more in admiration. It's like a star from the sky you can never reach but you can only see but whereas being an Asian in Asia ... I feel more vulnerable. They always say [ ] it means pretty lady, pretty lady. I always get street harassment. (Participant 2)

While many researchers consider a second (or third) language of benefit in the field, the same participant described the weight of understanding of multiple languages, even when pretending not to understand:

> They call me [ ] which means Chinese prostitute. So, they talk about me in a sexualised way. And because I understand and therefore, I feel really vulnerable because I look around at the beach with no-one else, just me and the two of them. (Participant 2)

Similar to the reported issues of understanding the language, participants reported difficulties with research in their native cultures. For example, a participant describes her failure to recruit participants as a result of mistaken identity:

> If I approached a local or Asian, people would just like wave to me [dismissively], like trying to avoid me because we have so many ... there are so many scams in Asia by Asians ... Why I was a failure was because I was seen as a scam. (Participant 2)

Another issue of mistaken identity was described by another Asian participant conducting research in a remote part of Australia:

> As I was about to leave, they [two Asian men] started talking, saying – hey, look, I didn't know this type of thing is actually legal in Australia. What's the price we have to pay? ... and also, the weird grinning on their face at that moment, the way they put it, it's in Mandarin ... immediately I thought – Oh my god, they thought I was soliciting [prostitution]. (Participant 3)

This participant fled instinctively as it was getting dark. Upon arrival at her accommodation, she described the impact of the incident: 'I was just literally frightened with my hands shaking. There's no other research assistant, just myself in the field so, that was one of the most extreme cases.'

The impact of race on research did not go unnoticed by other participants. For example, an experienced Western researcher commented about the interplay of race and gender in the field:

> I think that nationality trumps gender when working in Asia. I think that the influence that I had, the fact that people wanted to listen to me, the fact that people would answer my questions, the fact that I had access to whoever I wanted to speak to was trumped by my white skin over my gender. (Participant 7)

It is obvious that, apart from already reported general issues of sexual harassment experienced by female researchers, race and ethnicity can produce added physical and verbal risks for females conducting fieldwork. In addition, it can complicate fieldwork making some locations unsuitable or requiring researchers to adapt to online interviews (Participant 2). Our findings highlight the differences experienced by some female researchers as a result of race. Our data shows that the experience of being mistakenly identified as prostitutes or scammers is a reality for female Asian researchers. This differs vastly from the field experiences of Western women and is deserving of more attention. Ultimately, this led Participant 2 not being able to conduct her research as an Asian woman in Asia in the field but having to resort to Skype interviews instead. Our findings suggest the need for further exploration of the impacts of race and ethnicity as they relate to gendered violence and risk in the field.

4.4 Physical and Emotional Field Preparations

All of the previously described themes are largely intertwined. A recurrent concern for all the women interviewed was self-defence and maintaining physical and emotional safety in the field. The participants' responses demonstrated the thought, energy (both physical and emotional) and preparation required for a successful and safe field experience. Participants' responses indicated that it was commonplace to carry something for protection, such as a folded knife or pepper spray. Several participants mentioned that they take safety precautions, such as not going out in the evening or dining out alone; some participants had trained in martial arts and self-defence partly to protect themselves should the need arise. Exemplary comments of various methods related to physical and emotional field preparations included:

> I've always got a degree of reserve, a sort of professional veneer which in some ways gives me a safety bubble. (Participant 1)
> I'm a bit cautious … I never let my guard down. (Participant 2)
> I've got some pretty strong [local] language that I can throw at [men] if they overstep a line. (Participant 7)

Having to deal with unexpected politically, socially, and sexually risky situations by yourself in remote research places is not something a researcher gets prepared for or forms part of grant applications (Chiswell & Wheeler, 2016). Instances of unaccompanied research and/or the absence of preparation can lead to severe emotional implications for female researchers.

In addition to the risk of gendered violence, the isolation, and concerns about mental wellbeing, there are other risk factors that come to the fore when conducting research in remote places, such as on a Pacific island. A participant describes an incident that occurred during her fieldwork:

> The school burnt down, and they believed it was arson and there were only two Pakeha [white people] on the island, myself and a teacher at the school, so they figured no-one on the island would've burnt the school down because it's too important, so it had to be one of us. A police officer came to talk to me very, very early one morning and this little kid from the village ran in and said: Oh, you're in trouble! And I thought: Holy crap! Because back in those days there were only two telephones on the island, the flights only came a couple of times a week and if anything happened it would've been quite some time before anyone realized something had gone wrong because it's in the days before the internet and cell phones ... Oh my god, I'm going to end up in jail, I'm not going to have a job and I'm going to have to pay back this money [sizeable grant]. (Participant 1)

The inherent loneliness and feelings of isolation commonly experienced during fieldwork in foreign environments may exacerbate risks and dangers for female researchers. The risks of unaccompanied research and the lack of a safety net or support system are largely unacknowledged by the academy. As described by an experienced participant:

> When you are a researcher, you're very much kind of a lone researcher, especially for your PhD. It's not like you're doing it in a team … I don't think the Ethics Committee necessarily think about gender as a safety issue when you're doing say a survey. A survey often seems risk-averse, right, but actually you're a young female, potentially a young 20-year-old, on your own, standing in an environment with potentially no-one around you, with a clipboard and you have to approach people and you don't know who you are approaching … I think there's an absolute lack of support for female researchers. I don't think the academy fully appreciates the

> qualitative differences, shall we say, of being a female researcher and having to do fieldwork. You are vulnerable. At the end of the day, nobody really cares if you do get sexually assaulted. Who's going to care? (Participant 10)

According to participants' responses, strong local language, training in self-defence, self-defence gadgets and evasive actions represent current risk-minimization strategies being used in the field and might aid in keeping women safe during fieldwork. However, female researchers must carefully navigate the local and sexual politics of the field site while recruiting participants in the local community. Women are often described as having, and are possibly more conditioned to have, a nice and approachable demeanour. Previous researchers have been described as being 'easy on the eyes' (see Chiswell & Wheeler, 2016). The responsibility of being 'nice' enough to recruit participants and, thus, conduct successful research while being 'tough' enough to fend off harassment falls upon the female researcher. This concept was bluntly summarized by a participant: 'Don't get raped because you're too polite to get out of the way.' (Participant 1)

4.5 Strategies for Risk Minimization and Gender Equality

Strategies and training for how to keep safe in the field are seriously lacking in academia and more attention is needed to address the gendered risks specific to females in field experiences. The need for this was addressed among participants:

> I do think that you need to know or sort of have an idea of what you are putting yourself into because my experience is that I was being reckless and naïve. (Participant 2)

At present female researchers are largely limited to what risk-related information they can glean from one another (e.g., Hamilton & Fielding, 2018). Our participants suggested some strategies derived from their learnt experiences when it came to risk minimization, such as having awareness of cultural norms:

> I think it's really important to have a good sense of the culture that you're going into. It's very important to work within the cultural norms whether you agree with them or not. (Participant 1)

There were also suggestions for pre-fieldtrip workshops, support for planning exercizes, and accompanied research:

> Always have a couple of people that you know at the site rather than go in there by yourself. Come with a research assistant if the budget allows. (Participant 3)
> Don't go to the field cold, work with local people. (Participant 7)
> To have a plan B, to have a support network around you is really important. (Participant 10)

Then there was the suggestion for a female gender check list or plan which deals with how to create a sense of safety and mental wellbeing in the field:

> Plan ahead and put structures in place to create that sense of safety. That can be cultural safety, personal safety or physical safety. (Participant 1)
> How do you deal with being sexually harassed or abused, or having people constantly throwing comments at you of a sexual nature? … I suppose it's a check on your mental health as well as your physical health to constantly check that say – are your thoughts being positive to yourself? That's his attitude, not yours, you're ok, you are who you are, just get on with it, whatever it might be. So, there's that kind of emotional resilience. (Participant 10)

Despite the frequency of females conducting field research, our data suggests the need for immediate reform in how we prepare female researchers for a fieldwork experience and how we continue to support female researchers in the field. Some of the participants' experiences suggest that one option is beginning our researcher careers with physically safer methods, such as through virtual interviewing or passive data collection on social media sites. Other options suggested in this data set and elsewhere include accommodating and supporting accompanied research (Chiswell & Wheeler, 2016; Porter & Schänzel, 2018b). Also notable were the feelings of unpreparedness among early career researchers; thus, emphasising the need to include supervisors in training. Collectively, participant responses suggest the need for fieldwork-specific resilience training. This idea is often referred to as a 'resilience toolbox', or a method that includes responses and/or steps for comprehending and processing unpleasant events, reframing focus, and adapting to a dynamic situation.

5. Conclusion

Our research documented field work experiences from 13 female researchers. In doing so it provided shared female perspectives about negotiating risk and dangers when in the field. Through these perspectives, we explored some of the factors impacting the female researcher in the field. The results from this exploratory study affirm that women field researchers engage in risk-taking. While on the surface, this risk-taking may be considered 'voluntary', for some female researchers, the pressures of conforming to the expectations of academia make these engagements less than voluntary. The findings from this study add to the growing body of literature on the obvious impact of gender on the field experience and assert the importance for gender-based positionality in research.

Our findings reaffirmed the political nature of fieldwork and the need to challenge sexual politics and patriarchal domination (Cai, 2019; Warren, 1988). Although the tourism agenda has long considered gender equality an area in need of attention (UNWTO, 2011), to achieve this, the academy must be able to safely support researchers, and more specifically women, involved in tourism research. There remains an urgent need to normalize gender positionality in research (Chiswell & Wheeler, 2016; Porter & Schänzel, 2018), to continue the discussion of fieldworker safety and wellbeing and to actively support safer ways of researching. As the field of tourism research evolves and global connectivity advances (perhaps, more rapidly as a result of the COVID-19 pandemic), our adaptability as researchers must also transform. The findings from this study have added to the albeit small but existing body of knowledge on female researcher safety in the field. Through this study and the continuation of similar explorations we can expand the limited knowledge base on how to reduce gender-based risk in the field.

We should be at a point where we are able to prioritize personal safety. Many of the solutions are immediately feasible and straightforward. The forthcoming discussions will be uncomfortable; however, as noted by one of our participants, 'If everyone was more open about their vulnerabilities and we brought more vulnerability into the workplace, it might actually be a nicer place.'

Our recommendations for immediate action are:

- Need for a 'Resilience toolbox';
- Need to normalize safer ways of doing research (e.g., Zoom, video interviewing, social media);
- Need to train both researchers and supervisors in planning future fieldwork;
- Need for more collaborative research opportunities;
- Need for increased research funding;
- Need for ongoing mental health support;
- Acknowledgement of the impacts of gender-based positionality;

- Need for a continuing discussion to further gender equality in the tourism agenda.

Gender-based violence and risk in tourism field research are important and serious issues that deserve not only immediate action, but also further research into their scale and the emotional effects they can have on female researchers. Acknowledging violence in the field, therefore, emerges as a crucial political, social and ethical task in academia that raises questions about access to knowledge and knowledge production in tourism.

References

Aquino, R.S. (2021). Performing and negotiating Filipino masculinities in the field. In Porter, B.A., Schänzel, H.A., & Cheer, J.M. (2021). *Masculinities in the field: Tourism and transdisciplinary research* (pp. 71–84). Bristol, UK: Channel View.

Bondestam, F., & Lundqvist, M. (2020). Sexual harassment in higher education: A systematic review. *European Journal of Higher Education, 10*(4), 397–419.

Braun, V., & Clarke, V. (2006). Using thematic analysis in psychology. *Qualitative Research in Psychology, 3*(2), 77–101.

Cai, Y. (2019). Confronting sexual harassment in the field. *Made in China Journal*, October, 25.

Carson, D. (2001). *Qualitative marketing research*. Thousand Oaks, CA: Sage.

Chiswell, H.M., & Wheeler, R. (2016). 'As long as you're easy on the eye': Reflecting on issues of positionality and researcher safety during farmer interviews. *Area, 48*(2), 229–35.

Clark, I., & Grant, A. (2015). Sexuality and danger in the field: Starting an uncomfortable conversation. *Journal of the Anthropological Society of Oxford, 7*(1), 1–14.

Criado Perez, C. (2019). *Invisible women: Exposing data bias in a world designed for men*. London: Chatto & Windus.

Eger, C. (2021). Gender matters: Rethinking violence in tourism. *Annals of Tourism Research, 88*, 103143.

Frohlick. S.E. (2002). 'You brought your baby to base camp?' Families and field sites. *The Great Lakes Geographer, 9*, 49–58.

Gibbons, A. (2014). Sexual harassment is common in scientific fieldwork (16 July). Science. https://www.sciencemag.org/news/2014/07/sexual-harassment-common-scientific-fieldwork (accessed 20 November 2021).

Green, G., Barbour, R.S., Barnard, M., & Kitzinger, J. (1993). 'Who wears the trousers?' Sexual harassment in research settings. *Women's Studies International Forum, 16*(6), 627–37.

Hamilton, J., & Fielding, R. (2018). Safety first: The biases of gender and precaution in fieldwork. In Porter, B.A. & Schänzel, H.A. (eds), *Femininities in the field: Tourism and transdisciplinary research* (pp. 10–22). Bristol, UK: Channel View.

Huang, M. (2016). Vulnerable observers: Notes on fieldwork and rape. *The Chronicle of Higher Education*, 12 October. https://www.chronicle.com/article/Vulnerable-Observers-Notes-on/238042accessed 20 November 2021.

Jordan, F., & Gibson, H. (2004). Let your data do the talking: Researching the solo travel experiences of British and American women. In Phillimore, J. & Goodson, L. (eds), *Qualitative research in tourism: Ontologies, epistemologies and methodologies* (pp. 215–35). Milton Park: Routledge.

Kaspar,, H. & Landolt, S. (2016). Flirting in the field: Shifting positionalities and power relations in innocuous sexualisations of research encounters. *Gender, Place & Culture, 23*(1), 107–19.

Kloß, S.T. (2017). Sexual(ized) harassment and ethnographic fieldwork: A silenced aspect of social research. *Ethnography, 18*(3), 396–414.

Martinez, E., & Peters, C. (2018). Gender bias and marine mammal tourism research. In Porter, B.A. & Schänzel, H.A. (eds), *Femininities in the field: Tourism and transdisciplinary research* (pp. 109–25). Bristol, UK: Channel View.

Moreno, E. (1995). Rape in the field: Reflections from a survivor. In Kulick, D. & Willson, M. (eds), *Taboo: Sex, identity, and erotic subjectivity in anthropological fieldwork* (pp. 219–50). Milton Park: Routledge.

Mügge, L.M. (2013). Sexually harassed by gatekeepers: Reflections on fieldwork in Surinam and Turkey. *International Journal of Social Research Methodology, 16*(6), 541–6.

Neuman, W.L. (2014). *Social research methods: Qualitative and quantitative approaches.* New York: Pearson.

Ooi, C.-S. (2021). How masculinity creeps in: Awkward field encounters of a male researcher. In Porter, B.A., Schänzel, H.A., & Cheer, J.M. (eds), *Masculinities in the field: Tourism and transdisciplinary research* (pp. 85–98). Bristol, UK: Channel View.

Porter, B.A. (2018). Early motherhood and research: From bump to baby in the field. In Porter, B.A. & Schänzel, H.A. (eds), *Femininities in the field: Tourism and transdisciplinary research* (pp. 68–83). Bristol, UK: Channel View.

Porter, B.A., & Schänzel, H.A. (2018a). Conclusion – gender: A variable and a practice. In Porter, B.A. & Schänzel, H.A. (eds), *Femininities in the field: Tourism and transdisciplinary research* (pp. 200–8). Bristol, UK: Channel View.

Porter, B.A., & Schänzel, H.A. (eds). (2018b). *Femininities in the field: Tourism and transdisciplinary research.* Bristol, UK: Channel View.

Porter, B.A., Schänzel, H.A., & Cheer, J.M. (eds). (2021). *Masculinities in the field: Tourism and transdisciplinary research.* Bristol, UK: Channel View.

Pritchard, A., & Morgan, N.J. (2000). Constructing tourism landscapes – gender, sexuality and space. *Tourism Geographies, 2*(2), 115–39.

Rinkus, M., Kelly, J.R., Wright, W., Medina, L., & Dobson, T. (2018). Gendered considerations for safety in conservation fieldwork. *Society & Natural Resources, 31*(12), 1419–26.

Ross, K. (2015). 'No sir, she was not a fool in the field': Gendered risks and sexual violence in immersed cross- cultural fieldwork. *The Professional Geographer, 67*(2), 180–6.

Schänzel, H. (2018). Motherhood within family tourism research: Case studies of New Zealand and Samoa. In Porter, B.A. & Schänzel, H.A. (eds), *Femininities in the field: Tourism and transdisciplinary research* (pp. 185–99). Bristol, UK: Channel View.

Swanson, S.S. (2018). The married life (as a marine tourism researcher). In Porter, B.A. & Schänzel, H.A. (eds), *Femininities in the field: Tourism and transdisciplinary research* (pp. 37–52). Bristol, UK: Channel View.

Sundberg, J. (2003). Masculinist epistemologies and the politics of fieldwork in Latin Americanist geography. *The Professional Geographer,55*(2), 180–90.

Thomas, R.J. (2019). Sources of friendship and structurally induced homophily across the life course. *Sociological Perspectives, 62*(6), 822–43.

Thornhill, T. (2021). Lonely Planet travel guides accused of 'downplaying' the harassment that women travellers suffer from men in countries such as Argentina, Egypt and Thailand. *Daily Mail Australia*, 20 March. https://www.dailymail.co.uk/travel/travel_news/article-9380905/Lonely-Planet-travel-guides-accused-downplaying-harassment-women-travellers-suffer-men.html?fbclid=IwAR3grp7hH3fjJkPNVWcctd00cagXdrQQSJO5hEI2SBbph1ShiyScjmXQWGQ (accessed 20 November 2021).

UNWTO. (2011). Tourism: A vehicle for gender equality and women's empowerment – UN reports. https://www.unwto.org/archive/europe/news/2011-03-11/tourism-vehicle-gender-equality-and-women-s-empowerment-un-reports# (accessed 20 November 2021).

Usher, L.A. (2018). 'Dale chica!': A surfer chick's reflections on field research in Central America. In Porter, B.A. & Schänzel, H.A. (eds), *Femininities in the field: Tourism and transdisciplinary research* (pp. 53–67). Bristol, UK: Channel View.

Vizcaino-Suárez, P., Jeffrey, H., & Eger, C. (2020). *Tourism and gender-based violence: Challenging inequalities*. CABI.

Warren, C.A. (1988). *Gender issues in field research* (Vol. 9). London: Sage.

Yang, E.C.L., Khoo-Lattimore, C., & Arcodia, C. (2018). Constructing space and self through risk taking: A case of Asian solo female travelers. *Journal of Travel Research, 57*(2), 260–72.

10 The importance of friendship: the lived experience of female delegates at association conferences

Elspeth Frew and Judith Mair

Attending a conference is a bonding experience ... we're ... not travelling to be together, but we are using that opportunity to be together.

1. Introduction

Tourism is a vitally important sector for women's employment and entrepreneurship opportunities (Pritchard, 2018). A range of researchers have considered gender and tourism from several perspectives, such as female employment which can lead to empowerment particularly in developing countries (Foley et al., 2018) but can also lead to inequality (Maliva et al., 2018), and patriarchal and dominant gender stereotypes (Yudina et al, 2018). Similarly, recent research in the conference and events sector has considered gender and the events sector in regard to (in)equality in the meetings sector, and career options and mentoring (Werner, 2021). Conferences are big business, yet research investigating the gendered nature of conference attendance is relatively scarce. As early as 2005, Jago and Deery highlighted the importance of doing more, in practice, to address the needs of female convention delegates. However, despite the call for gender-aware frameworks that acknowledge the significance of gender and power in tourism (Harris & Ateljevic, 2003), a similar approach in conference research has not been forthcoming. As Ramirez et al. (2013) point out, although attendees' gender (sex) is a fundamental element of market segmentation, and that conferences are experienced differently by women than by men, little exploration of how this plays out in terms of the attendance experience has been published in academic journals.

Conferences are considered to be an important part of the (predominantly) male academic career model, where networking, presenting one's work and gaining an academic reputation are seen as the prerequisites to success and promotion (White, 2014). Mair and Frew (2018) found evidence of issues particular to female delegates, including the importance of having strong female role models, the significance of fun and friendship, the prominent role of emotions, challenges associated with carer responsibilities, safety concerns, harassment and the need for women to have an 'academic persona'. This latter point relates to concerns that women have about their professional image and being judged on how they look.

As early as 1933, Bassett highlighted the way that conferences allowed people to meet face-to-face, get to know each other and exchange ideas, and noted that 'firm bonds of fellowship' can be established and preserved when personal contacts are made (Bassett, 1933, p. 562). In 1954, Cook noted that meeting people at conferences could 'ripen into lasting friendships' (Cook, 1954, p.4). Foley et al. (2014, p.53) consider that 'friendships forged through business events have been a cornerstone of scientific meetings for many years', suggesting that conferences and friendship go hand-in-hand. Mair and Thompson (2009) also highlight the role of friendship, noting that both meeting old friends and making new friends are important in the conference attendance decision. Similarly, Fjelstul et al. (2009) examined differences in attendance motivations between generational cohorts and found that meeting and making new friends emerged as important for all the cohorts in their study. Hahm et al. (2016) note that networking at a conference, both at formal social events and during less structured leisure time, can lead to building, or enhancing a sense of community, and as such is an important component of satisfaction with a conference. Ramirez et al. (2013) highlighted that the importance of networking and socialising was particularly significant for female delegates, reflecting the study by Venkatesh et al. (2000) which suggested that this may be a function of women's tendency to be more relationship-oriented than men.

Friendships have particular significance in our busy and stressed lives because they are regarded as potential contributors to improved health and wellbeing, mostly because friendships are linked with the notion of social support, which has been recognized as being associated with health benefits of all kinds (Glover & Parry, 2008). Several authors have examined the importance of making business contacts and maintaining and expanding one's networks during conferences (Mair et al., 2018; Severt et al., 2007). However, the importance of the friendships that can develop as a result of these continually reaffirmed contacts has not been considered in the same depth. Despite the long-recognized fact that friendships can be formed at conferences, very little research attention has been directed towards understanding how academic conferences can help to establish and maintain these friendships. This chapter aims to contribute to developing a more nuanced approach to understanding academic conferences with the research objective being to examine the role of such conferences in maintaining supportive friendships among female academics.

2. Literature Review on Friendship

Friendships are a core aspect of our lives, yet as Fehr (1996, p. 5) points out, 'everyone knows what friendship is... until asked to define it'. Friendship cannot be easily defined or analysed – it almost defies definition. However, there are certain attributes of friendship that can be recognized, including affection, confiding, receiving assistance, trust and shared activities (Fehr, 1996). Tang (2010) highlights the informal and voluntary nature of friendship, and suggests that it offers a range of social support mechanisms, from having fun and enjoying time together, to providing information to enable informed decisions and emotional aid in times of distress or crisis. Social support in this context has two main elements – feeling cared for by others, and a perception that should support be needed from others, it will be available (Coleman & Iso-Ahola, 1993). Individuals in stressful situations and events often turn to friends for social support to assist them to 'buffer the negative effects' of the stressor (Glover & Parry, 2008).

Forming friendships happens in a variety of ways, and friendships can be simple or complex (Tang, 2010). Fehr (1996) highlights potential theoretical frameworks to understand friendships, suggesting that reinforcement theory, social exchange theory and equity theory can help to explain why individuals like other people in terms of the reward that one (or both) party accrues as a result of the friendship. However, this appears to be a rather instrumentalist approach, reducing the complex nature of friendship to an exchange of rewards. Cognitive consistency theory, on the other hand, helps to explain friendship by positing that we are attracted to people who are similar to us, or who have attitudes and values that we share (Fehr, 1996). This appears to provide a deeper understanding of who we choose to have as friends.

Maintaining friendships can be challenging, particularly when there are spatial or temporal distances between friends. Online maintenance of friendships is becoming more commonplace, particularly in the era of the COVID-19 pandemic, and friendships can be performed in the online space in a way that allows continuance of the social support reciprocated between friends (Tang,

2010). However, physical meetings reinforce friendships in way that online interaction does not (Tang, 2010). Friendships are significant elements in the performance of identity (Cover, 2012) and so when there are gaps between face-to-face meetings, the opportunities to reinforce and perform one's identity are correspondingly reduced. Thus, seeking opportunities for physical meetings is arguably a vital part of maintaining friendships.

Several authors have highlighted gender differences in relation to friendships and have found that friendship tends to operate differently between men and women (Ermer & Matera, 2021). For example, Block and Greenberg (2002, p. 3) found that friendships between women are often 'deeper, more enduring and more plentiful than those between men'. They suggest that women often offer support for each other during times of crisis, they admit weaknesses and faults to each other and will share defeats as well as victories. In addition, female friendship has been shown to be linked more closely to emotional wellbeing compared with male friendship (Ermer & Proulx, 2020) with women being more likely than men to note that friendships create affective aspects (e.g., feelings) (Adams et al., 2000).

The rise of feminism and a range of other social changes such as geographic mobility and the increasing number of women working both inside and outside the home, the so-called 'balancing babies and briefcases' challenge (Bordeaux Silverstein, 2014), have been implicated in a transformation of the way that society views women's friendships (Tummala-Narra, 2014). Fehr (1996) suggests that women seem to prefer friends with whom they can talk about feelings and relationships, while men are more likely to prefer friends with whom they can undertake activities. While this may appear to be a generalization, and it is likely that friendship differences between genders are much more finely grained, nonetheless, it is argued that friendships between women may be more empowering than friendships between men (Comas-Diaz, 2014). Such empowerment relates to the fact that friendships between women appear to provide the emotional support needed to help women increase their resilience, self-efficacy and agency (Comas-Diaz, 2014) and to cope with oppression such as sexism (Tummala-Narra, 2014). As Comas-Diaz and Weiner (2016) explain, women offer each other security, refuge, hope and solace.

3. Conceptual Model

In the leisure literature, Glover and Parry (2008) developed a conceptual model to explain the social process associated with friendship and its connection to health and wellbeing outcomes. The model illustrates how friendship can have positive health benefits as friendships can offer emotional support and provide material resources that individuals are able to use directly to 'improve their care and reduce their stress'. However, they note that such friendships may also come 'with strings attached, and the obligations that come with maintaining friendships can add stressors and reduce personal well-being' (Glover & Parry, 2008, p. 221).

The Glover and Parry (2008) conceptual model, which was developed in the context of women facing fertility problems, appears appropriate as a framework in this chapter as it is concerned with friendship based on a shared social identity and considers that friendships are built, maintained and sustained within a sphere of sociability. The shared social identity highlighted by Glover and Parry (2008) reflects a social connection shared with others who could relate to the stressful life event with which they are dealing. They suggest that 'friendships based upon a shared social identity (interest friendships) develop into deep friendships as friends invest in the relationship through routine social contact, primarily within leisure contexts' (2008, p. 222). The sphere of sociability in the conceptual model reflects that the friendships were 'formed and most often maintained and sustained' within 'leisure-oriented social contexts' with the example given of friendships formed and maintained via such activities as 'on the walking track' and 'in waiting rooms'. These women attended a variety of leisure events which allowed them to maintain friendships recognising that 'joint leisure participation reaffirmed the sociable bonds among friends' (Glover & Parry, 2008, p. 223).

Glover and Parry (2008, p. 224) suggest that such social capital is crucial to an individual's health because it can facilitate three forms of action, namely, '*expressive* (getting by), *instrumental* (getting ahead), and *obstructive* (falling behind)'. These are described collectively as 'products of friendships'. In the Glover and Parry (2008, p. 224) case, the first form of action is *expressiveaction* – since the women were dealing with similar experiences, they were able to empathize with each other as they had 'experienced or were experiencing similar challenges themselves … reflecting group solidarity' which can be 'cemented by a common experience of adversity'. The second form of action, namely *instrumental action*, is tied to the material dimension of friendship, which gives friends access to resources and valuable information from friends. Respondents in the Glover and Parry (2008, p. 225) study felt that they were able to receive information that helped them feel empowered and 'in greater control of their situations'. The third form of action, referred to as *obstructive action*, acknowledges that there can be ill-effects generated by friendships, for example, when individuals feel obligated to engage in activities with these friends which they are not comfortable with, such as attending leisure events which reminded the participants of their personal situation and could create stress. The Glover and Parry (2008, p. 225) study found that the 'social norms and sanctions embedded in their friendships compelled them to continue to support their friends under stressful circumstances' even though their participation was, to some extent, detrimental to their own health.

Finally, the Glover and Parry (2008, p. 226) model recognizes that each individual has a choice and must decide whether to exit the relationship or remain loyal to it. Their study found that some friendships 'can become sources of angst, whereas others are comforting and therefore indispensable to wellbeing'. They propose that the positive by-products associated with friendship can lead to 'feelings of indebtedness, which strengthen relationships and reinforce loyalty' (Glover & Parry, 2008, p. 227). However, by contrast they also acknowledge that when the dynamics of a friendship change, the friendship can sometimes dissolve, perhaps because, as they argue, 'empathetic identification is perceived to cease'. This chapter considers friendship within the framework of Glover and Parry (2008) and considers the components and dimensions of friendships among academic women, forged and strengthened during academic conference attendance.

4. Methodology

The method used in this chapter is duoethnography. Originating from the notion of autoethnography, a method where an author uses their own knowledge and experiences to elucidate a given phenomenon (Holt, 2003), duoethnography involves co-constructing a narrative based on a dialogue between two (or more) researchers. The participants become both the researchers and the researched (Norris, 2008). During the dialogue, which usually takes the form of a conversation, the researchers engage with each other to discuss their personal experiences, each informed by their own personal histories, and come together to make sense and meaning of the topic being discussed (Denshire, 2014; Zazkis & Koichu, 2014). Indeed, duoethnography has been described as a scholarly conversation whereby the topic is viewed through the researcher's eyes and communicated via a written dialogue (Gómez, 2013). This method allows for each individual to create their own narrative about events and experiences, and can help find a range of meanings, some of which may be shared with the other researcher; others of which may be unique to the individual (Norris & Sawyer, 2012). It is in the discussion, the comparison of experiences and the coming together of meanings that the emergent explanations and underpinnings of the phenomenon under study becomes clear.

As a qualitative method informed by social constructivism, duoethnography, similar to autoethnography, does not rely on the traditional positivistic notions of truth and validity (Norris & Sawyer, 2012). Indeed, universal truths are not sought. Rather, duoethnography provides knowledge that is fluid rather than being fixed, and provides opportunities for the researchers to reflect, deliberate and conclude in a non-judgemental way (Higgins et al., 2018). As such, it is the rigour of the dialogic process and collaborative enquiry that should be judged (Norris & Sawyer, 2012).

Whilst it is a relatively novel approach in the field of tourism and hospitality, the method has been used consistently for several years, particularly in education research, including childhood education (Ceglowski & Makovsky, 2012); Indigenous education (Madden & McGregor, 2013); mathematics education (Rapke, 2014); postcolonial education (Sawyer & Liggett, 2012); and post graduate supervision (Higgins et al., 2018; Kidd & Finlayson, 2015). The method is now gaining some traction among scholars in a range of other disciplines including health studies (Grant & Radcliffe, 2015), industrial psychology (Meier & Geldenhuys, 2017), mathematics (Eaton & Bailey, 2018) and tourism (Mair & Frew, 2018; Tan & Teoh, 2019). In addition, a range of feminist authors have used duoethnography as a methodology including pioneers in the technique such as Spencer and Paisley (2013). Other recent examples include Benjamin and Schwab (2021) who considered solo women travellers, and Almanssori and Hillier (2020) who considered the personal lived experiences of mothering, teaching and academic-related tasks during initial stages of the COVID-19 pandemic. In particular, the method is proving to be a valuable tool in intersectional research (see e.g., Brown & Mogadime, 2017; Wagaman & Sanchez, 2017).

The two authors of this chapter have known each other for around 15 years. They initially met at a university seminar and then became friends after attending several conferences together. They both work in the university sector in Australia, although at different universities, teaching and researching in tourism and events. Their friendship moved from occasional catch-ups at conferences to regularly spending time together, meeting at a range of work-related and personal events. They have supported each other through work challenges (e.g., promotion applications, difficult meetings, faculty and university re-structuring) and personal challenges (such as moving house and raising children) and have also enjoyed many fun occasions together over the years. In order to undertake this research, the two researchers met in 2019 and had a free ranging conversation which reflected on their experiences at the most recent discipline (tourism, hospitality and event) academic association conference that they had attended together. The conversation was recorded, transcribed verbatim and then analysed for the themes of friendships, using manual coding, and taking the elements of Glover and Parry (2008) as *a priori* codes.

The findings of this research are presented in the form of a conversation, or script, allowing the voices of the researchers to come through, demonstrating to the reader how the identities and lives of the researchers are situated socially and culturally via the dialogic text (Norris & Sawyer, 2012). Each conversational excerpt represents a particular element of the Glover and Parry (2008) model as illustrated by the headings below.

5. Findings and Discussion

The findings suggest that networking is an important reason for women to attend academic conferences. Encounters with already established and proven friends appear to be important to the researchers as a means of reinforcing these friendships. The face-to-face component of the interaction was important to allow the sharing of experiences at the academic conference, to provide the opportunity to chat about individual home university working environments, and to reflect on changing careers and families. The online follow-up of sharing photos and reflections was important, but the face-to-face interaction appeared to be paramount. Indeed, the opportunity to catch up face-to-face appears to be one of the major motivations for travel to attend this academic conference, a fact that has important ramifications for maintaining friendships amidst the challenges wrought by the COVID-19 pandemic.

This building of a friendship community and socialising with those friends is shown to be very important as a means of helping in terms of both career development and sense of wellbeing. There was evidence of fun and enjoyment during the conference which appeared to reinforce the friendship and provided further impetus to maintain this friendship in the intervening time before the next get together (given the wide geographical dispersal of the friendship group). As Ramirez et al. (2013) demonstrated, socialising at a conference seems to be more important for women than men, and the findings of this study certainly emphasize that the social opportunities available were valued and utilized.

5.1 Friendships Based on Shared Social Identity

For Glover and Parry (2008), the shared social identity was of women undergoing fertility treatment; in this case, the shared social identity was of female academics attending an academic conference. In this case, both the researchers have similar roles within national universities, being engaged in teaching, research and administrative responsibilities in the same discipline, in the male dominated world of academia. The shared nature of the experience appeared to act as a conduit for discussions around issues of mutual importance – highlighted in particular by this exchange, which revolves around the importance for individuals of developing an appropriate academic brand to fit in with their social identity and the importance of maintaining a positive personal image at an academic conference:

> There's the whole idea that every individual academic is their own brand, and that you're portraying ideally your best self anywhere, where other people are going to see you. You rely on your reputation and people knowing you. You don't want to be remembered as that one that did the presentation with spinach in their teeth. You want to be remembered as that one that did the really interesting presentation on whatever.
>
> True. I like that expression of you as a brand, I hadn't really thought about it recently. I have thought about it in the past, but it's great to revisit that because, what is your brand? How do you reinforce your brand? So there's a brand that you have within your department as being the work horse, or the one that gets good teaching marks, or the one that takes on roles in committees and speaks out. But there's also the brand that you have among your research-related peers, or your peers in your discipline, which is slightly different, it's more like your research persona.

Being able to share such ideas and concerns and express them with other women who understand and who are going through exactly the same things is a vital function of friendship and meeting face-to-face makes sharing of such notions much easier. This finding supports Hahm et al. (2016) and the sense of community created by attending a business event and the enhancing of community between attendees, particularly at academic annual meetings. The personal interactions while staying in a shared apartment with other female academic friends, and the conversations and experiences shared, helped to reinforce these friendships.

5.2 Sphere of Sociability: Relationships Built, Maintained and Sustained

As Glover and Parry (2008) point out, the sphere of sociability relates to the fact that friendships are both formed and maintained within social contexts. For the researchers, this sphere of sociability related not only to physical attendance at the academic conference, and the time available to socialize during the formal conference program, but also the fact that they shared an apartment, providing opportunity for informal socialising during leisure time too. This underpins the suggestion that, as highlighted by several authors (e.g., Fjelstuhl et al., 2009; Foley et al., 2014; Opperman & Chon, 1997; Yoo & Chon, 2008), attending a conference is a social experience.

The exchange noted below highlights the importance of the time spent renewing and maintaining existing friendships. It also stresses that the absence of friends can have a negative impact on the attendee experience:

> Attending a conference is a bonding experience, but … we're all travelling from different places in Australia to be together – not travelling to be together, but we are using that opportunity to be together, and it's the sort of thing that you do with friends. It's the sort of thing that you don't do with your colleagues. For the most part, if I went to a conference and there was nobody there I knew, I wouldn't have that opportunity to feel validated about what I had chosen to do or to say, or to wear or to think, and I think that's really that reinforcement and validation of your choices, I think it's quite important.
> Agreed. I have a colleague who has just come back from a conference of a thousand people in New York, and she said it was very isolating, she was quite lonely. She only knew two people in the whole conference because there just wasn't that feeling of togetherness and so on that we associate with good conferences.

5.3 Expressive Action: Empathy and Group Solidarity (Getting By)

Much of the discussions between the female academics reflected their similar experiences and how they had overcome issues and difficulties (reflecting Glover and Parry's expressive action). The following exchange highlights the importance of being able to relax with people the attendees are comfortable with, to relieve some of the pressure and stress of being 'on duty' for long days, and is an example of what Glover and Parry (2008) refer to as expressive action – sympathising and empathising regarding some of the harder aspects of performing academic work, and mutual support:

> When we were sharing the apartment, we bought some nice stuff so that we could sit down and have a nice breakfast together. Actually, that's one of the nice things about having an apartment, is that you don't have to go down to the hotel dining room for breakfast. So the last conference I was at, in the Hilton, beautiful hotel, but you wake up in the morning and you've got let's say maybe 10, 11, maybe 12 hours with

some of these people. You don't actually want to have to talk business at breakfast as well. It's tiring.
It IS tiring. Even just your ability to remember everybody's names, the pronunciation of the names. I'm very impressed by that.
Thank you! [Laughs]. I just deeply appreciate having people around me when I am under pressure a little bit, to be the face of the association. So when I go to the conference I have to go to everything, and I have to be smiling at everything, and I have to speak at most things. I just really appreciate having people around who get that, and that are all supportive. So when we go back to the apartment, or when we go out for drinks – I'm not the Chair of the Association anymore, I'm just somebody having a drink. Whereas when I'm at the conference I feel I have to network, I have to talk to people, I have to have my smiley face on, and it's quite wearing.
'You're right, you have to be seen to be the right type of person, you've got to look the part, you've got to talk the part because also as members of the association, we want you to be like that. We expect the Chair to represent what we think.

This exchange supports Fehr's (1996) findings that friendships have certain attributes and can involve affection, confiding, receiving assistance, trust and shared activities. This also provides further evidence for Tang's (2010) findings that friends can provide a social support mechanism and can involve having fun while engaging in time together, as well as providing information and enabling informal decisions and emotional aid in times of hardship.

5.4 Instrumental Action: Sharing of Resources (Getting Ahead)

Glover and Parry (2008) note that one of the key dimensions of friendship is instrumental action – where friends provide each other with valuable information, which helps them to feel empowered. As Mair and Frew (2018) suggest, many women in academia are concerned with their appearance and grooming, and derive a certain level of confidence from presenting their best self. The following exchange reinforces how friends can support each other in terms of their appearance:

Do you remember doing things like checking on peoples' food or lipstick on their teeth? Now, I wouldn't do that with – there are many, many people I wouldn't do that with! I wouldn't necessarily do it with a man. I would probably only do that with friends.
[Laughs] Yeah, I think that goes to a deeper level of better connection with somebody, so it's not just colleagues, and it's not even just acquaintances, it's you have to know somebody pretty well before you feel up to doing that.
It reinforces that when you're at a conference, you're in the public eye, you are basically trying to make the best impression on the people around you, you don't

> want to look a fool, you don't want to look stupid. You want to look professional and appear in a professional manner at all times.
> That was a bonding experience, wasn't it, because it made us feel that we're all part of this – we were there together, sharing an apartment together, and going out into the world to have this experience, but we're supporting each other.

This exchange reinforces the intimate relationship that can be created between friends, supporting each other to allow the individual to develop a professional image and assist in the public portrayal of that image. The sharing of resources reflects the occasional feelings of inadequacy among female academics and resonates with the notions of the babies and briefcases dilemma highlighted by Bourdeaux Silverstein (2014) and the dual roles of caregiver and conference attendee (Henderson, 2018).

Mention was also made with regard to advice about handling situations that arose at their home institutions and suggestions on strategies for applying for promotion. There was also the sharing of academic resources such as articles or links to web pages related to issues raised in discussions. Although the friendship itself may not necessarily provide solutions for these difficult issues, nonetheless, it offers the opportunity to discuss issues of mutual concern, and provide empathy and sympathy as well as potential strategies for addressing these issues:

> Everyone knows your position within your own university, everyone knows where you are in the hierarchy, and so everyone deals with you in that way. So when you're out of your normal situation at the conference you're dealing with people from your own discipline and you do feel you have a bond with them.
> You also hear some real war stories from other people who are just surviving by their fingertips, hanging on with relation to their organization, and the downsizing … And you can be supportive of them.
> It reinforces the importance of attending this conference, and we look at potential PhD examiners, you're looking at people to review, to work collaboratively with in the future, and you're looking for friendship and support.

5.5 Obstructive Action: Comparison of Each Other's Success (Falling Behind)

While the majority of themes identified relate to the positive aspects of friendships, it is important to recognize that there can be negative aspects too. As Glover and Parry (2008) point out, individuals may feel obliged to privilege the friendship over personal wishes. In this case, the female academics remained as friends, and simply noted that others had not been able to maintain friendships where one individual became considerably more successful than others. In this exchange, it can be seen that the researchers recognize the dangers inherent in comparing self with others – although people are quick to congratulate others for achieving success, the longer-term impacts of potential discontent, and even jealousy, can be damaging to friendships and working relationships:

> Now, one of the things that I've noticed that when I go to these conferences, I often compare my career to others, and reflect on what stage I'm at in my career compared to others. So it makes me reflect on my career, colleagues and my work/life balance. You can start to see the type of people who are successful in academia, and they're very, very focused and they're very political as well, they do a lot of moving and shaking. But from a female perspective, the triple combo of being a professor, having children and a partner, the three things often don't go together. I call it the three P's of professoriate, partner and progenies – there's often one thing that's sacrificed. So if you think about the professors that we know, they often either have no children or they're single.
> I don't think there are very many single mum professors in our discipline. That's a really tough gig.
> True. And we do congratulate each other, as friends, we do see that when other people become successful.

On the whole there appeared to be support of friends in their careers. Perhaps a person gaining promotion or moving into a new role at an overseas university could be deemed to be uncomfortable for other members of the group and so the friendship may be challenged, but this did not appear to be the case in this friendship.

5.6 Outcomes of Friendships: Loyalty or Exit

The importance of the friendships in the decision to attend the conference appears to be significant. Not only do the researchers choose which conferences to attend based (at least partly) on which of their friends will be attending, these conferences also provide the face-to-face space to stay loyal friends throughout the rest of the year when face-to-face meetings may not be viable, and the friendships have to be maintained by telephone, email, social media or other methods. The following exchange highlights the importance of meeting friends at conferences and the desire to maintain the friendships over the long term:

> So conferences don't just happen, you've got to have planning. So there'll be calls for papers and there'll be the accommodation booking, and there'll be all the chat amongst us as to where we're staying, and who's staying where. It's just part of the anticipation, it's like any holiday I suppose, not that it's a holiday of course! [Laughs] But similar to a holiday, there's a sense of anticipation, and then there are all the recollections afterwards, like we're doing now. But even if it's just on Facebook or with sending photos round afterwards. So it's more than just the experience at the time.

However, as has been noted, friendship is a complex construct and one that has no guarantee of continued success. Glover and Parry (2008) even suggest that in some cases, friendships can become a source of angst. If this becomes the case, then each individual has the choice of whether or not to sustain the friendship or dissolve it. The following exchange reflects a situation where a lack of coordination of social and leisure activities led to bad feelings about how much they missed out on by not being aware of an important social situation:

> I had a bad, bad experience. I got in a taxi with three other people and we ended up in this restaurant that was really, really horrible. But I found out the next day that most of my friends had ended up in a karaoke bar, and it could've been a really good night, but we ended up all dispersed. I felt really put out.
> I didn't even go out that night because I didn't know where everyone was going – I ended up back at the apartment with a cup of tea!
> Yeah, I had to leave by myself, which is very unusual, got a taxi by myself.

In this instance, there was no problem with the friendship of the female academics, but it illustrates how these sorts of things can have a damaging effect on relationships established at the academic conference, which in extreme cases may lead to exiting the friendship.

6. Conclusion

> I feel like moving forward I have a group of female friends that I can trust, you can hang out with and you know that if everyone's going to the next conference you can have friendship year to year going forward ... You come back rejuvenated.

Academic conferences play an important part in the life and journey of an academic, as a means of networking with a community of like-minded individuals but also to establish and maintain friendships among fellow academics. For women this is particularly important given the often male-dominated environment they work in at their home institutions and the challenges of maintaining and developing an academic career while balancing family responsibilities. This resonates with the issues highlighted by White (2014) relating to the challenges for women trying to emulate the (predominantly) male academic career model, with its focus on networking, presenting one's research and developing an academic reputation.

This chapter has demonstrated that attending conferences with existing friends is a vital part of maintaining these friendships over time, and that attending conferences can be a bonding activity for friends. There is also evidence that the benefits of academic conference attendance go beyond personal enjoyment. Indeed, the friendship examined in this chapter (along with others that we are familiar with) straddles the boundary between the personal and the professional, by providing a source of social support (Coleman & Iso-Ahola, 1993) and providing advice and information on managing academic workloads and balancing academic and personal lives. As Cover (2012) notes, friendships are a key part of the performance of identity, in this case that of an academic woman. Thus, the findings of this study suggest that friendships appear, as posited by Glover and Parry (2008), to be a significant contributor to the wellbeing of female academics, as well as providing support to help women increase their resilience, self-efficacy and agency (Comas-Diaz, 2014). Therefore, maintaining and nurturing these relationships is likely to prove advantageous for both the individuals concerned, and by extension, their university employers. This chapter supports Hixson (2012) in regard to events facilitating face-to face discussions as a means to help improve collaboration and cooperation over time.

Academic conference managers can facilitate the development and maintenance of friendships by including mention of apartments close to the conference venue on their web pages and by building in free time into the conference programme to facilitate engagement as a means of facilitating the establishment of new friendships among academic attendees and, the maintenance of old friendships. These easily achievable amendments to a conference programme may make the event appear more appealing to potential attendees who are seeking the face-to-face engagement and interaction with their current and future academic friends. This chapter supports the suggestion from Foley, et al. (2014, p. 64) that business event planners should provide the 'social space required for the development of relationships' but suggest in addition that the event planners need to provide opportunities for delegates to nurture and maintain friendships via associated leisure activities and social engagements.

The limitation of this research is that the research focuses on the lived experiences of two female academics at one annual tourism, hospitality and event academic conference. There is recognition that other types of events may have different outcomes in relation to friendships, for example if the event is a trade or sales event where there may be more competition between delegates to secure sales. In other words, the camaraderie experienced at an academic conference among females may not be as prevalent in a different environment.

Future research into the role of friendships at academic annual conferences could consider the differences in event experiences between males and females during the critical moments of friendship establishment, development, strengthening and maintenance. Such research would further illuminate the variety of needs of the delegates, recognising that attendees are not homogenous and may have vastly different experiences of the same event. Such future research would build on recent work in the area of the dual roles of care-giver and conference attendee and the need to accommodate and assist attendees to ensure higher levels of satisfaction and encourage return intentions.

Finally, the impact of the COVID-19 pandemic on how we maintain friendships needs considerable further research. While we have noted that face-to-face meetings are a key way to maintain friendships, physical meetings have become much more difficult and in some cases impossible. The efficacy of attempts to maintain friendships online (via Teams catch-ups or virtual drinks) with associated Zoom fatigue is as yet unknown, and research is required to see if the absence of physical meetings leads to longer-term issues with previously long-established friendships. It is to be hoped that existing friendships are strong enough to withstand long periods of not catching up face-to-face, but more junior women may be missing out on important opportunities to make new friends and cement existing friendships, thus creating yet more potential disadvantages for those trying to make their way in academia.

References

Adams, R.G., Blieszner, R., & De Vries, B. (2000). Definitions of friendship in the third age: Age, gender, and study location effects. *Journal of Aging Studies, 14*(1), 117–33. https://doi.org/10.1016/S0890-4065(00)80019-5

Almanssori, S. & Hillier, K.M. (2020). Frontline workers from home: A feminist duoethnographic inquiry of mothering, teaching, and academia during the initial stages of the COVID-19 pandemic. *Journal of the Motherhood Initiative for Research and Community Involvement.* Available at: https:// jarm .journals .yorku .ca/ index .php/jarm/article/view/40613 (accessed 26 September 2021).

Bassett, L.E. (1933). Why conventions? *Quarterly Journal of Speech, 19*(4), 561–6.

Benjamin, S. & Schwab, K. (2021) Navigating the waves of feminism(s): A duoethnography of two feminist travellers. *Annals of Leisure Research.* https://doi.org/10.1080/11745398.2021.1938155

Block, J.D. & Greenberg, D. (2002). *Women and friendship.* Gretna, LA: Wellness Institute.

Bordeaux Silverstein, L. (2014). A complicated friendship. In L. Comas-Diaz & M.B. Weiner (eds), *Women psychotherapists' reflections on female friendships: Sisters of the heart* (pp. 76–85). Abingdon, UK: Routledge.

Brown, H. & Mogadime, D. (2017). Advocacy for diversity begins with the self: Unleashing silenced stories: A duoethnographic account. *Understanding and Dismantling Privilege, 7*(2), 15–38.

Ceglowski, D. & Makovsky, T. (2012). Duoethnography with children. *Ethnography and Education*, *7*(3), 283–95. https://doi.org/10.1080/17457823.2012.717197

Coleman, D. & Iso-Ahola, S.E. (1993). Leisure and health: The role of social support and self-determination. *Journal of Leisure Research*, *25*(2), 111–28. https://doi.org/10.1080/00222216.1993.11969913

Comas-Diaz, L. (2014). SisterHeart: How intimate friendships empower and transform women. In L. Comas-Diaz & M.B. Weiner (eds), *Women psychotherapists' reflections on female friendships: Sisters of the heart*, (pp. 139–46). Abingdon, UK: Routledge.

Comas-Diaz, L. & Weiner, M.B. (eds). (2016). *Women psychotherapists' reflections on female friendships: Sisters of the heart*. Abingdon, UK: Routledge.

Cook, H.P. (1954). The annual conference marches on. *The Tax Executive*, *10*, 3–5.

Cover, R. (2012). Performing and undoing identity online: Social networking, identity theories and the incompatibility of online profiles and friendship regimes. *Convergence*, *18*(2), 177–93. https://doi.org/10.1177/1354856511433684

Denshire, S. (2014). On auto-ethnography. *Current Sociology*, *62*(6), 831–50. https://doi.org/10.1177/0011392114533339

Eaton, C.D. & Bailey, L.M. (2018). Revealing luz: Illuminating our identities through duoethnography. *Journal of Humanistic Mathematics*, *8*(2), 60–89. https://doi.org/10.5642/jhummath.201802.08

Ermer, A.E. & Matera, K.N (2021). Older women's friendships: Illuminating the role of marital histories in how older women navigate friendships and caregiving for friends. *Journal of Women & Aging*, *33*(2), 214–29.

Ermer, A.E., & Proulx, C.M. (2020). Wellbeing among older adult couples: The role of social networks and neighbors. *Journal of Social and Personal Relationships*, *37*(4), 1073–109. https://doi.org/10.1177/0265407519886350

Fehr, B. (1996). *Friendship processes: Sage series on close relationships*. Thousand Oaks, CA: Sage Publications.

Fjelstul, J., Severt, K., & Breiter, D. (2009). An analysis of the motivators and inhibitors affecting association meeting attendance for generation X and baby boomers. *Event Management*, *13*(1), 31–41. https://doi.org/10.3727/152599509789130575

Foley, C., Edwards, D., & Schlenker, K. (2014). Business events and friendship: Leveraging the sociable legacies. *Event Management*, *18*(1), 53–64. https://doi.org/10.3727/152599514X13883555341887

Foley, C., Grabowski, S., Small, J., & Wearing, S. (2018). Women of the Kokoda: From poverty to empowerment in sustainable tourism development. *Tourism, Culture & Communication*, *18*(1), 21–34. https://doi.org/10.3727/109830418X15180180585158

Glover, T.D., & Parry, D.C. (2008). Friendships developed subsequent to a stressful life event: The interplay of leisure, social capital, and health. *Journal of Leisure Research*, *40*(2), 208–30. https://doi.org/10.1080/00222216.2008.11950138

Gómez, G.S. (2013). Book review: Joe Norris, Richard D Sawyer & Darren Lund, Duoethnography: Dialogic methods for social, health, and educational research. *Qualitative Research*, *13*(4), 474–5. https://doi.org/10.1177/1468794113484440

Grant, A.J. & Radcliffe, M.A.C. (2015). Resisting technical rationality in mental health nurse higher education: A duoethnography. *The Qualitative Report*, *20*(6), 815–25.

Hahm, J.J., Breiter, D., Severt, K., Wang, Y., & Fjelstul, J. (2016). The relationship between sense of community and satisfaction on future intentions to attend an association's annual meeting. *Tourism Management*, *52*, 151–60. https://doi.org/10.1016/j.tourman.2015.06.016

Harris, C. & Ateljevic, I. (2003). Perpetuating the male gaze as the norm: Challenges for 'her' participation in business travel. *Tourism Recreation Research*, *28*(2), 21–30.

Henderson, E.F. (2018). Academics in two places at once: (Not) managing caring responsibilities at conferences. In R. Finkel, B. Sharp, & M. Sweeney(eds), *Accessibility, inclusion, and diversity in critical event studies* (pp. 218–29). Abingdon, UK: Routledge.

Higgins, M., Morton, A.E., & Wolkenhauer, R. (2018). (Re) conceptualizing preservice teacher supervision through duoethnography: Reflecting, supporting, and collaborating with and for each other. *Teaching and Teacher Education, 69*, 75–84. https://doi.org/10.1016/j.tate.2017.09.020

Hixson, E. (2012). *The psychological benefits of attending conventions*. Paper presented at the Global Events Congress V, Stavanger, Norway, 13–15 June.

Holt, N.L. (2003). Representation, legitimation, and autoethnography: An auto-ethnographic writing story. *International Journal of Qualitative Methods, 2*(1), 18–28. https://doi.org/10.1177/160940690300200102

Jago, L.K. & Deery, M. (2005). Relationships and factors influencing convention decision-making. *Journal of Convention & Event Tourism, 7*(1), 23–41.

Kidd, J. & Finlayson, M.P. (2015). She pushed me, and I flew: A duoethnographical story from supervisors in flight. *Forum Qualitative Sozialforschung/Forum: Qualitative Social Research, 16*(1). https://doi.org/10.17169/fqs-16.1.2217

Madden, B. & McGregor, H.E. (2013). Ex(er)cising student voice in pedagogy for decolonizing: Exploring complexities through duoethnography. *Review of Education, Pedagogy, and Cultural Studies, 35*(5), 371–91. https://doi.org/10.1080/10714413.2013.842866

Mair, J. & Frew, E. (2018). Academic conferences: A female duo-ethnography. *Current Issues in Tourism, 21*(18), 2152–72. https://doi.org/10.1080/13683500.2016.1248909

Mair, J. & Thompson, K. (2009). The UK association conference attendance decision-making process. *Tourism Management, 30*(3), 400–9. https://doi.org/10.1016/j.tourman.2008.08.002

Mair, J., Lockstone-Binney, L., & Whitelaw, P.A. (2018). The motives and barriers of association conference attendance: Evidence from an Australasian tourism and hospitality academic conference. *Journal of Hospitality and Tourism Management, 34*(58–65). https://doi.org/10.1016/j.jhtm.2017.11.004

Maliva, N., Bulkens, M., Peters, K., & Van der Duim, R. (2018). Female tourism entrepreneurs in Zanzibar: An enactment perspective. *Tourism, Culture & Communication, 18*(1), 9–20. https://doi.org/10.3727/109830418X15180180585149

Meier, C. & Geldenhuys, D.J. (2017). Co-constructing appreciative inquiry across disciplines: A duo-ethnography. *SA Journal of Industrial Psychology, 43*(1), 1–9. https://doi.org/10.4102/sajip.v43i0.1400

Norris, J. (2008). Duoethnography. In L.M. Given(ed.), *The Sage encyclopedia of qualitative research methods* (pp. 233–6). Thousand Oaks, CA: Sage.

Norris, J. & Sawyer, R.D. (2012). Towards a dialogic methodology. In J. Norris, R.D. Sawyer, & D. Lund(eds), *Duoethnography: Dialogic methods for social, health and educational research* (pp. 9–39). Walnut Creek, CA: Left Coast Press.

Oppermann, M. & Chon, K.S. (1997). Convention participation decision-making process. *Annals of Tourism Research, 24*(1), 178–91.

Pritchard, A., (2018). Predicting the next decade of tourism gender research. *Tourism Management Perspectives, 25*, 144–6.

Ramirez, D., Laing, J., & Mair, J. (2013). Exploring intentions to attend a convention: A gender perspective. *Event Management, 17*(2), 165–78. https://doi.org/10.3727/152599513X13668224082503

Rapke, T.K. (2014). Duoethnography: A new research methodology for mathematics education. *Canadian Journal of Science, Mathematics and Technology Education, 14*(2), 172–86. https://doi.org/10.1080/14926156.2014.903317

Sawyer, R.D. & Liggett, T. (2012). Shifting positionalities: A critical discussion of a duoethnographic inquiry of a personal curriculum of post/colonialism. *International Journal of Qualitative Methods, 11*(5), 628–51. https://doi.org/10.1177/160940691201100507

Severt, D., Wang, Y., Chen, P.J., & Breiter, D. (2007). Examining the motivation, perceived performance, and behavioral intentions of convention attendees: evidence from a regional conference. *Tourism Management, 28*(2), 399–408. https://doi.org/10.1016/j.tourman.2006.04.003

Spencer, C. & Paisley, K. (2013). Two women, a bottle of wine, and the bachelor: Duoethnography as a means to explore experiences of femininity in a leisure setting. *Journal of Leisure Research, 45*(5), 695–716. https://doi.org/10.18666/jlr-2013-v45-i5-4370

Tan, E. & Teoh, S. (2019). A nostalgic peranakan journey in Melaka: Duo-ethnographic conversations between a Nyonya and Baba. *Tourism Management Perspectives, 32*, 100570.

Tang, L. (2010). Development of online friendship in different social spaces: A case study. *Information, Communication and Society, 13*(4), 615–33. https://doi.org/10.1080/13691180902998639

Tummala-Narra, P. (2014). Growing at the hyphen: Female friendships and social context. In L. Comas-Diaz & M.B. Weiner(eds), *Women psychotherapists' reflections on female friendships: Sisters of the heart,* (pp. 35–50). Abingdon, UK: Routledge.

Venkatesh, V., Morris, M. G., & Ackerman, P.L. (2000). A longitudinal field investigation of gender differences in individual technology adoption decision-making processes. *Organizational Behavior and Human DecisionProcesses, 83*(1), 33–60. https://doi.org/10.1006/obhd.2000.2896

Wagaman, M.A. & Sanchez, I. (2017). Looking through the magnifying glass: A duoethnographic approach to understanding the value and process of participatory action research with LGBTQ youth. *Qualitative Social Work, 16*(1), 78–95. https://doi.org/10.1177/1473325015595855

Werner, K. (2021). The future is female, the future is diverse: Perceptions of young female talents on their future in the (German) event industry. *Journal of Policy Research in Tourism, Leisure and Events.* https://doi.org/10.1080/19407963.2021.1975289

White, J.N.K. (2014). Australasian university management, gender and life course issues. *Equality, Diversity and Inclusion: An International Journal, 33*(4), 384–p95.

Yoo, J.J.E. & Chon, K. (2008). Factors affecting convention participation decision-making: developing a measurement scale. *Journal of Travel Research, 47*(1), 113–22. https://doi.org/10.1177/0047287507312421

Yudina, O., Grimwood, B.S., Berbary, L.A. & Mair, H. (2018). The gendered natures of polar bear tourism. *Tourism Culture & Communication, 18*(1), 51–66.

Zazkis, R. & Koichu, B. (2014) A fictional dialogue on infinitude of primes: Introducing virtual duoethnography. *Educational Studies in Mathematics, 88*(2), 163–81. https://doi.org/10.1007/s10649-014-9580-0

11 Conclusion to *A Research Agenda for Gender and Tourism*

Donna Chambers and Erica Wilson

1. Introduction

The collection of chapters in this book have touched upon issues that are pertinent to current and future contemplations of research in gender and tourism. The interdisciplinary discussions have covered a range of geographical and cultural contexts from Saudi Arabia and Iran in the Middle East, Macao in South-East Asia, Colombia in Latin America and on to the continent of Australia. There is also a novel conceptualization of islands as involving gendered encounters between tourists and residents. The discussions in these chapters have also been wide-ranging and are comprised of several critical, though under-researched areas in the canon of gender and tourism research – including gender-based violence and risk in tourism field research, how friendships between women are engendered at academic tourism conferences, issues of power inherent in women's experiences of tourism work during the COVID-19 pandemic and the exploitation of migrant women in hospitality settings. Methodologies have primarily been qualitative involving both primary and secondary sources of data.

This concluding chapter draws its inspiration from the discussions in this book but goes further to suggest other fruitful avenues for research. In doing so, what we present below is in no way comprehensive, but rather we hope that we will provoke some critical discussions on the future for gender and tourism research in terms of theory and method(ology). While we discuss these two concepts separately for heuristic purposes, this is perhaps a false distinction as both are intimately intertwined.

2. Theoretical Directions for Gender and Tourism Research

The authors of the nine chapters implicitly embrace feminist approaches and here we wish to highlight the value of feminist theorizing to discussions of gender and tourism starting with the relevance of Black feminist theory. We suggest that in tourism studies, the voices of Black women have traditionally been muted and any future agenda for tourism gender research must contemplate the voices of Black women.

2.1 Black Feminist Theorizing

In her seminal text titled *Ain't I a woman: Black women and feminism*, renowned Black feminist bell hooks expresses the marginalization and subjugation of Black women:

> As far back as slavery, white people established a social hierarchy based on race and sex that ranked white men first, white women second, though sometimes equal to black men, who are ranked third, and black women last.(hooks, 1981 [2015], p. 78)

The hierarchy described by hooks is implicitly based on an understanding of human evolution that is based on eugenics and encapsulates not just the historic but the current situation of Black women in our contemporary society and consequently in tourism. Our contention is that in traditional discourses and practices of tourism, Black women's voices have been largely silenced due to the intersecting factors of racism and sexism. Today, this is still relevant despite emerging evidence in tourism studies of the presence of some counter-narratives and practices, for example, through publications like that by Emma Lee on the manufacture of Black women's bodies (Lee, 2017) and discussions around the Black Travel movement in the United States, as narrated by Stefanie Benjamin and Alana Dillette (Benjamin & Dilette, 2021).

According to Chambers (2022), Black women in tourism are affected by a double negation – they are frequently erased from discourses of both sexism and racism. Black women in tourism have primarily been the objects of research and too often (re)presented by white men and women as socio-culturally, economically, and politically vulnerable and thus in need of 'empowerment' (Arnfred, 2004; Syed, 2010).Chambers (2022)argues that where Black women's voices are 'heard', it is often through the interpretive lens of Western scholars and (re)producers of culture in a range of popular media.

In the context of leisure studies, Mowatt et al. (2013) suggest that Black women in research are represented according to two juxtaposing positions – invisibility and hypervisibility. Black women are invisible both as research participants and as researchers. The body of the Black woman only appears when conceptions of sexual-subjection or social disparities are discussed. Mowatt et al. (2013) go further to contend that in leisure spaces Black women's bodies are stereotyped as abnormal, hypersexual, and their social location highlighted as deviant. And this stereotypical representation of Black women is used to justify and excuse exploitation and violence. Indeed, Mendoza argues 'The racializing logic that Europeans imposed on the colonized robbed non-Europeans ... of their status as gendered beings. Devoid of humanity and gender, non-Europeans were endlessly exploitable, as well as eliminable' (2016, p.118). The way Black women are represented because of the colonial project thus requires the recognition of race in conjunction with gendered body politics (Mowatt et al., 2013).

Yet, in tourism studies there are scarcely any publications which draw on Black feminist theory. This absence reflects and reinforces tourism's coloniality and the colonizing discourses of white feminism. Coloniality, as defined by Maldonado-Torres (2007) means:

> [L]ong-standing patterns of power that emerged as a result of colonialism that define culture, labour, intersubjective relations, and knowledge production well beyond the strict limits of colonial administrations. *Thus, coloniality survives colonization*[our emphasis]. It is maintained alive in books, in the criteria for academic performance, in cultural patterns, in common sense, in the self-image of peoples, in aspirations of self, and so many other aspects of our modern experience. (p. 243)

To bring this argument on coloniality more firmly into the sphere of Black feminism, Mendoza (2016) adopts the concept of the 'coloniality of gender' as articulated in the work of Maria Lugones (2007). Mendoza (2016) argues that:

> From an anticolonial feminist perspective, theories advanced by women of color are subjected to recolonization as their central ideas and concepts slowly disappear or reappear whitewashed and devoid of their critical impetus. (p. 103)

In this context, Mendoza argues that the notion of intersectionality, which emerged from the Black feminist movement in the United States, diverges significantly from the anticolonial struggles of women in other parts of the world. This is because intersectionality as articulated by Black feminists in the United States, embraces 'liberal inclusion as a political project' and thus fails to realize the criticality and radical nature of anticolonial struggles.

Indeed, Kimberlé Crenshaw, a Black legal scholar from the United States, is attributed with coining the term 'intersectionality'. Crenshaw observed the marginalization of African American women in both the legal and the public spheres and for her, intersectionality refers to the way in which race, class and sexual subordination are intimately intertwined (Crenshaw, 1989). According to Mendoza (2016):

> [I]ntersectionality illuminated ties between epistemic location and knowledge production, and offered analytic strategies that linked the material, the discursive, and the structural. Demonstrating the inadequacies of 'either/or' (binary) ways of thinking and the futility of efforts to rank oppressions, intersectionality reflects lessons that US black feminist theorists drew from black women's lived experiences of enslavement, uprootedness and dispossession, economic and reproductive exploitation, and Jim Crow segregation, share cropping and domestic labor, lynching, rape, and race riots, second-class citizenship, and systemic racism under the guise of formal equality. (p. 106)

The point here is that Black feminist theorizing emerged from a particular geo-political and historical context, and as such often excluded the experiences of women of colour from the non-Anglophone world whose struggles against coloniality should be contextualized but are often ignored due to Anglo-centrism. The question that arises then in tourism gender research is how can we access and include the knowledges from those women that are located outside of the dominant Anglo-centric paradigm? Indeed, discussions of colonialism in tourism tend to focus on British colonial experiences, often ignoring the voices of women from other colonial contexts such as those from French, Portuguese and Spanish locales which are often not articulated in English. Black feminist theorizing can also exclude the voices of indigenous women of colour within settler colonial contexts such as Australia, New Zealand, and North America whose experiences of the coloniality of power must also be contextualized. It is important for tourism researchers, in thinking about future research agendas for gender and tourism, to consider the pervasiveness of the coloniality of power, its racialized and gendered dimensions, and its material effects not only in the Anglophone world, but across multiple historical and geo-political contexts. While Black feminist theory with its origins in the experiences of African American women might not be entirely suitable for all women racialized as Black, Crenshaw's (1989) notion of intersectionality can certainly be applied in a wider range of contexts and highlights the fact that Black women's experiences, while multidimensional, are nevertheless intrinsically intertwined through the coloniality of power.

2.2 Theorizations of Sex and Gender

White/Western feminism is argued to have failed to understand the link between sex and gender, thus leading to cisgender women's negation of trans-women's rights to be called 'women' (see Upadhyay, 2021). Indeed, bell hooks long ago dismantled the reductionist way in which (white/Western) feminism understood the category of woman:

> The efforts of black women and women of color to challenge and deconstruct the category 'woman' – the insistence on recognition that gender is not the sole factor for determining constructions of femaleness – was a critical intervention, one which led to a profound revolution in feminist thought and truly interrogated and disrupted the hegemonic feminist theory produced primarily by academic women, most of whom were white. (hooks, 1994, p. 63)

Returning to the work of Maria Lugones (2007) on the coloniality of gender, Icaza and Vázquez (2016) discuss the notion of gender in global development paradigms and highlight how, by focusing on the binary social constructions of men and women, it erases diverse sexual identities. They argue that:

> … an untouched heterosexual order is also present in the promotion of girls schooling as a central goal in development policy (e.g. Malala Yousafai's case). The underlying assumption is that education is one way through which gender-based discrimination against women in society, especially in the global south can counter the re-emergence of fundamentalisms around the world. However, this assumption is based upon the idea that male and female sexual identities are a given. This impacts on how access to education is conceived as related to a pre-established sexual order in which any other identities are not fully considered/thought (e.g., lesbian, gay, transgender, intersex kids). (Icaza & Vázquez, 2016, p. 65)

With this in mind, we now consider a strand of recent often visceral and polarizing debate that has arisen within the feminist movement and has been described as gender-critical feminism or sometimes more derogatively termed 'trans-exclusionary radical feminism' (TERF). It has long been accepted that gender is a social construct and should therefore be distinguished from biological sex categories (see, for example, West & Zimmerman, 1987). Indeed, reflecting the fluid nature of gender, Judith Butler famously spoke of the 'performance' of gender (see Butler, 1988). Gender-critical feminism arose out of radical feminism and supports the notion that gender results from social norms and expectations *but* that these are fundamentally underpinned by biological sex categories. In this sense, gender cannot be divorced from sex, the latter seen as fixed and unchangeable. According to Lawford-Smith (2022, p. 13),'gender-critical feminism is both a continuation of radical feminism and distinct from it.'For gender-critical feminists, gender cannot be understood as simply an identity, as this erases the notion that humans can be divided into biological sex categories. For adherents to gender-critical feminism, divorcing gender from biological sex categories undermines the historic and current struggles for women's rights (see Lawford-Smith, 2022). For gender-critical feminists it is important to re-centre women within feminism and to argue for the protection of sex-based rights (Lawford-Smith, 2022; Stock, 2021).

The arguments between those who see gender as identity (therefore denying the existence of categories of biological sex) and those who see gender as a 'set of social norms and expectations imposed on the basis of sex' (Lawford-Smith, 2022, p. x) (the gender-critical feminists or TERFs) has played out in our universities, in social media, in sport, and across our cultural institutions, often with deleterious effects. One of the most prominent members of gender-critical feminists is, arguably, JK Rowling who in a 2020 tweet declared:

> If sex isn't real, there's no same-sex attraction. If sex isn't real, the lived reality of women globally is erased. I know and love trans people but erasing the concept of sex removes the ability of many to meaningfully discuss their lives. It isn't hate to speak the truth. (@jk_rowling, June 6, 2020, 11:02 pm)

Gender-critical feminists or TERFs have been renounced for what are deemed to be transphobic views. According to Hotine (2021):

> The rhetoric being espoused by such figures as Rowling is particularly abhorrent and dangerous as it feeds into anti-trans rhetoric and stigma that trans individuals already face. By shrouding their anti-trans dogma behind various dog whistles and a veneer of respectable concern and pseudo-science, TERFs are working to further de-stabilize trans' [sic] peoples standing in society and their safety. (Hotine, 2021, n.p.)

This debate around the category of 'woman' has also led to serious questions about who is, or can be a feminist, what feminism means and who and what feminism is for. It has also led to questions about the status of transwomen, as for gender-critical feminists, transwomen cannot be women as this would deny the inextricable connection between sex and gender. While gender-critical feminists appear to make a logical argument, this denies the fact that it is not biology that creates female vulnerability and oppression but:

> ... our social interpretation of the body and our preconceived biases and gender norms that are responsible. Biology has been used to justify the narrative that women are 'natural caregivers' and that their responsibilities to provide unpaid care are therefore justified, but this exploitation of female labour does not arise purely because women give birth. It arises because of social biases that create the link between the female body and gender norms. (Hotine, 2021, n.p.)

This is not to deny the importance of biology but to highlight its lack of fixity and its arbitrary, socially contextual nature. Gender-critical feminist perspectives on the innateness of biology also raises questions about their views on Black women. Race has long been debunked as a biological category and is instead now widely accepted as a social construct but with deleterious material implications for Black women. Yet it appears that gender-critical feminists are silent on, and even reject, intersectional feminist analyses as distractions from the core function of feminism which is perceived to be the protection of essentialist sex-based rights (see Lawford-Smith, 2022).

In mainstream tourism studies there is a dearth of research which seeks to critically unpack these problematics in contemporary feminist scholarship and how these affect the treatment of transgender people in tourism. That said, there have been several publications which have focused on transgender tourists - many have explored their travel experiences but have not examined these through feminist/intersectional theoretical lenses. For example, Monterrubio et al. (2021) looked at the constraints affecting trans individuals from engaging in tourism in Mexico using leisure constraints theory. Further, Olson and Reddy-Best (2019) examined the travel experiences of transgender and non-gender-conforming tourists. More recently Ong et al. (2022) undertook a systematic literature review on publications in tourism which examined LGBTQI issues, and this revealed a lack of focus on transgender people, and where this was discussed, Global North contexts predominated. Ong et al. (2022) suggested that this elision of the Global South perhaps pointed to the fact that in these countries issues of sexuality were more problematic and there might be risks involved for researchers and research participants.

While the trans community constitutes a minority population, increasing publicity in the sporting and celebrity arenas has resulted in growing visibility to the problematics associated with sex and gender. However, the discourse on gender and tourism has not done enough to provide critical problematizations of the concept of gender, its geo-historical origins, and its material effects on tourists' embodied experiences. We suggest that spaces exist for more critical inter/post/cross disciplinary theoretical discussions on gender and sex, and how these are problematized in travel and tourism in different geographical contexts.

2.3 Feminist Theorizing: Fourth Wave Feminism

Another aspect of feminist theorizing that has been under-researched in tourism studies is the impact of what has, arguably, been deemed as 'fourth wave' feminism in travel and tourism domains. It is not our intention to go into a discussion here of the concept of feminist 'waves' as this has been expertly covered elsewhere (see for example Parry & Fullagar, 2013). The point that we continue to make here is that there is a dearth of studies in tourism gender research that focuses on more recent feminist theorizing – certainly tourism gender scholars should have much to say about the ubiquity of social media in our contemporary societies and its implications for the discourse and practice of gendered relationships in travel and tourism contexts.

What distinguishes fourth wave feminism is the use of social media as a platform for activism or what is more broadly known as technological mobilization. According to Parry et al. (2019, p. 3), 'social media has returned feminism to the realm of public discourse and as such fourth wave feminism is "an everyday feminism".' Fourth wave feminism situates women's 'individual lived experiences within broader global discourses' (Parry et al., 2019, p. 1) using social media channels such as Instagram, Twitter, Facebook, Snapchat, Tik Tok etc. The issues of particular focus in fourth wave feminism are the representation of women in popular cultural forms, and violence and harassment against women as witnessed in the use of popular hashtag campaigns like #Metoo, #TimesUp, #everydaysexism and #SayHerName. It is debatable whether technological mobilization can do more than merely highlight individual concerns around sexism and misogyny and issues faced by specific communities, rather than lead to wider structural and global change. Indeed, many of the hashtag campaigns are seen to be dominated by white feminists and to further neo-liberal agendas through the promotion of consumerist cultures. According to Fullagar et al. (2019):

> Questions remain about how we disentangle fourth wave feminism and post-feminism within online spaces as digital feminisms have emerged alongside the global dominance of neoliberal rationalities, markets, and modes of governing selfhood. (p. 45)

There have been a few publications in tourism and hospitality research which examine digital activism but several focus only on a single hashtag – #Metoo (see Min et al., 2021; Pearlman & Bordelon, 2022; Ram, 2021; Yang et al., 2020) and do not provide critical analyses of wider movements or any theoretical unpacking of the problematics associated with this aspect of fourth wave feminism. Heimtun and Morgan (2012) suggest that feminist tourism researchers have yet to engage with fourth wave feminism and we argue that this remains the case a decade later. We contend that more work in tourism needs to engage with theoretical concerns around fourth wave feminism and the extent to which it provides radical alternatives to the structural complexities of what is a globalized neo-liberal heteronormative domain. Importantly we need to question the extent to which hashtag campaigns continue to give prominence to white feminism while simultaneously marginalizing the voices of women of colour. Indeed, Trott (2021) suggests that there are:

> ... power dynamics within digital feminist networks that reproduce colonial violence and oppression within mainstream neoliberal feminism and academia, [and] digital networks do not empower marginalized voices equitably. (2021, p. 1125)

And this is despite the contention that intersectionality is a central tenet of fourth wave feminism (see Cochrane, 2013).

2.4 Theorizing Gender and the Environment

Finally, in our brief overview of theoretical lacunas in research on tourism and gender, we argue that it is also important to theorize the relationship between gender and the environment (and sustainability more widely) especially in the context of current discussions about the achievement of the 17 United Nations Sustainable Development Goals (SDGs). Indeed UNSDG No. 5 is aimed at achieving gender equality and 'empowering all women and girls' although it is understood that gender equality is fundamental to achieving all the other SDGs. The link between gender and environmental sustainability has been documented in tourism research most recently in the Special Issue of the *Journal of Sustainable Tourism* edited by Eger, Munar and Hsu (2022). In their editorial, they argue that gender theorizing and feminist epistemologies are necessary to understandings of sustainability and in the context of tourism (see Eger et al., 2022). We want to suggest here that theorizations of the link between gender and environmental sustainability are still underdeveloped in tourism studies. And here we point to eco-feminist and feminist political ecology theories which are pertinent in this context.

Eco-feminists believed that an essential aspect of the colonial project was the domination of other races and nations as well as parts of nature. Central to the problematics of Western colonization was the association of women and other subordinated groups with nature (thus more primitive) while male elites were associated with reason and culture – White Man was the master subject in this scenario (see discussions in Plumwood, 2004). However, the establishment of this kind of dualistic structure of man/culture and woman/nature led to other dualisms such as men/rationality, women/emotional, men/competitive and women/nurturing. In the context of these socially constructed dualisms, feminists accepted the idea that women are closer to nature, and with the rise of the environmental movement, argued that women therefore inherently had a superior understanding of the importance of environmental protection. According to Nightingale (2006, p. 166) 'this ecofeminist thinking was premised on the idea that the domination of women was linked to environmental destruction and other problematic social inequalities such as racism.' Nightingale further contended that:

> This work was incredibly important in promoting the idea that uneducated people (especially women) could have a better understanding of environmental protection than scientists and policymakers. It was also important in advocating a global women's movement, linked together by threats to women's home environments. (2006, p. 166)

Eco-feminists thus argued that to reverse the destruction of the environment it was important that women be emancipated. Unfortunately, this eco-feminist position promoted an essentialist idea of women, based largely on gender as biological sex, and this belief pervaded feminism at that time. Other feminists (such as Black feminists) argued that such essentialist conceptualizations of women ignored very real differences between women and even more problematic was the notion of an essential female nature (Nightingale, 2006). While there is indeed a relationship between women and their desire to protect the environment, this relationship is not based on any essentialist link between women and nature, but rather is associated with women's material realities, recognising that these differ according to cultural and politico-geographical location. As such feminist political ecology seeks to demonstrate how gender (conceptualized as culturally defined male/female sex roles) 'structures access to particular types of knowledge, space, resources and social-political processes' (Nightingale, 2006, p. 169). By focusing on such structural issues an argument can be made that the opportunities and challenges regarding environmental change and development are different for men and women. However, there is a danger here in returning to the belief that gender is synonymous with 'women' and reproducing essentialist understandings of women's innate connection to the land. Nightingale argues that:

> This kind of essentialism masks a variety of political-economic, cultural, and symbolic processes by which gender is produced by environmental issues as well as being implicated in the construction of the 'issue' itself. In short, what is still not sufficiently highlighted is a clear understanding of how gender has come to be relevant in these contexts at all. (2006, p. 169)

One answer to this problematic according to Nightingale (2006) is to recognize how gender and the environment are mutually constituted and 'this requires an engagement with the relationships between development projects, subjectivities, and (re)productive activities, as well as material transformations of ecosystems' (p. 170). We have found some limited application of feminist political ecology in tourism studies chiefly by Cole (2016, 2017) who examined the link between gender and the problems with water resources in the emerging tourism destination of Labuan Bajo in Indonesia. Another publication by Mkono et al. (2021), while it integrated a political ecology approach and was focused on women's empowerment, gender-justice and gender-equity, did not embrace a specifically feminist political ecology approach. Similarly, Kato (2019) used a political ecology approach to examine the link between gender and the sustainability of the ocean through a case study of traditional women divers in Japan. However, rather than drawing on feminist political ecology, Kato (2019) adopted an ecohumanist approach.

Thus, a feminist approach to political ecology is fairly limited in tourism studies although there has been more research on the political ecology of tourism (see, for example, LaVanchy, 2017; Mosedale, 2015; Mostafanezhad et al., 2016; Nepal & Saarinen, 2016; Stonich, 1998, and a special issue on the political ecology of tourism in the *Journal of Sustainable Tourism* edited by Mostafanezhad & Norum, 2019). We propose that given the prominence of environmental sustainability and the importance of the achievement of the UNSDGs by 2030, more research in tourism that critically explores feminist political ecology would contribute to our knowledge and understanding of the power structures and intersectionalities underpinning the gender/environment nexus.

3. Method(ological) Directions for Gender and Tourism Research

The papers within this book primarily utilized traditional qualitative methodologies and methods (semi-structured interviews, document analysis, qualitative content analysis) and to a lesser extent quantitative methods (quantitative systematic literature review). The use of duoethnography (Frew & Mair, Chapter 10, this volume) to examine the role of academic conferences in maintaining supportive friendships among female academics presented an interesting departure. Our research revealed that while duoethnography as a dialogic research methodology has long been used in other fields of study such as education and nursing (see an extensive discussion of duoethnography in Sawyer & Norris, 2012) it has only attracted limited attention in tourism and leisure studies (see for example, Benjamin & Schwab, 2021; Pung et al., 2020).

3.1 Overview of Feminist Methodologies

We believe that there is scope for innovative approaches to gender and tourism research which draw on what can be deemed as 'feminist methodologies'. Recognizing that there are different feminisms, it is possible to discern some broad propositions underpinning feminist methodologies which include:

- A reflexive understanding that gender pervades all aspects of our social world;
- The importance of 'consciousness-raising' both as a way of seeing and a methodological tool;
- Challenging objectivity and embracing the legitimacy of subjectivity and value-laden, creative research;
- A concern with ethics and the treatment of women as subjects, and not objects of research;
- An understanding that research is necessarily a political activity;
- A view that all knowledge is socially constructed;
- A view of the (social) sciences as inherently patriarchal and Euro/Anglo-centric (adapted from Stanley & Wise, 1990 [2013]).

So overall, feminist methodologies see all knowledge as contextually located and resulting from the conditions of its production. We argue that any agenda for gender and tourism research should draw on the tenets of feminist methodologies, or feminist standpoints as outlined above, and tourism researchers should make these explicit in their research. There have, admittedly, been tourism scholars who have argued explicitly for the use of feminist standpoint methodologies (see for example, Aitchison, 2005; Almela & Calvet, 2021; Figueroa-Domecq & Segovia-Perez, 2020; Heimtun & Morgan, 2012; Humberstone, 2004; Munar, 2017). We recognize that the tenets we have outlined above are broad epistemological stances that underpin feminist methodologies and questions remain about *how* to creatively *do* gender research in a tourism context. In the following, we seek to outline two methods that can be adopted to interrogate the gendered nature of our tourism social world. The first is feminist participatory action research (FPAR) and the second is the counter-narrative/storytelling approach adopted by Critical Race Theorists (the latter closely aligned to Black feminist theory). We believe that both methods are under-served in tourism and gender research but can make important contributions to critical work in this area that is suitable for addressing contemporary global and local concerns around social justice.

3.2 Feminist Participatory Action Research

Feminist participatory action research (FPAR) combines feminist epistemologies with participatory action research (PAR) and aims at involving women as co-creators of research, activism, and social critique for the purpose of emancipation. According to Gatenby and Humphries (2000, p. 89) 'the emphasis of PAR has been on liberating oppressed groups through research as praxis.' Certainly, PAR draws inspiration from the works of Paulo Freire in terms of its dialogic methods and its philosophy of liberation of marginalized knowledges and groups (see Freire, 1970, [1996]). PAR does not have defined methods, and techniques are often diverse and experimental. However, what is central to PAR is dialogue amongst the community/ies involved which normally takes place in community meetings with participants identifying issues and problems, reflecting on the research process, and developing liberatory solutions themselves. Researchers in this scenario are not detached from the process but work together with the community/ies as co-participants. The techniques and ethos of PAR fit well with feminist epistemologies and their well-established belief in the political, value-laden nature of research and the purpose of research as leading to women's empowerment (Gatenby & Humphries, 2000). FPAR is thus a critical approach that focuses on:

> ... democratizing the research process, acknowledging lived experiences, and contributing to social justice agendas to counter prevailing ideologies and power relations that are deeply gendered, classed, and racialized. (Reid & Frisby, 2008, p. 93)

It is important to note that doing FPAR:

> ... inevitably changes the researcher, sometimes painfully, sometimes in exciting, sustaining ways. The self-reflexivity such changes engender is a feature of all feminist scholarship in some way. (Gatenby & Humphries, 2000, p. 90)

Despite the liberational potentialities of FPAR, there are some challenges with this approach, and these include critical considerations of:

> ... who is privileged epistemologically and how this affects the representation of voices and the interpretations of findings. Questions about how and who can speak for women of colour, lesbians, working-class women and postcolonials [*sic*], for example, continue to be pivotal in helping feminists clarify the links between theory, method, and action. (Reid & Frisby, 2008, p. 96)

While PAR has been used in tourism studies (see for example Goebel et al., 2020; O' Leary & Coghlan, 2022; Perkins et al., 2021; Schmitz et al., 2016; Wang et al., 2019), there is limited, if any, application of FPAR and indeed we were only able to discern one study that applied PAR to investigate women in a tourism setting. The study we refer to here is that by Merkel Arias and Kieffer (2022) who used PAR to develop a community based sustainable tourism initiative with a group of women in rural Mexico. This study, while it focused on women, did not explicitly include feminist epistemologies.

We believe that FPAR can be an innovative and important approach for gender research in tourism but researchers who wish to adopt this approach must be cognizant that:

> ... participatory approaches can impose rather than alleviate entrenched power relations, especially if communities are wrongly assumed to be homogeneous ... local knowledge has been romanticized through participatory approaches that leave broader exclusionary processes and institutions unchanged. (Reid & Frisby, 2008, p. 98 citing Cooke & Kothari, 2001)

Further, FPAR requires a high level of reflexivity on the part of the researcher to address tensions

> ... inherent in representing women's voices and experiences because questions are continually raised about 'who has the authority to represent women's voices and to what end', 'what forms of the representation will best capture the dynamics involved', 'who decides whether they are credible', and 'do representations reinscribe rather than transcend dominant power relations?' (Reid & Frisby, 2008, p. 99)

Multiple data sources can be used in FPAR studies such as diaries, journals, participatory workshops, poetry, visual methods (such as photography, film and art), and practices such as co-writing (Reid & Frisby, 2008). What is important to note here is the creativity and flexibility involved in techniques of FPAR.

3.3 Critical Race Theory: Counter-Narratives/Storytelling

Finally in this section we propose counter-narrative/storytelling, a central liberatory method(ology) used in Critical Race Theory (CRT) which is very much aligned with Black feminism. While this method has been widely used in educational research particularly in the United States (see for example, Liu, 2015; Miles, 2019; Solorzano & Yosso, 2002) it has relevance for intersectional studies in tourism which seek to expose race, class, and gender oppression in a range of geographical settings. Counter-storytelling draws on the main tenets of CRT which, while it does not represent a cohesive theoretical approach (Bell, 1995), includes the following principles: racism is inherent in our societies; racism is intersectional and must be understood also in the context of other inequalities such as gender, class and sexuality; race is a historically contingent social construct; challenge to traditionally dominant ideologies that subscribe to objectivity and colour blindness; commitment to social justice that is both liberating and transformational; adherence to the central role of marginalized voices and a concomitant methodological approach that draws on the notion of 'cultural intuition' which includes storytelling and counter-storytelling; and finally, the embrace of trans disciplinarity (Carbado & Roithmayr, 2014; Solorzano & Yosso, 2001).

Yet, the application of CRT's method(ology) of counter-narrative/storytelling in tourism has been very limited and even less so in gender and tourism research (although see for example Chambers, 2022; Lee, 2017). Counter-narrative storytelling is described by Solorzano and Yosso thus:

> ... a method of telling the stories of those people whose experiences are not often told (i.e., those on the margins of society). The counter-story is also a tool for exposing, analyzing, and challenging the majoritarian stories of racial privilege. Counter-stories can shatter complacency, challenge the dominant discourse on race, and further the struggle for racial reform. (2002, p. 32)

It is important to recognize that counter-narratives need not only respond to majoritarian narratives as this can further reinforce the centrality of dominant discourses. There are many unheard counter-narratives in the histories of Black women and other marginalized groupings and their telling of these stories can help 'strengthen traditions of social, political, and cultural survival and resistance'(Solorzano & Yosso, 2002, p. 32). Narratives (stories) can exist in various forms, three of which are described here. First, personal autobiographical reflections on incidents of exploitation or exclusion. Second, composite narratives which utilize several source materials (these can be from film, music, visual art, literature, theatre) and the researcher's voice to recount collective experiences of oppression that are brought together by the researcher and placed in their historical or cultural context. A good description of composite counter-storytelling is provided by Miller et al. who suggest that:

> In this method, researchers construct literary narratives based on the experiences of the participants and the researchers themselves, creating composite 'characters' that represent the collective voice of a marginalized group ... once the data have been compiled, the researchers create composite characters to help tell the counterstory. Thus, although grounded in the voices of the participants like other forms of counter-narrative, the resulting counterstory puts those voices in dialog with the researchers' knowledge and experience, including their own experiences as members of a marginalized group. The result, although created through literary procedures and with literary devices, is not intended to be taken as 'fiction' ... composite characters may also protect the privacy – and therefore safety – of participants. (2020, pp. 279–80)

Third, cultural intuition, that is the multiple sources of knowledge that researchers from marginalized groups bring to their research in a highly reflexive process, is also an important technique of counter-storytelling. There are four sources of cultural intuition – the personal experience of the researcher; our academic experiences which include how we understand and interpret the literature relevant to the topic; our professional experiences as researchers; and the analytical research process itself recognizing that our experiences inform our approach to the research, the data collection, analysis, and interpretation (see Bernal, 1998). According to Bernal (1998, p. 568) cultural intuition refers to 'a complex process that is experiential, intuitive, historical, personal, collective and dynamic'. Solorzano and Yosso (2002) are keen to reject claims of the lack of rigour of counter-storytelling as a research technique by contending that:

> Counter-storytelling is different from fictional storytelling. We are not developing imaginary characters that engage in fictional scenarios. Instead, the 'composite' characters we develop are grounded in real-life experiences and actual empirical data and are contextualized in social situations that are also grounded in real life, not fiction. (p. 36)

Counter-storytelling as a liberatory process must also result in action and in this sense, Miller et al. (2020, p. 274) posit that this 'sharing, reflection, and action constitute a hermeneutic process' because 'by reflecting on one's actions there can be new knowledge and illumination of one's interests that can, in turn, inform new action' (Liu, 2015, p. 140).

As indicated previously there have been very limited studies in gender and tourism research that draw on counter-storytelling. Exceptions include Lee (2017), a Māori researcher, who in a very powerful article used counter-storytelling as an indigenous methodology to highlight how Black female bodies were performed against and exploited by 'Establishment men' during the colonial encounter. Lee locates herself as integral to this narrative along with the Black women from tebrakunna country. According to Lee:

> To dislodge the western voice, then, as superior, and universal I refrain from a third-person narrative of being 'Indigenous' and instead speak of 'us' and 'ours' … to centrally locate our Black female bodies and tebrakunna country as powerful agents of decolonization. This methodology of grounding ourselves as material storytellers helps shield us against becoming a spectacle … As the tellers, speakers and actors of our own stories and experiences, we create the culturally safe spaces to examine the intersections … by which we are colonized and devise the pathways towards emancipation. Our Black female bodies then become a positive assertion of the ethic of tebrakunna country, where kinship and custodianship are the basis for identity and connection. (2017, pp. 95–6)

Chambers (2022) drew on her own positionality as a Black woman in tourism to analyse a fictional film (Heading South) to highlight the way that Black women from the postcolonial context of Haiti had been robbed of agency and represented in stereotypical ways as vulnerable and submissive.

It should become clear by now that counter-storytelling is both a methodology (a way of thinking that draws on the tenets of CRT) and a method (drawing on unconventional and creative primarily qualitative techniques) to tell the stories of those who have been marginalized in society from their own lived experiences and memories. Counter-storytelling is therefore useful for bringing to the fore voices that have traditionally been silenced in gender and tourism research. Gender and tourism scholars should ask themselves 'what do counter-narratives reveal about how gendered power operates in tourism settings?'

4. Concluding Remarks

In this concluding chapter we have presented a research agenda for gender and tourism which seeks to add to the theoretical and method(ological) discussions in the nine chapters that comprise this book, and in gender and tourism research more widely. We recognize that our discussions in this chapter are necessarily selective and perhaps reflect the interests and positionalities of the editors of this book. Admittedly, these discussions can only be partial and there are more theories and method(ologies) that can be applied to tourism and gender research. However, we hope that what we have articulated here can act as a provocation, and a stimulus for more critical, and theoretically informed explorations of tourism and gender.

As we were finalizing this conclusion, the news emerged that the Supreme Court in the United States had revoked Roe v Wade, that constitutional right that had existed for 50 years and which legalized abortion across the country (see BBC, 2022 for an overview of this legislation). We believe this to be regressive and a setback for women in the United States which robs them of their right to choose what happens with their reproductive health. Indeed, we question how these restrictions on women's freedom over their bodies will affect women (particularly at the intersection between class and race) and their mobilities including their tourism mobilities. The United States is not the only country that has witnessed a return to restrictions over women's freedoms – another example is the re-ascendance of the Taliban to government in Afghanistan in 2021 which has led to a return to the severe restrictions on the right to education for women and girls and their freedom to inhabit the public sphere (for context, see Ahmed-Ghosh, 2003 for a history of women in Afghanistan). Both examples point to the power of governments and legislatures over women's bodies and mobilities. The implications for women's experiences of tourism and leisure are yet to be determined but we hope that future gender and tourism research will explore these and related avenues.

In addition, it is generally acknowledged that the negative effects of climate change are felt more acutely by women and girls (see Eastin, 2018) largely because of gender inequality in social, economic, and political spheres. Climate change has an impact on tourism (and tourism also impacts on climate change) with the effects more deleterious for women. Clearly, there are several avenues opening up for more critical discussions on gender and the political economy of tourism, gender and tourism mobilities, and gender, justice and human rights in a tourism context. We would urge researchers at the nexus between tourism and gender to contemplate more critical, reflexive and innovative approaches that can contribute to social justice agendas in our tourism world.

References

Ahmed-Ghosh, H. (2003). A history of women in Afghanistan: Lessons learnt for the future or yesterdays and tomorrow: Women in Afghanistan. *Journal of International Women's Studies*, *4*(3), 1–14.

Aitchison, C.C. (2005). Feminist and gender perspectives in tourism studies: The social-cultural nexus of critical and cultural theories. *Tourist Studies*, *5*(3), 207–24.

Almela, M.S., & Calvet, N.A. (2021). Volunteer tourism and gender: A feminist research agenda. *Tourism and Hospitality Research*, *21*(4), 461–72.

Arnfred, S. (2004). Introduction: Re-thinking sexualities in Africa. In S. Arnfred (ed.), *Re-thinking sexualities in Africa* (pp. 7–29). Sweden: Almqvist Wiksell Tryckeri AB.

BBC (2022). Roe v Wade: What is US Supreme Court ruling on abortion? Available from https:// www .bbc .co .uk/ news/ world -us -canada -54513499 (accessed 7 July 2022).

Bell, D. (1995). Who's afraid of critical race theory? *University of Illinois Law Review*, 4, 893–910.

Benjamin, S., & Dillette, A.K. (2021). Black travel movement: Systemic racism informing tourism. *Annals of Tourism Research*, *88*, 103169.

Benjamin, S., & Schwab, K. (2021). Navigating the waves of feminism (s): A duoethnography of two feminist travellers. *Annals of Leisure Research*, 1–18.

Bernal, D.D. (1998). Using a Chicana feminist epistemology in educational research. *Harvard Educational Review*, *68*(4), 555–83.

Butler, J. (1988). Performative acts and gender constitution: An essay in phenomenology and feminist theory. *Theatre Journal*, 40(4), 519–31.

Carbado. D.W., & Roithmayr, D. (2014). Critical race theory meets social science. *The Annual Review of Law and Social Science*, 10, 149–67.

Chambers, D. (2022). Are we all in this together? Gender intersectionality and sustainable tourism. *Journal of Sustainable Tourism, 30*(7), 1586–601.
Cochrane, K. (2013). *All the rebel women: The rise of the fourth wave of feminism*. Vol. 8. New York: Guardian Books.
Cole, S. (2016). A gendered political ecology of tourism and water. In M. Mostafanezhad, R. Norum, E.J. Shelton, & A. Thompson-Carr (eds), *Political ecology of tourism* (pp. 49–67). New York: Routledge.
Cole, S. (2017). Water worries: An intersectional feminist political ecology of tourism and water in Labuan Bajo, Indonesia. *Annals of Tourism Research, 67*, 14–24.
Crenshaw, K. (1989). Demarginalizing the intersection of race and sex: A black feminist critique of antidiscrimination doctrine, feminist theory and antiracist politics. *University of Chicago Legal Forum, 1*(8), 139–67.
Eastin, J. (2018). Climate change and gender equality in developing states. *World Development, 107*, 289–305.
Eger, C., Munar, A.M., & Hsu, C. (2022). Gender and tourism sustainability. *Journal of Sustainable Tourism, 30*(7), 1459–75.
Figueroa-Domecq, C., & Segovia-Perez, M. (2020). Application of a gender perspective in tourism research: A theoretical and practical approach. *Journal of Tourism Analysis: Revista de Análisis Turístico, 27*(2), 251–70.
Freire, P. ([1970], 1996). *Pedagogy of the oppressed*. London: Penguin.
Fullagar, S., Pavlidis, A., & Francombe-Webb, J. (2019). Feminist theories after the poststructural turn. In D. Parry (ed.), *Feminisms in leisure studies: Advancing a fourth wave* (pp. 34–57). London: Routledge.
Gatenby, B., & Humphries, M. (2000, January). Feminist participatory action research: Methodological and ethical issues. *Women's Studies International Forum, 23*(1), 89–105.
Goebel, K., Camargo-Borges, C., & Eelderink, M. (2020). Exploring participatory action research as a driver for sustainable tourism. *International Journal of Tourism Research, 22*(4), 425–37.
Heimtun, B., & Morgan, N. (2012). Proposing paradigm peace: Mixed methods in feminist tourism research. *Tourist Studies, 12*(3), 287–304.
hooks, b. (1981/2015). *Ain't I a woman: Black women and feminism*. New York: Routledge.
hooks, b. (1994). *Teaching to transgress: Education as the practice of freedom*. New York: Routledge.
Hotine, E. (2021). Biology, society and sex: Deconstructing anti-trans rhetoric and trans-exclusionary radical feminism. *Journal of the Nuffield Department of Surgical Sciences, 2*(3), 1–5.
Humberstone, B. (2004). Standpoint research: Multiple versions of reality in tourism theorising and research. In J. Phillimore & L. Goodson (eds), *Qualitative research in tourism. Ontologies, epistemologies and methodologies* (pp. 137–54). London: Routledge.
Icaza, R., & Vázquez, R. (2016). The coloniality of gender as a radical critique of developmentalism. In *The Palgrave handbook of gender and development* (pp. 62–73). London: Palgrave Macmillan.
Kato, K. (2019). Gender and sustainability – exploring ways of knowing: An ecohumanities perspective. *Journal of Sustainable Tourism, 27*(7), 939–56.
LaVanchy, G.T. (2017). When wells run dry: Water and tourism in Nicaragua. *Annals of Tourism Research, 64*, 37–50.
Lawford-Smith, H. (2022). *Gender-critical feminism*. Oxford: Oxford University Press.

Lee, E. (2017). Performing colonisation: The manufacture of Black female bodies in tourism research. *Annals of Tourism Research, 66*, 95–104.
Liu, K. (2015). Critical reflection as a framework for transformative learning in teacher education. *Educational Review, 67*(2), 135–57.
Lugones, M. (2007). Heterosexualism and the colonial/modern gender system. *Hypatia, 22*(1), 186–219.
Maldonado-Torres, N. (2007). On the coloniality of being. *Cultural Studies*, 21(2–3), 240–70.
Mendoza, B. (2016). Coloniality of gender and power. In L. Disch & M. Hawkesworth (eds), *The Oxford handbook of feminist theory* (pp. 100–21). Oxford: Oxford University Press.
Merkel Arias, N., & Kieffer, M. (2022). Participatory action research for the assessment of community-based rural tourism: A case study of co-construction of tourism sustainability indicators in Mexico. *Current Issues in Tourism*, 1–18.
Miles, J. (2019). Historical silences and the enduring power of counter storytelling. *Curriculum Inquiry, 49*(3), 253–9.
Miller, R., Liu, K., & Ball, A.F. (2020). Critical counter-narrative as transformative methodology for educational equity. *Review of Research in Education, 44*(1), 269–300.
Min, J., Lee, H., Lema, J., Agrusa, J., & Linnes, C. (2021). The #MeToo movement in paradise: An assessment of the restaurant industry. *Journal of Foodservice Business Research*, 1–19.
Mkono, M., Rastegar, R., & Ruhanen, L. (2021). Empowering women to protect wildlife in former hunting tourism zones: A political ecology of Akashinga, Zimbabwe. *Journal of Sustainable Tourism*, 1–21.
Monterrubio, C., Mendoza-Ontiveros, M.M., Rodríguez Madera, S.L., & Pérez, J. (2021). Tourism constraints on transgender individuals in Mexico. *Tourism and Hospitality Research, 21*(4), 433–46.
Mosedale, J. (2015). Critical engagements with nature: Tourism, political economy of nature and political ecology. *Tourism Geographies, 17*(4), 505–10.
Mostafanezhad, M., & Norum, R. (2019). The anthropocenic imaginary: Political ecologies of tourism in a geological epoch. *Journal of Sustainable Tourism, 27*(4), 421–35.
Mostafanezhad, M., Norum, R., Shelton, E.J., & Thompson-Carr, A. (eds). (2016). *Political ecology of tourism*. New York: Routledge.
Mowatt, R.A., French, B.H., & Malebranche, D.A. (2013). Black/female/body hypervisibility and invisibility: A Black feminist augmentation of feminist leisure research. *Journal of Leisure Research, 45*(5), 644–60.
Munar, A.M. (2017). To be a feminist in (tourism) academia. *Anatolia, 28*(4), 514–29.
Nepal, S., & Saarinen, J. (2016). *Political ecology and tourism*. New York: Routledge.
Nightingale, A. (2006). The nature of gender: Work, gender, and environment. *Environment and Planning D: Society and Space, 24*(2), 165–85.
O'Leary, D., & Coghlan, D. (2022), Action research in hospitality and tourism research. In F. Okumus, S.M Rasoolimanesh, & S. Jahani (eds), *Contemporary research methods in hospitality and tourism* (pp. 237–51). Bingley, UK: Emerald Publishing.
Olson, E.D., & Reddy-Best, K. (2019). 'Pre-topsurgery, the body scanning machine would most likely error': Transgender and gender nonconforming travel and tourism experiences. *Tourism Management, 70*, 250–61.
Ong, F., Vorobjovas-Pinta, O., & Lewis, C. (2022). LGBTIQ+ identities in tourism and leisure research: A systematic qualitative literature review. *Journal of Sustainable Tourism, 30*(7), 1476–99.

Parry, D.C., & Fullagar, S. (2013). Feminist leisure research in the contemporary era. *Journal of Leisure Research, 45*(5), 571–82.

Parry, D., Johnson, C.W., & Wagler, F-A. (2019). Fourth wave feminism: Theoretical underpinnings and future directions for leisure research. In D. Parry (ed.), *Feminisms in leisure studies: Advancing a fourth wave* (pp. 1–12). London: Routledge.

Pearlman, D.M., & Bordelon, B.M. (2022). How the #MeToo movement affected sexual harassment in the hospitality industry: A US case study. *International Journal of Hospitality Management, 101*. https://doi.org/10.1016/j.ijhm.2021.103106

Perkins, R., Khoo-Lattimore, C., & Arcodia, C. (2021). Collaboration in marketing regional tourism destinations: Constructing a business cluster formation framework through participatory action research. *Journal of Hospitality and Tourism Management, 46*, 347–59.

Plumwood, V. (2004). Gender, eco-feminism and the environment. *Controversies in Environmental Sociology, 1*, 43–60.

Pung, J.M., Yung, R., Khoo-Lattimore, C., & Del Chiappa, G. (2020). Transformative travel experiences and gender: A double duoethnography approach. *Current Issues in Tourism, 23*(5), 538–58.

Ram, Y. (2021). Metoo and tourism: A systematic review. *Current Issues in Tourism, 24*(3), 321–39.

Reid, C., & Frisby, W. (2008). Continuing the journey: Articulating dimensions of feminist participatory action research (FPAR). *Sage handbook of action research: Participative inquiry and practice*. Vol. 2 (pp. 93–105). London: Sage.

Sawyer, R.D., & Norris, J. (2012). *Duoethnography*. Oxford: Oxford University Press.

Schmitz, S., & Lekane Tsobgou, D. (2016). Developing tourism products and new partnerships through participatory action research in rural Cameroon. *Geographical Research, 54*(2), 143–52.

Solorzano, D.G., & Yosso, T.J. (2001). Critical race and LatCrit theory and method: Counter storytelling. *Qualitative Studies in Education, 14*(4), 471–95.

Solórzano, D.G., & Yosso, T.J. (2002). Critical race methodology: Counter-storytelling as an analytical framework for education research. *Qualitative Inquiry, 8*(1), 23–44.

Stanley, L., & Wise, S. (1990/2013). Method, methodology and epistemology in feminist research processes. In L. Stanley (ed.), *Feminist praxis*. Vol. 3 (pp. 20–60). London: Routledge.

Stock, K. (2021). *Material girls: Why reality matters for feminism*. London: Little Brown.

Stonich, S.C. (1998). Political ecology of tourism. *Annals of Tourism Research, 25*(1), 25–54.

Syed, J. (2010). Reconstructing gender empowerment. *Women's Studies International Forum, 33*(3), 283–94.

Trott, V. (2021). Networked feminism: Counterpublics and the intersectional issues of #MeToo. *Feminist Media Studies, 21*(7), 1125–42.

Upadhyay, N. (2021). Coloniality of white feminism and its transphobia: A comment on Burt. *Feminist Criminology, 16*(4), 539–44.

Wang, Y.C., Yang, J., & Yang, C.E. (2019). Hotel internal branding: A participatory action study with a case hotel. *Journal of Hospitality and Tourism Management, 40*, 31–9.

West, C., & Zimmerman, D-H. (1987). Doing gender. *Gender and Society 1*(2), 125–51.

Yang, E.C.L., Chen, Y., & Ho, C-H. (2020). #Metoo: A feminist hashtag analysis of gender based violence against solo female travellers. In P. Vizcaino, H. Jeffrey, & C. Eger (eds), *Tourism and gender-based violence: Challenging inequalities*. (pp. 159–72). Wallingford: ABI.

Index